TREVOR'S KITCHEN GARDEN

This book is dedicated to
Neidín, my niece and godchild.

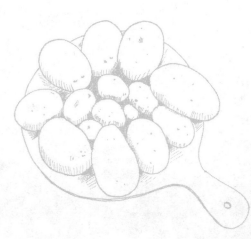

Trevor's Kitchen Garden

*A Week-by-Week Guide
to Growing Your Own Food*

TREVOR SARGENT

ORPEN PRESS

Orpen Press
Lonsdale House
Avoca Ave
Blackrock
Co. Dublin
Ireland

e-mail: info@orpenpress.com
www.orpenpress.com

ISBN 978-1-871305-39-5

Printed in the UK by the MPG Books Group

Preface

I HOPE YOU ENJOY using this book as much as I enjoyed writing and illustrating it. The idea for a weekly guide to growing food organically in a small garden began as a blog which is still going strong: www.trevorskitchengarden.ie.

This website came about as a response to people asking me, 'What should I be doing now in the garden, as I want to grow more food for me and my family?' At the time, I was Minister for Food and Horticulture, so I had little time for gardening, except very early in the morning or very late at night. Thankfully, my garden is small and manageable, and therefore not overly time consuming. With the help of Lorcan O'Toole and Ciarán Finn, two photographers, we put up video clips and pictures to illustrate the weekly text on the blog.

After a couple of years of blogging, I was delighted to receive a call from Orpen Press with a request to write this book. I set out to write a practical weekly handbook for anyone wishing to grow food organically on a small scale. Along with weekly tips, there are also food-related thoughts and ideas appropriate to each specific week. This book is for kitchen gardeners who want to grow locally, while being mindful of how this earth must feed all humanity. In essence, this is the book I would have wanted by my side when I began growing food over thirty years ago.

Since then, I have been a teacher, a founder of Sonairte, the ecology centre near Laytown, Co. Meath, leader of the Green Party (An Comhaontas Glas), a member of Dáil Éireann and Minister for Food and Horticulture. This book is, in a way, a continuation of the work I began in the Department of Agriculture, Fisheries and Food. In 2008, the UN International Year of the Potato gave me the idea, in partnership with Agri Aware (the charitable agricultural awareness trust), to send potato-growing kits and advice to every primary school in the country. Thanks to the sponsorship of many generous groups, such as Bord Bia, the Irish Farmers' Association, An Post, Safe Food Ireland, and many fruit and vegetable companies, this mammoth task was successfully undertaken. The following year, we expanded the programme countrywide, so schools could grow five crop varieties in an Agri Aware programme called 'Incredible Edibles'.

School and home kitchen gardens are now commonplace as a result of the 'Incredible Edibles' programme. The Grow It Yourself (GIY) Ireland movement has also helped many new kitchen gardeners to get growing. Thankfully, all of us can now visit publicly accessible kitchen gardens too, where the novice gardener can see what grows well in the local climate and soil conditions. In many cases, these are organic gardens attached to environmental education centres which run horticulture and related courses for schools and adults alike. SEED (Schools Environ-mental Education Development) is a network of these organic centres around Ireland. To date, the network includes The Organic Centre, Co. Leitrim, Sonairte at Laytown, Co. Meath, the Irish Seed Savers Association near Scarriff, Co. Clare, the Kerry Earth Education Project near Tralee, Co. Wexford Organic Centre near New Ross and the Nano Nagle Centre near Mallow, Co. Cork. I have attended courses run by these centres and I recommend them. The centres are often good places to get gardening experience and advice, so drop in to your nearest one.

If SEED had more money, these centres could provide more hands-on kitchen gardener training. With this in mind, the royalties from this book are going to provide more courses in organic horticulture through SEED. So enjoy the book, sow some seed and then drop in to your nearest organic centre to see how their crops are doing.

Contents

Introduction

I HAVE ALWAYS ASPIRED to grow as much as possible of my
own food, ever since as a teenager I read *The Complete Book of
Self-Sufficiency* by John Seymour. Although I was too young to
realise it as a child, the tomatoes, peas, blackcurrants and the
famous 'everlasting cabbage' grown by my father in the back
garden instilled in me an appreciation of kitchen gardening being
a pleasurable part of family life.

My enthusiasm for self-sufficiency lost the run of itself, however,
when I went to live in West Cork to take up my first job at The
Model School, Dunmanway, which in the nineteenth century
cultivated enough land to feed the monitors (apprentice teachers)
who were living there while they undertook their training. In my
second year teaching there, I was fortunate to be asked to mind my
friends' house on 1 acre, as they were going to England to seek
employment. The acre was a fallow meadow which I imagined
could be a productive kitchen garden. I tried to turn some of it into
a vegetable patch and soon realised why the gardening books
suggest that the beginner starts on a small scale. The weeds got the
better of me on that scale. I would have had to give up teaching to
get the time to properly maintain an acre of fruit and vegetables.

When I took up the job of Principal of St George's National
School in Balbriggan, Co. Dublin in 1983, I put my eye on the
school lawn as a prospective vegetable patch. All went well for a
while, but the lack of pathways and the mucky shoes meant I was
very unpopular with the school cleaner! In due course I had the
garden landscaped with permanent pathways and divided into beds

1

so the pupils could help tend it without having to stand on the soil.

By the time I had saved up enough money to put a deposit on a house in Balbriggan in 1987, I had learned the hard way that you do not need a large space in which to grow a wide range of fruit and vegetables. The back garden of the house I bought was 20 ft wide by 40 ft long. More significantly, it was a south-facing garden, which was a decisive factor in my buying the location for what has become known as Trevor's Kitchen Garden.

GROWING FOOD IN A SMALL GARDEN HAS ITS ATTRACTIONS

I know that some houses have smaller gardens or no gardens at all. Having worked in larger plots growing fruit and vegetables, it was a relief to be able to micro-manage this smaller space. The wonders of nature can be appreciated at any scale – visiting a rainforest or contemplating a radish plant.

Take, for example, the tiny woodlice which inhabit the compost bin. They are detritivores, conveniently feeding on dead plant matter, and their faeces in turn sustains a myriad of soil microbes which are vital if soil is to grow healthy plants. They are also called 'armadillo bugs' (from the Spanish meaning 'little armoured one') as they look like that larger forest animal, the armadillo. Their relatives during the Permian and Triassic Ages, around 230 million years ago, included the Typothorax, but this creature was the size and shape of a Volkswagen Beetle, with a crocodile's tail, and weighed the same as a car. The Typothorax only ate plant material, just as the woodlouse does now. However, today the tiny modern look-a-like of the Typothorax could be tidying up your window box and keeping your soil fauna and flora healthy. As the Swedish botanist Carl Linnaeus (1717–1778) observed so eloquently in Latin, 'Natura in minimis maxime miranda' or 'Nature is at its most awesome in miniature form.'

Even in a small growing area, one is never done with learning about and experimenting with techniques, planting times and varieties of seeds to sow. I had a notion when I began my suburban kitchen garden that, some day in the future, I would not have a 20 ft x 40 ft patch but instead a larger 200 ft x 400 ft holding of growing space, perhaps in the form of an allotment. In other words, if I could learn how to grow a wide diversity of food crops in a small garden, then I would have the knowledge to scale up this diversity of produce on a larger holding. Instead of having space for one apple tree and two blackcurrant bushes, I imagined someday having space for ten apple trees and twenty blackcurrant bushes.

However, I am now very happy where I am. Over the years, I have developed an appreciation for the particular attraction which comes with growing a diverse range of food in a small space just outside the kitchen door. For a start, it does not take as much time as would a larger plot. Second, many people who visit are surprised that such a variety of food crops can be grown in such a small space while still leaving space for a patio, a pond, roses, paths, a garden shed, a wood store, various compost containers and a lawn (a very small one, mind you).

Having very few specimens of a wide variety of fruit and vegetables, many of which are just not stocked in the supermarkets, is more than interesting. It also points to maintaining a diverse diet and good health.

KITCHEN GARDENING IS A KEY TO MORE DIVERSITY IN OUR DIET

The human species evolved long before agriculture as we know it. Our digestive systems are the result of thousands of years of eating a multitude of available berries, nuts, plants and only rarely meat or fish, whenever we could catch or trap an animal or a fish. Once populations grew and there were too many of us to roam around foraging, agriculture became the next best way of feeding ourselves.

Anthropologists have examined human skeletons of hunter-gatherers and found they were larger, suggesting they had healthier diets compared to our more modern agricultural ancestors. What this tells me is that it is not enough to have good fresh unprocessed organic food, as the first farmers enjoyed; what is also important is the diversity of food types which would naturally be eaten if you were foraging rather than cultivating crops and keeping livestock.

Below is a table showing a time line of the human diet:

500,000 BC	early man using stone implements
50,000 BC	first use of fire by man
20,000 BC	animal skins used for clothing
8,000 BC	agriculture begins in the Middle East
7,000 BC	first humans in Ireland foraging, hunting and living near lakes and rivers
4,000 BC	first records of agriculture in Ireland when Neolithic farmers arrive
3,000 BC	farming communities organised enough to build Newgrange

I am not suggesting we live like hunter-gatherers. However, kitchen gardening can help in extending the diversity of foods in our diet, since supermarkets carry a limited range of fresh produce, as any seed catalogue will testify.

KITCHEN GARDENING HELPS US TO APPRECIATE FARMING

Large-scale commercial farming is a very different discipline from small-scale kitchen gardening. The farmer buys seeds and plant plugs (seedlings in modules of compost) in bulk, whilst the kitchen gardener sows individual seeds, little and often. For example, just because a packet of rocket contains 1,000 seeds does not mean they must all be planted at once. Over the years I have tried and tested ways to grow exactly what I need and I store unused seeds for the next time or, better still, give them away or swap them with another kitchen gardener. Our own health and future food security requires that everyone should to some extent be familiar and ideally involved in how food is produced. This book is a handbook to help more of us enjoy growing some of the food we like to eat.

IF WE HAVE TO GROW FOOD, WE MAY AS WELL ENJOY OURSELVES

Without sounding too dramatic, we are a people in transition. How we keep warm, travel, learn or re-learn life skills, and feed and enjoy ourselves are all parts of that transition. In some respects we are voyaging into the unknown. In other ways, not too much imagination is required to picture life in a post-fossil-fuel society.

Take an old map of any town or village in the 1700s. Rob Hopkins, the founder of the Transition Towns movement, recently tweeted about a 1793 map of Guildford (see below), the county town of Surrey in England, with the introduction 'What it looks like when food grows everywhere' (www.transitionculture.org).

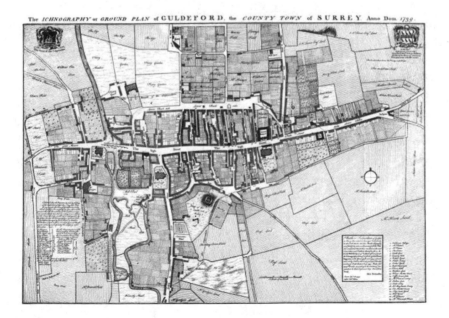

After noting the housing and roadways, the map shows the next greatest land use was an extensive tapestry of gardens and orchards attached to schools, hospitals, prisons, monasteries and behind every domestic dwelling. Placenames often reflected this gardening land use. My favourite on that map is 'Walnut Tree Close'.

ABOUT THIS BOOK

The story behind each month

I was surprised, when I did some research, at how the names we use for each month often originated from farming activity or a festival related to food and farming. Each month in the book begins with a look at why the month ahead is so named, in various languages, including Irish.

Work each week in the garden

Each week in the garden has its own chapter, beginning with the First Week in February, the start of spring in Ireland (Lá 'le Bríde). The first part of each chapter describes a seasonal task which I undertake at that time in my own garden, either composting, seed sowing, pruning, chopping and storing firewood, etc.

Weekly food-related topics

The second half of each chapter, 'The Bigger Picture', takes a look at a topical food-related issue which I am reminded of at that particular time of year, for example, the tradition of planting potatoes on St Patrick's Day in the Second Week in March or, in the Third Week in December, how your kitchen garden can save you money around Christmas.

Thoughts from other kitchen gardeners

At intervals throughout the book, at the end of each month, two other kitchen gardeners answer questions about their own gardens, the tools they use and the food they like to grow. These growers are from around the country and are locally renowned and sometimes internationally known personalities. Their contributions add a sense of community to the book, as well as offering different perspectives on the motivations and pleasures of maintaining a kitchen garden.

Call to action

No longer are kitchen gardening and allotmenteering pastimes only. They are fast becoming ways for families to save money, for communities to become more resilient and for countries to be more prepared for threats to food security. Now is the time to take more action. We must not be caught unawares, as happened when the financial bubble burst. As sure as eggs are eggs, the food bubble will burst too. Growing more of our own food and supporting local farmers and food producers is the obvious way to make our communities resilient and ensure that Ireland is nutritionally secure. This book sets out to help make that transition to a food secure and healthier future.

Visiting other kitchen gardens

This book also indicates places to visit around Ireland where you can see fruit and vegetables growing in the conditions which are typical in that locality. The best places are often organic centres, where courses are run on topics from designing a kitchen garden to pruning fruit trees. Many such gardens and organic centres are marked on a map printed towards the end of the book in the 'Bigger Picture' section of the First Week in November.

Planning a garden

T O PLAN a new garden is to be part of a sacred tradition going back over 20,000 years. The Ancient Egyptians believed that the garden was where heaven and earth were joined, where people could converse with each other and with their gods. Plans of those early Egyptian gardens can still be seen today.

I recall the excitement of acquiring a patch of land about twenty years ago, measuring it, noting the dimensions and roughly drawing on paper a garden map to the scale of the garden-to-be. In my case, I needed two maps, so I could plan a front and a back garden.

On a separate sheet of paper, I listed the desirable components of the garden for me: four vegetable patches for a four-year rotation of annual crops, fruit patches, a garden shed site, a compost bin location, and so on.

A SHORT CUT FOR EARLY RESULTS

If this all-in-one grand plan cannot be undertaken in one go, then be selective. For example, one or more raised beds can be started, taking up no more than 1 sq. m. If you have space for a 4 sq. m. raised bed, then better still. Four planks, at least 1 m long each, can be nailed together to make the square boundary of a raised bed. Put this square on a patch of soil or on part of the lawn which gets good light. To kill off the grass at the base, layer some cardboard or some sheets of newsprint on the grass and fill the raised bed with soil. Mix in the compost if the soil needs organic matter. Even a small child could reach in to the centre of such a raised bed, so there is no need to walk on, and compress, the soil in it. A good crop to begin with is potatoes. If space is available for four such raised beds, then a diversity of crops can be cultivated organically. I have four such raised beds, each 4 sq. m. in area (see my back garden plan below). Year by year, your productive garden can be developed. Some folks I know have enough raised beds to operate a five-, nine- or twelve-year rotation. I have only space for a four-year rotation, and organic researchers tell me a four-year system is the minimum to avoid any build-up of plant diseases. (See the Second Week in February for more information about rotating crops.)

PLANNING THE BACK GARDEN

Sunshine

Before taking out a mortgage to buy my home, I checked to see which parts of the garden got the most and least sunshine. Lucky for me, the larger garden at the back was south facing. In due course, my friendly neighbour and I had a dividing wall built. On my side, the wall is west facing and useful for fruit trees. The fig and plum trees which grow against it benefit from the sun's heat, both during the day and at night when the warmth is slowly released.

Pathways

Every couple of days, when I get to empty kitchen peelings and tea leaves, etc. in the compost tumbler beside the wood store, I am thankful for the paths I laid over twenty years ago. Likewise, weather does not deter me when I venture out to collect firewood or ingredients for a meal. Gardening can be mucky, but with durable paths harvesting can be as clean as the aisle of any supermarket, with the added bonus of fresh air and birdsong.

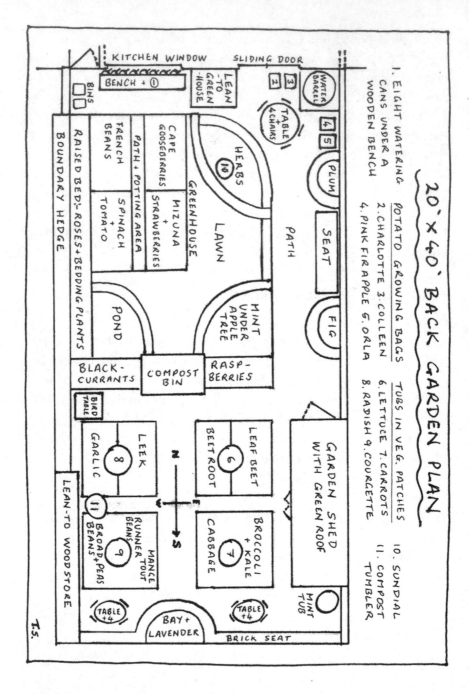

20' x 40' BACK GARDEN PLAN

1. EIGHT WATERING
   CANS UNDER A
   WOODEN BENCH

   POTATO GROWING BAGS
   2. CHARLOTTE 3. COLLEEN
   4. PINK FIR APPLE 5. ORLA

   TUBS IN VEG. PATCHES
   6. LETTUCE 7. CARROTS
   8. RADISH 9. COURGETTE

   10. SUNDIAL
   11. COMPOST
       TUMBLER

KITCHEN WINDOW   SLIDING DOOR

BENCH + ①

BINS

LEAN
-TO GREEN
-HOUSE

WATER BARREL

②
③

TABLE + 4 CHAIRS

④ ⑤

PLUM

BOUNDARY HEDGE

RAISED BED:- ROSES + BEDDING PLANTS

FRENCH BEANS

PATH + POTTING AREA

CAPE GOOSEBERRIES

MIZUNA + STRAWBERRIES

SPINACH + TOMATO

GREENHOUSE

HERBS ⑩

LAWN

PATH

SEAT

FIG

POND

MINT UNDER APPLE TREE

BLACK-CURRANTS

COMPOST BIN

RASP-BERRIES

BIRD TABLE

GARLIC ⑧

LEEK

BEET ROOT ⑥

LEAF BEET

GARDEN SHED WITH GREEN ROOF

LEAN-TO WOODSTORE

⑪

BROAD BEANS + PEAS

RUNNER BEANS ⑨

MANGE TOUT

N
W   E
S

CABBAGE

BROCCOLI + KALE ⑦

MINT TUB

TABLE + 4

BAY + LAVENDER

TABLE + 4

BRICK SEAT

T.S.

10

Aesthetics

Garden design is, for me, primarily a matter of practicalities, but I enjoy symmetry too. The curved edging around some beds softens the straight lines elsewhere. These curved lines are laid as red brick borders. This red brick also complements the red brick from which the central compost bin is built.

Compost

Initially, the compost bin was made of wood, which lasted about seven years before it started to disintegrate. The more recent brick structure both looks well and will not need replacing any time soon, hopefully.

The greenhouse

Another recent addition is the greenhouse. Initially my lean-to greenhouse (also called the 'telephone box' by local wits!) was sufficient for growing two tomato plants in boxes of fresh soil each year. Fortune smiled on me when I turned fifty, as some Green friends clubbed together for my birthday and bought me a state-of-the-art greenhouse with an automatic ventilation system built in. This has increased the garden's productivity and given me an indoor potting area too.

Shed and wood store

Other structures like the garden shed and wood store were later additions also. They are described further in the Fourth Week in July and the Fourth Week in December respectively.

PLANNING THE FRONT GARDEN

The front garden is more often in shade as it is on the north side of the house. As it is also three quarters the size of the back garden, it is less productive in terms of growing food.

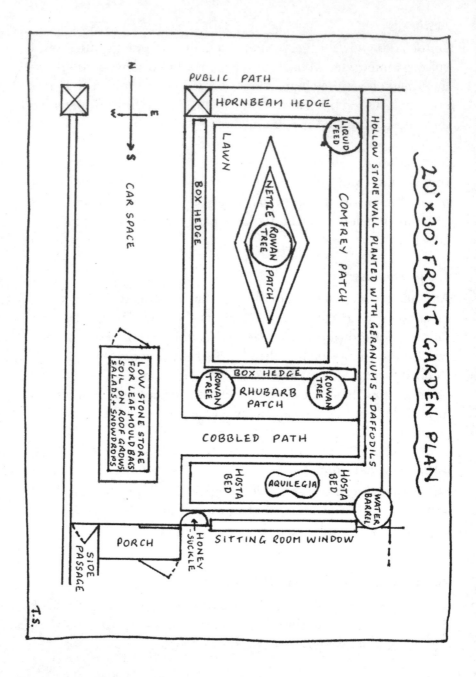

20' x 30' FRONT GARDEN PLAN

PUBLIC PATH

HORNBEAM HEDGE

N
W — E
S

CAR SPACE

LAWN

BOX HEDGE

LIQUID FEED

COMFREY PATCH

HOLLOW STONE WALL PLANTED WITH GERANIUMS + DAFFODILS

NETTLE PATCH

ROWAN TREE

BOX HEDGE

ROWAN TREE

RHUBARB PATCH

ROWAN TREE

LOW STONE STORE FOR LEAF MOULD BAGS SOIL ON ROOF GROWS SALADS + SNOWDROPS

COBBLED PATH

HOSTA BED

AQUILEGIA

HOSTA BED

WATER BARREL

SIDE PASSAGE

PORCH

HONEY-SUCKLE

SITTING ROOM WINDOW

T.S.

12

Trees

However, wildlife has good food sources in the form of three rowan trees, which generously produce red berries in the autumn. This little copse attracts sparrows, starlings, blackbirds, thrushes, bullfinches, chaffinches, several species of tits, including long-tailed tits, and the occasional sparrow hawk. The hornbeam hedge, nettle patch and even the fragrant honeysuckle at the front door are alive with birdlife, especially when I replenish the bird feeders and hang new fat balls from the trees.

Food

In essence, the front garden is more of a wildlife garden, but it also complements the main food production area at the back. Rhubarb does reasonably well here, although it is growing in a shady patch. Lamb's lettuce and rocket self-seed on any bare patches of soil. Foraging in the front garden can therefore yield interesting additional ingredients for salads.

Water

The water barrel collects rain water, just as the barrel in the back garden collects water from the south-sloping half of the roof. The other barrel near the hornbeam hedge is for making liquid feed for both gardens.

Comfrey

The comfrey patch is decorative when it produces purple flowers much loved by bees. Its main role, however, is as a compost ingredient. It grows so fast it can be harvested three times a year. The leaves are stuffed in the liquid feed barrel and soaked in water (see Third Week in February).

Leaf mould

The best looking type of natural mulch to suppress weed growth is leaf mould (see Second Week in December). Bags of fallen leaves are bagged and stored away in what was a stone built small trailer garage. The roof is flat and covered with soil. This curious structure in the front garden looks like a raised bed at first glance. Some passers-by have wondered if it is a nuclear fall-out shelter – it is not!

Feabhra ❧ February

The Month of Februa, the Roman Festival of Purification

THE ANCIENT ROMANS celebrated the festival of Februa or Februatio, which was a time of ritual washing, purging and purification on the fifteenth of the month. It is this festival which is recalled by the name of the month in both Irish and English. The Anglo-Saxons may have felt the need for some ritual washing at this time of year as their name for February was Solmonath, which translates as 'mud month'.

In Ireland, Lá 'le Bríde (St Brigid's Day), celebrated on 1 February, is the foremost festival of the month. More than any other Irish saint, Brigid was revered by both the pagan and later Christian traditions. The older goddess Brigid is associated with the gifts of poetry, healing and smith craft. She is also identified with nurturing, fertility and fire. Brigid, the saint, established her abbey and church in Cill Dara (Kildare), meaning 'the church of oak', in around 480 AD. This was an acclaimed centre of worship, culture and hospitality, with a farm and kitchen garden big enough to feed many residents and visitors alike.

The Celtic festival of Imbolc also falls at the start of February and marks the time to emerge from darkness and begin working outdoors. Brigid, as goddess of fire, heralds this new beginning to the agricultural year. There was a strong tradition of babies being born at this time, their conceptions having taken place at the previous festival of Bealtaine (1 May). Chances of survival were stronger for children born at this time as their births coincided with the first sheep's milk of the year. With a higher fat content than

15

cow's milk, this new food was a welcome delicacy for lactating mothers. Some translate *Imbolc* as 'in the belly of the mother', while others say it means 'ewe's milk'. One thing we all hope is that Mother Earth is stirring again for another year of growing.

An overview of the work ahead in the garden this month:
Sow out: early peas, broad beans, spinach, Jerusalem artichokes.
Sow under glass: lettuce, carrots, radish, turnips.
Harvest: winter cabbages, cauliflowers, Brussels sprouts and leeks.

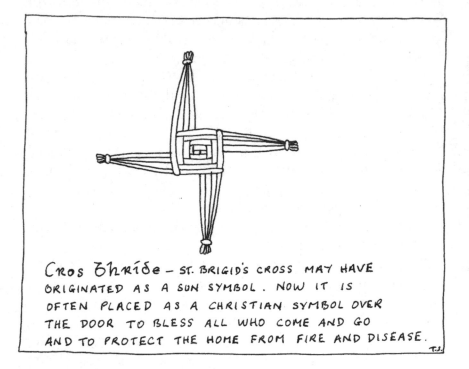

Cros Bhríde – ST. BRIGID'S CROSS MAY HAVE ORIGINATED AS A SUN SYMBOL. NOW IT IS OFTEN PLACED AS A CHRISTIAN SYMBOL OVER THE DOOR TO BLESS ALL WHO COME AND GO AND TO PROTECT THE HOME FROM FIRE AND DISEASE.

🍂 FIRST WEEK IN FEBRUARY 🍂

A new year in the kitchen garden

'Anois teacht an Earraigh, beidh an lá ag dul chun síneadh,
Agus tar éis na Féile Bríde, ardóidh mé mo sheol.'
(Ó Raifteirí, 1784–1834)

THE song 'Cill Aodáin' by Ó Raifteirí, the blind poet, tells us that St Brigid's Day, 1 February, heralds the coming of spring. This may be hard to accept as the garden can appear a little dismal and many trees are still not in leaf at this time. However, there are certain jobs that can be done before the really busy period arrives later in spring.

GET A CROP OF EARLIER THAN NORMAL RHUBARB BY 'FORCING'

If you have no rhubarb yet in your garden, then identify a patch for growing it, and beg or buy a crown for planting this spring. This you should grow without harvesting the first year to let it become established. In the second year some modest harvesting of a few stalks can begin. In year three the plant should be robust enough to withstand 'forcing', but don't force the same crown every year as the plant may become weakened if it is not rested for a year or two. Having a few rhubarb crowns means a different crown each year can be chosen for forcing.

'Forcing' is the term for fooling a plant into thinking it is so far underground that it musters all its energy to reach light by growing faster than usual. By doing this, fresh shoots are produced which are useful at this time (and sweeter than later stalks), when there is little else fresh from the garden. In the days before plentiful transport and heating fuel, and abundant importation of fresh and not-so-

17

fresh fruit and vegetables, 'forcing' was a necessary part of year-round production in the kitchen garden. The iconic 'forcing pot' was a common sight in Victorian times to bring on early harvests of rhubarb and sea kale. Likewise, crowns of asparagus and chicory were lifted from outside and brought into darkened sheds where they put on a spurt of growth.

If you are not in the way of acquiring a forcing pot, then an upturned black bucket or bin will do the job just as well. Cover a sprouting rhubarb crown with the bucket and block out any chinks of light by earthing up around the pot. After a couple of weeks check progress by lifting the pot. Harvest the pale pink shoots when they are 15–30 cm (6 inches to a foot) high. If left in the dark longer than a month, the plant will suffer and the precious early harvest will deteriorate.

OTHER JOBS FOR THE WEEK THAT IS IN IT:

This may take longer than a week, but now is a good time to acquire or construct a garden shed. I designed mine on paper first, and bought the rough wood and other fixtures, as I liked the idea of building a lean-to structure with a living roof. All the plants growing on the roof arrived there naturally; nothing was planted by human hands. It is therefore a fascinating reservoir of local biodiversity. It includes ivy, which is probably not a good idea as the roots of ivy are renowned for wrecking buildings. However, I am keeping the ivy in check and the shed has been waterproof for over fifteen years now, so fingers crossed for the future. A coat of non-toxic water-based wood preserver on all exposed surfaces greatly prolongs the life of any outdoor wooden structure in our temperate climate. Ideally, this should be applied annually to exposed wood after it has enjoyed some fine weather for a few days so the wood is dry enough to soak up the preservative.

Whether you have a shed or not, now is the time to assemble

seed trays, pots (used coffee-to-go cups work fine also), seed compost, etc. In the next few weeks, this equipment will be put to good use.

🌿 Sow broad beans and an early pea cultivar such as 'Early Onward'.

🌿 Arrange main crop potatoes in egg boxes, 'rose end' up, on windowsills indoors to sprout.

GRASS
ROOFED
SHED
CRÓ
CEANN
TUÍ

The Bigger Picture:
Some inspirational growers I have met

John Peterson: I met John in Modena, Italy, at the Organic World Congress in June 2008. Born in 1949 in Illinois, USA on a conventional farm – in other words, a farm wholly dependent on agricultural chemicals – the Peterson farm went the expansion route until financial calamity arrived in the 1980s and almost closed the farm down for good. While deep in despair, John heard from city folk in Chicago (a two-hour drive away) that they wanted to be partners with an organic farmer who could supply them with fresh fruit and vegetables. John set about becoming that partner and has not looked back. About ninety families now pay John the seed capital he needs in the spring to sow the crops they will be eating. This co-operative venture is known as Community Supported Agriculture (CSA). Hundreds of farmers in the USA are becoming CSA partners. CSAs are starting up elsewhere too. For instance, Skerries in Co. Dublin now has a vibrant CSA project. John has diversified by producing a documentary about his odyssey called *The Real Dirt on Farmer John* which I bought and enjoyed. He has also published *Farmer John's Cookbook – The Real Dirt on Vegetables*, which is a great read and full of seasonal recipes. His CSA website is www.angelicorganics.com.

Joy Larkcom: I met Joy at Waterford Institute of Technology, Ireland, where both of us were making presentations at the inaugural Grow It Yourself (GIY) Ireland Conference in 2009. Joy, who is from Wellesbourne in Warwickshire, England, but now lives in Co. Cork, is truly a pioneering grower and writer. In 1974, she published *Vegetables from Small Gardens*, the first of many books. In 1976, she and her husband Don and their two children embarked on a 'grand vegetable tour' of Europe, from Holland to Hungary, sampling vegetables and collecting seeds, which were added to the Vegetable Gene Bank at Wellesbourne when they returned to England. As a result of this work, rocket salad and Lollo Rosso lettuce from Italy are widely available. It is fair to say that Joy popularised the 'cut-and-come-again' salads (i.e. the leaves can be picked and the plant left to continue growing), after travelling worldwide to countries like China and Australia. In 1993, Joy won the Royal Horticultural Society Garden Writer of the Year Award.

John Seymour: I met John in Trinity College Dublin (TCD) in 1992. I had been inspired to get involved in growing food when I read his famous book *The Complete Book of Self-Sufficiency* as a teenager in the 1970s. Now that John has passed on, my copy, signed when we met in TCD, is a most treasured possession. A graduate of agricultural college in England, John began farm work in 1930 in Essex when 100 acres employed five extra hands; in other words, six families were supported. By 1992, the farm had expanded to 700 acres but sadly only employed three men and the old farmhouse had been sold. By 1992 just wheat and barley were grown there using artificial fertilisers and sprays. John worked around England and Africa before settling in Co. Wexford, Ireland with his wife. Will Sutherland continues his pioneering work in Ireland, teaching and empowering people to be more self-reliant.

Iain Tolhurst: I met Iain on his organic farm in Oxfordshire, England when I made an appointment to visit his enterprise along with horticulturalist Stiofán Nutty and photographer Ciarán Finn, who were both working with me in the Department of Agriculture, Fisheries and Food at the time. Iain has been farming since 1976 and his current eighteen-acre holding has been leased since around 1990. His is the first farm in the world to adopt the Stockfree Organic Standard, administered by the UK Soil Association. This requires extensive crop rotations, using green manures for building fertility and retaining nutrients. At any given time, one third of the land is in resting mode. Iain told me that he sees himself as a compost maker who grows food as a sideline. If he takes out 100 tonnes of vegetables a year, 100 tonnes of compost has to be returned to the soil. His customers buy a box of seasonal vegetables every week. A scientific study of the carbon footprint of the farm showed his produce to be 90 per cent more efficient than conventional supermarket vegetables (according to Professor Tim Jackson, *Newsnight*, BBC, March 2007). See www.tolhurstorganic.co.uk.

Klaus Laitenberger: I met Klaus at the launch of his book *Vegetables for the Irish Garden* at the Cultivate Centre in Andrew St, Dublin. His book is a valuable resource for growers in Ireland as

21

the advice is based on local conditions of soil and climate. For instance, Klaus advises that sowing times are later in Ireland than recommended in most non-Irish gardening books and on seed packets. Klaus grows on a 20 m x 10 m patch in the north-west of the country. This is adequate for all his family's needs. Klaus came to Ireland in 1999 and had an important part in developing the Organic Centre at Rossinver, Co. Leitrim, helping it to become the centre for organic horticulture training and demonstration it is today. He is now, along with Joy Larkcom and others, a patron of the exciting new Grow It Yourself (GIY) movement. For more information, see www.giyireland.com and www.milkwoodfarm.com.

Geraldine O'Toole and Laura Turner: I have known Laura for many years as both of us were involved in the establishment of the National Ecology Centre, called Sonairte, near Laytown, Co. Meath in the 1980s. Geraldine has been very involved in Sonairte over the last number of years as well. Both Laura and Geraldine are fantastic at sowing seed and nurturing plants. I sell many of these vegetable, fruit and flowering plants and herbs at Balbriggan Fish and Farmers' Market in George's Square, Balbriggan every Friday morning. I am always relieved and delighted to get reports from customers to say the plants they bought previously are growing better than they would normally expect. Apart from the horticultural skills of Laura and Geraldine and all who work at Sonairte, I do believe the root development of plants reared organically has to be strong and robust, as artificial fertilisers are not permissible on an organic holding. I would be interested in any scientific comparison between organic and non-organic nursery stock root development. See www.sonairte.ie.

Time to prune, keep the bird table in order and plan rotation

'Parlement of Foules
For this was on seynt Volantynys day
When euery bryd comyth there to chese his make.'
(Geoffrey Chaucer, 1382)

MOST, BUT NOT ALL, FRUIT CAN BE PRUNED BEFORE LEAVES APPEAR

PRUNING is not a complicated job. Such a range of tools and 'tricks of the trade' have developed that the basic skill of pruning is sometimes lost. If you answer yes to any of the questions below, then pruning is called for:

🍂 Do I need to reduce the spread of the tree or bush?

🍂 Do I need to remove branches to make fruit picking easier?

🍂 Could the tree do with a prune to give it a more pleasant shape?

🍂 Are there dead branches or diseased boughs which cannot be treated?

🍂 Do I want to stimulate new growth by removing raspberry canes which fruited last year, etc.?

However, if you have a plum tree or any member of the cherry family, the only time to prune these trees is in mid-summer when the sap has risen and the trees are in leaf. I made the mistake of pruning a plum tree in February. It developed silver leaf and died. However, the apple tree, blackcurrant bushes and raspberry canes need pruning now, so they do not spread too much in my small garden.

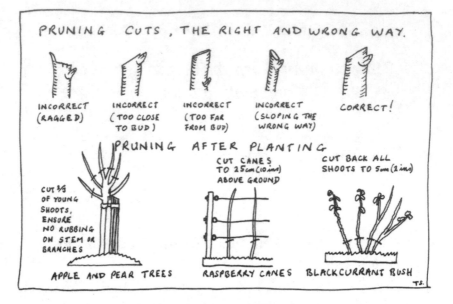

PRUNING CUTS, THE RIGHT AND WRONG WAY.

INCORRECT (RAGGED)

INCORRECT (TOO CLOSE TO BUD)

INCORRECT (TOO FAR FROM BUD)

INCORRECT (SLOPING THE WRONG WAY)

CORRECT!

PRUNING AFTER PLANTING

CUT ⅓ OF YOUNG SHOOTS, ENSURE NO RUBBING ON STEM OR BRANCHES

CUT CANES TO 25cm (10ins) ABOVE GROUND

CUT BACK ALL SHOOTS TO 5cm (2ins)

APPLE AND PEAR TREES

RASPBERRY CANES

BLACKCURRANT BUSH

OTHER JOBS FOR THE WEEK THAT IS IN IT:

🍃 There are various views on feeding the birds once spring arrives and their natural food supplies increase. In my experience, the continuous feeding keeps the insectivore- and mollusc-eating birds in the garden and they feed on aphids, etc., as well as visiting the bird table. The feeding in spring also helps parent birds to keep their strength up so they can rear a good brood of chicks, who in turn will become allies in the garden. In Sonairte's walled garden, we have noticed a reduced aphid problem ever since we continued feeding the birds there, even in summer.

The Bigger Picture:
A Valentine's message which helps plan a crop rotation

There is no denying 'People love bunches of roses', especially if you grow them yourself. These words also form a useful acronym

24

and concentrate the mind when planning a rotation:

1. **P**eople – potatoes (tomatoes and peppers are also members of this family)
2. **L**ove – legumes (peas and beans)
3. **B**unches – brassicas (cabbage, kale, Brussels sprouts, radish, turnip, swede, kohlrabi, etc.)
4. **O**f – onions (also garlic, leeks, shallots, scallions)
5. **R**oses – roots (carrots, parsley, parsnips, beetroot)

In my small garden, I can manage four plots, which I am told is the minimum. Even so, other people get away with a three-plot rotation, i.e. potatoes, brassicas and then all other vegetables. Some key factors include giving ground which grew potatoes a break from that crop so that pests like eelworm are prevented from multiplying. Likewise, ground which grew brassicas needs a break to thwart the disease clubroot, which takes about twenty years to eradicate if it gets a hold in a garden. Imagine not growing cabbage for twenty years! Onions need to be rotated to avoid white rot.

Peas and beans seem to be disease resistant, but they are rotated because they leave behind nitrogen in the soil, which they harnessed naturally from the air. This benefits the nitrogen-hungry brassicas, which are grown where the legumes had grown the previous year.

Potatoes are listed first because the potato plot is the first to be sown. Most of the compost is dug in before the potato seed is planted. Potatoes are hardy and are better at dealing with composted soil than other crops. Root crops especially need fine soil to prevent their roots forking. This is why root crops are at the end of the rotation acronym.

Although pest and disease control is the main benefit of crop rotation, there are other important advantages. Not all crops require the same types of soil preparation and cultivation, while compost and lime applications also vary. Brassicas sometimes need some lime sprinkled on their plot before planting as they do better in alkaline soil.

After a while, all gardeners develop their own particular rotation depending on what crops grow well and what crops they like to eat. In my case, I grow potatoes in bags filled with soil from the potato patch, which in my case grows onions, garlic and leeks. In the last plot, I fill large pots from the fourth plot – the roots plot – to grow carrots and salads. Meanwhile, I grow beetroot, chard and spinach in the roots plot.

The basic rule is to start simply and to allow your taste buds and common sense guide you over time.

Happy Valentine's Day!

The freshest, tastiest leafy vegetables will be in your garden

'Of all the changes to our food system that go under the heading "The Western Diet", the shift from a food chain with green plants at its base to one based on seeds may be the most far reaching of all.'

(Michael Pollan, *In Defence of Food*, 2008)

WESTERN people's reliance on a globalised food system has reduced our choices. Gone are the crop varieties (numerous varieties of apples, tomatoes, peas, beans, salads, potatoes, courgettes, etc.) which do not satisfy the long shelf-life requirements of international wholesalers and retailers. One hundred and twenty years ago there were one hundred and twenty varieties of tall garden pea available in Ireland and Britain; today you would be lucky to find fresh garden peas of any variety in a shop. Half of all broccoli in the USA is the one variety – 'Marathon' – grown mainly for its uniformity of shape and size.

Another trend has been that less and less leafy vegetables are stocked in shops because they wilt more quickly than other fresh produce like onions or carrots. Humans have evolved to require leafy vegetables for good health. They provide anti-oxidants, phytochemicals, fibre and essential omega-3 fatty acids. Total reliance on shop-bought food provides a rich mainly seed- or grain-based diet. Meat is often grain fed, bread is made from grain and all soya products in effect come from seeds. Growing and eating many leafy vegetable varieties in your own food-growing area is more than interesting; it is vital for optimum health.

Heads of cabbage can be easily grown with some care, but in my small space a 'come-and-cut-again' variety ensures I have a fresh green vegetable in the quantity I want when I want it. My favourite variety, 'everlasting cabbage', was obtained by post from www.irishseedsavers.ie.

BUY OR 'BORROW' A CUTTING OF EVERLASTING CABBAGE

I have lost count of the number of everlasting cabbage cuttings I have given away. Former President of Ireland Mary McAleese was happy to get a cutting to plant when we met at the GIY Ireland stand at Bloom* in 2011. I have not used rooting powder, which promotes root growth, but one could. After sticking the cutting where you want it to grow outdoors (or in a pot of soil if the final planting spot is not ready yet), firm it in and keep the soil moist but not too wet. Do not worry when you see the outer leaves wilt initially. After a week or two the inner centre of the cutting will

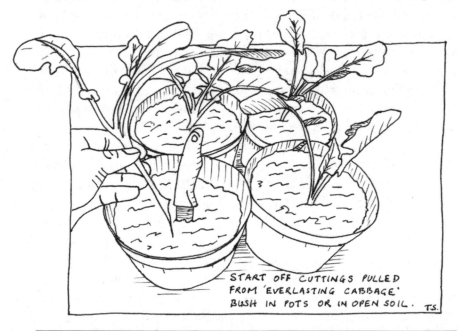

START OFF CUTTINGS PULLED FROM 'EVERLASTING CABBAGE' BUSH IN POTS OR IN OPEN SOIL. T.S.

---

* Ireland's largest gardening and food event, held annually in Dublin.

start to grow new leaves and this shows that roots are forming from the cutting below the surface. Let the plant establish itself as a 2 ft-high bush at least before harvesting a few leaves for cooking.

To cook, I steam the leaves for around the same length of time I would steam potatoes, maybe slightly less. Personally, I like a few drops of soya sauce when serving this very sweet-tasting leafy green vegetable, which goes well with any meal.

OTHER JOBS FOR THE WEEK THAT IS IN IT:

- Sow onion seeds and tomato seeds in a seed tray on a windowsill, ideally in a heated propagator.
- Take cuttings of hardwood herbs like rosemary to pot up as gifts for friends.
- Continue planting fruit trees, bushes and canes.
- If the weather is mild, early sowing of parsnip seed and onion sets can happen now.

The Bigger Picture:
Role of comfrey in organic growing

I am very grateful to Kathryn Marsh, a neighbour and organic growing pioneer, for giving me some root pieces of 'Bocking 14', a variety of comfrey which gives me a regular supply of potash and some nitrogen and phosphorus, whether I use the leaves in compost, as a mulch or make a comfrey liquid feed.

In case you are wondering, Bocking is a town in Essex, England, which, up to 1985, was the location of the Henry Doubleday Research Association trial ground (known today as Garden Organic and based at Ryton in Warwickshire). A number of Russian comfrey cultivars were grown there and tested for qualities such as levels of potash, general yield and manageability for a grower. Each cultivar had a number. Bocking 4 has good potash levels, with thick stems and violet flowers. Bocking 14 has good potash levels also, but thinner stems and mauve flowers. By the way, bees love the flowers, which is reason enough to grow it, I would say.

THE COMFREY CALENDAR

Comfrey dies down and is dormant from late November to late January in my garden. Once the root is dormant, it can be planted in well-composted soil. Keep the bed weed free until the comfrey leaves are big enough to block out light and so suppress weeds. Not everyone leaves it to flower before cutting each plant back to the ground, from where it quickly sprouts up again. Once the flowers wilt, I harvest the leaves from the five plants in my front garden, where they grow perennially alongside a stone wall, about three times during each growing season.

MAKING LIQUID FEED

Comfrey roots are so deep that they essentially 'mop up' many soil nutrients which have been leached away due to rainfall. Shallower rooted plants cannot reach deeply enough to benefit from these leached nutrients. The comfrey leaves are therefore rich in these nutrients in a form which other plants find easy to take up as the comfrey decomposes. My preferred use of comfrey is as a comfrey liquid feed. I bought a water butt, but not to collect rainwater. It lives on a pedestal beside the comfrey patch behind a hornbeam hedge in the front garden. I pile the comfrey leaves into this barrel, which has a tap. I top it up with water (generally rain water from another water butt), and leave it for a month or so with the lid in place, as it would not appeal as a perfume, shall we say. A full barrel gives me more than enough liquid feed for the year. I drain off the liquid feed into empty plastic bottles and store it. Before I water plants with rainwater, I add half a litre of liquid feed to each 8-litre watering can and stir with a stick.

OTHER USES FOR 'BOCKING 14' COMFREY

After the earlier spring batch of liquid feed, with two more harvests of comfrey leaves left in the growing year, I have comfrey leaves to spare. Some are used as mulch around fruit bushes and on vegetable plots. If slugs are around, they can be caught and expelled easily as they like to 'hide' under these comfrey leaves. The comfrey is a good addition to the compost heap, of course. Some growers make a comfrey leaf mould compost, but I have yet to try this. There are books written about this wonder plant. A place to start enquiring would be www.gardenorganic.org.uk.

🍂 FOURTH WEEK IN FEBRUARY 🍂

Time to kick back and enjoy nature's work on the ground

'Down by the glenside I met an old woman;
A-plucking young nettles, she ne'er saw me comin'
I listened a while to the song she was hummin' –
"Glory-o, glory-o to the Bould Fenian Men."'

(Peadar Kearney)

SOMETIMES it pays not to be too fastidious in the kitchen garden, denying anything which grows wild a chance to develop. After all, those vegetables on which we lavish such care were, in the past, wild and went unnoticed, unless a hungry forager, or hunter–gatherer, stumbled upon a specimen like wild cabbage or wild strawberry or any number of wild plants we cultivate today as herbs, fruit and vegetables.

It pays to do some homework about the edibility of what are often dismissed as 'weeds'. The most overlooked wild plant is the nettle, of which there are three species in Ireland. But it is the common stinging nettle which deserves more attention. The tender shoots are at their best now and through March and April. Aside from their health-giving properties like 'cleansing the blood', nettle soup or any other nettle dish brings with it the taste and satisfaction of gathering food from the wild, especially when there is a bit of a 'hungry gap' amongst locally cultivated fruit and vegetables.

Just remember, before you don those Marigold rubber gloves to harvest your stinging nettle tips, to leave enough behind for some of our rarest and most colourful butterflies. Some butterflies depend exclusively on nettle leaves to lay their eggs, such as the Red Admiral, the Small Tortoiseshell, the Peacock and the

Comma, which is rare but is making a welcome recovery.

A TASTY SPRING DISH USING NETTLES AND SPAGHETTI

I would like to thank Tatiana Smart, a fellow stallholder at Balbriggan Fish and Farmers' Market on a Friday morning, for the recipe for this exotic dish which I have made and enjoyed several times using nettles from the garden.

- Boil nettles (enough to fill a small shopping bag) in a little water until they are just soft and then take them off the heat.
- Heat a pan and melt some butter or use olive oil.
- Add crushed garlic (1 clove) and a chopped onion.
- Add chopped chilli according to taste.
- When the vegetables are soft, add a cup of vegetable stock.
- Once the pan is boiling, add the nettles and simmer for five minutes while you boil the spaghetti.
- Drain the spaghetti and nettles.
- Fold nettles into spaghetti and serve (grated parmesan cheese optional).

33

OTHER JOBS FOR THE WEEK THAT IS IN IT:

🌿 Check out recipes for furze (wine), dandelion (salad, soup) and charlock (vegetable broth). Coming in March will be primrose (syrup, tea) and in April cowslip and hawthorn (syrup, tea, wine). May brings the addition of meadowsweet (tea flavouring, wine) and June elder (thirst-quenching cordial, wine). From then on there should be plenty from your own cultivated crops to keep you going, but every month brings with it the potential for some foraging and a wild harvest.

🌿 Identify, so they can be protected, any self-seeded plants starting to appear in the garden. In my garden I get a great return on self-seeded lamb's lettuce, borage (for the flowers in salads), nasturtium (for leaves and flowers) and fennel (salads). Every spring yields a few surprises, so weed with care.

🌿 If you have more space than me, consider planting Jerusalem artichokes now. A good variety is Fuseau. Having an organically certified garden, I would buy the tubers from an organic seed supplier. Otherwise, those sold in the shops can be planted as the plant is quite trouble free. It is not prone to any major virus or disease problems. Plant them 30 cm (1ft) apart and 12.5 cm (5 inches) deep. The new crop can be lifted from early November onwards. Save a couple of tubers then for the subsequent year's seed tubers.

The Bigger Picture:
The impact of GMOs on food security

Growers of food should take an interest, not just in what genetically modified organisms (GMOs) in food involves, but, equally important, why such food is being pushed by the largest corporations on an apathetic public. If I look, I can easily find large labels declaring food to be 'GM free'. I have yet to find anything more than small print declaring 'contains GMOs'. It is just not a selling point. The public is understandably risk averse.

Nonetheless, the GM advocates assert that the public has no choice other than to accept GMOs for the sake of 'feeding the world'. This claim has been around since GMOs were first commercialised in 1996, and a billion people still go to bed each night hungry while another billion are dying of obesity-related illnesses.

Genetic modification of food has been a huge disappointment to those who were taken in by the propaganda and a cause of distress to farmers who do not have the hard currency and are continually required to raise money, often loans, to buy GM seed, fertiliser and pesticides. Before opting for GM cultivation, many farmers saved their own former non-GM seed from the previous season's crop. Nobel Prize winner Vandana Shiva has spoken on many occasions about the way Indian farmers, caught in the grip of GM corporation dependency, have been driven to commit suicide. If the GM agenda has brought change, it has succeeded in reducing the biodiversity of crop varieties as it is designed for monoculture cultivation. GM farming technology has also brought control of the food industry into fewer and fewer hands.

On the other hand, the International Assessment of Agricultural Science and Technology for Development (IAASTD) employed four hundred scientists for four years to determine what changes are needed worldwide to feed the growing human population. On 18 April 2008 the Institute of Science in Society reported on the conclusions of the IAASTD report as follows:

> A fundamental change in farming practise is needed to counteract soaring food prices, hunger, social inequities and environmental disasters. Genetically modified (GM) crops are highly controversial and will not play a substantial role in addressing the challenges of climate change, loss of biodiversity, hunger and poverty. Instead, small-scale farmers and agro-ecological methods are the way forward; with indigenous and local knowledge playing as important

35

a role as formal science. Furthermore, the rush to grow crops for biofuel could exacerbate food shortages and price rises.

Evidently we already have solutions to world hunger without GMOs. This is a good thing, as there is no time to wait around to see if the GM companies' extravagant claims and corporate propaganda about the future could ever be credible. As Minister of State for Food and Horticulture, I visited Ethiopia with Irish Aid and met with African Union representatives in Addis Ababa on 28 November 2008. Their focus in boosting food production is to train up farmers in organic methods which build up soil fertility and which ensure greater resilience to drought or floods. I witnessed how organic farming was empowering farmers and increasing crop yield substantially. Organic farmers in Africa were also not putting themselves in debt to foreign corporations by buying agri-chemical inputs and GM seeds.

Safety concerns about GM food have not been allayed after many tests. Laboratory rats fed on GM potatoes developed intestinal lesions during tests carried out at the prestigious Rowett Institute in the UK in 1996. I have details of over sixty other tests showing the effects of GMOs on humans and non-humans, how gene insertion disrupts DNA, ways in which GM crops can increase environmental toxins, and the risks of GM foods for children and newborns. Not surprisingly, perhaps, insurance companies are not prepared to insure GM farmers in Europe.

Without GM food labelling being mandatory in the EU yet, the only definite way to ensure food is GM free is to choose certified organic products. All non-organic fruit, vegetables and tillage crops are GM-free in Ireland, but without GM-free labelling, this is not apparent to the shopper. Organic farmers are not legally permitted to use manure from cattle which have eaten GM feed. Likewise, if cross-pollination with GM pollen occurs on an organic holding, then that organic farmer would lose their licence to sell produce as certified organic. Organic standards are strictly non-GM.

The marketing and exporting advantage of Ireland declaring itself a GM-free food island is clear as the vast majority of European shoppers that responded to numerous surveys do not want to eat GM food. Europe is Ireland's main food export market.

As the Dominic Behan song puts it, 'Thank God we're surrounded by water.' It is a geographical reality of which we have yet to take advantage, by declaring ourselves to be a GM-free food growing island.

Thoughts from other kitchen gardeners

PEADAR Ó RIADA

Peadar Ó Riada is a legend in Irish music circles. He lives in Cúil Aodha (Coolea), in the Irish speaking area west of Macroom in Cork known as Gaeltacht Mhúscraí. Peadar is also a renowned beekeeper, and grows much of his own food in the spectacular landscape where he lives with his talented family.

I first met Peadar at a bar in Bantry, West Cork in 1982. At that time, I was a teacher in nearby Dunmanway. In 2011, Peadar asked me to give a talk at a symposium about the future of employment entitled 'Tábhacht na Meithile sa Lá Inniu' during Féile na Laoch, the momentous festival which remembered the fortieth anniversary of the passing of the great Irish music composer, and Peadar's father, Seán Ó Riada.

Peadar, like his late father, continues to inspire others as an innovative composer and accomplished musician in this own right. In honour of one of his compositions, a reel called 'Feabhra', Peadar's experiences of growing his own food form a conclusion to the chapter on February.

Describe the location in which you grow your own food.

A southern aspect as near to the kitchen as possible. A stone wall protecting from the North and West is handy, as is good soil.

37

Which food do you look forward to harvesting most and why?

New potatoes or the first lettuce in spring

Which garden tool do you value most?

The spade (*an rámhainn*)

What motivates you to undertake the work involved in growing food?

Independence and time to think

What advice would you give to a person considering growing their own food?

Choose your plot with care. Then measure twice and dig once.

Have you an aspiration for the future in relation to food?

Self-sufficiency all year round

MARY WHITE

A former deputy leader of the Green Party (An Comhaontas Glas) and Minister for Equality, Mary is now running a local tourism business for walkers of all ages, www.blackstairsecotrails.ie. The walks start from Mary's family home near Borris, Co. Carlow, and her impressive kitchen garden is a major attraction for visitors before they set out on the pre-booked eco-trails.

Describe the location in which you grow your own food:

In South Carlow under the shelter of Mount Leinster. The site is sloping and very sheltered and perfect for growing fruit and vegetables.

Which food do you look forward to harvesting most and why?

All the brassicas. They include so many varieties, from early spinach and Swiss chard to the trickier cauliflowers and Brussels sprouts. I love cabbage of every kind: red cabbage, spring cabbage, particularly Hispi, and of course the great January King.

Which garden tool do you value most and why?

My hoe is my favourite implement. I have worn out so many Dutch hoes over the years. It is a brilliant tool and I cherish mine; in fact I am quite protective of my hoe!

What motivates you to undertake the work involved in growing food?

I believe good food is a vital part of good health. Home-produced food is the perfect way to ensure that you are getting the best food possible for the family.

We grow our food without chemicals, using all organic inputs. Our soil is in great condition and when you get the balance right between good fertile soils you can grow almost anything.

What advice would you give to a person considering growing their own food?

Just do it! The rewards are tremendous. It keeps you fit and the satisfaction of growing your own food is incalculable.

Have you an aspiration for the future in relation to food?

Yes, I would like to see as many people as possible in Ireland, even if they only have a very small garden, to get growing. We used to see gardens over the years bursting with fruit and vegetables. Then we lost that skill but it is coming back. I would love to see all children in school having school gardens and that growing our own food would be seen as the norm instead of just a small section of the population getting back to it. Our future is in growing our food, being sustainable and ensuring Ireland becomes the clean, green food island of Europe. We are on our way!

Márta ❧ March

The Month of the Roman God of War

THE SAYING 'mad as a March hare' comes to mind when I think back at the way, some years ago, I attempted to sow radish seeds out of doors in near freezing temperatures in early March. The seed packet blithely indicated that sowing can commence in March but made no mention of the temperature needed for germination. I now measure the temperature and make sure the soil is at least 7°C (45°F) before attempting to sow outdoors. As temperatures pick up and days lengthen, the growth of the seedlings accelerate, so an early sowing is not as much of a head start as I once thought.

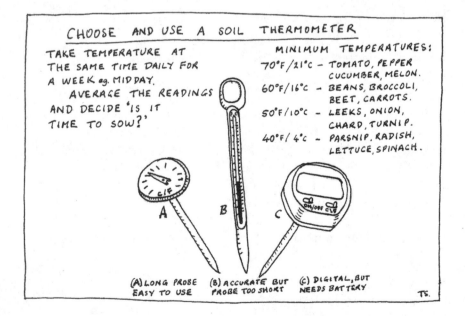

CHOOSE AND USE A SOIL THERMOMETER

TAKE TEMPERATURE AT THE SAME TIME DAILY FOR A WEEK eg. MIDDAY.
 AVERAGE THE READINGS AND DECIDE 'IS IT TIME TO SOW?'

MINIMUM TEMPERATURES:
70°F/21°C - TOMATO, PEPPER CUCUMBER, MELON.
60°F/16°C - BEANS, BROCCOLI, BEET, CARROTS.
50°F/10°C - LEEKS, ONION, CHARD, TURNIP.
40°F/4°C - PARSNIP, RADISH, LETTUCE, SPINACH.

A   B   C

(A) LONG PROBE EASY TO USE   (B) ACCURATE BUT PROBE TOO SHORT   (C) DIGITAL, BUT NEEDS BATTERY

TS.

The Romans, who decided to name this month after the god Mars, were also fixated on the weather at this time – but not for the purpose of sowing seeds only. March marked the end of cold weather, when the fighting legions could strike out again to conquer and expand their massive empire and quell rebellions. We do know there were soldiers who had an interest in kitchen gardening amongst those legions. Many of our common and less common vegetables were introduced to the Roman outpost of Britannica by these soldiers when they settled long enough to sow seeds. The Normans then brought those vegetable varieties to Ireland in the twelfth century. So, what did the Romans ever do for us? Well, for a start, they brought to Northern Europe garlic, onion, leek, lettuce, mustard, parsnip, skirret (a sweet-tasting edible root), turnip and radish.

Maybe the Saxons were sick of war and more interested in daylight for growing food when they named the month. They called it Lenctmonat, referring to the spring equinox and the lengthening of the days. This period is roughly the current season of Lent, the period in which Christians prepare for Easter. The Christian Romans called Lent Quadragesima and the Irish called it Carghas Earraigh, literally the Spring Fasting Time, or Carghas for short. With the winter stores of food so low in a time before one could buy food easily, fasting was as much a necessity as a choice.

An overview of the work ahead in the garden this month:

Plant: onion sets, early potatoes

Sow out: cabbages, Brussels sprouts, kale, turnips, leeks, onions, parsnips

Sow under glass: celery, celeriac, tomatoes, aubergines, peppers

Harvest: winter crops as in February, plus spring cabbage, kale and sprouting broccoli

❧ FIRST WEEK IN MARCH ❧

How to grow strawberries in any space available

'Instead of spreading out over more land, the farmer
concentrates on less land.'
(Gilbert Ellis Bailey, who coined the term 'vertical farming', 1852–1924)

THE strawberry varieties we enjoy today are a result, not of
cultivating the wild strawberry which one finds in the
mountains, but of crossing two American species that are widely
separated in nature. The strawberry is particularly suited to what
is termed 'vertical farming' (growing in tiers rather than on flat
ground) and the planter pictured below is one of many such
containers on the market which suits a strawberry grower like me
with a small garden.

I do not know anyone who does not look forward to the first
strawberries of the season. However, very few Irish-grown strawberries are grown in the open, as used to be the case. The pressure
to compete with out-of-season strawberry imports has driven Irish
strawberry growers to rely on 'protected cropping' more and more.
Strawberries grown in polytunnels are now *de rigueur.*

Having a few strawberry plants outdoors in the garden will yield
a taste of summer, a taste which commercial growers can no longer
afford to provide.

WHAT TO PLANT

Strawberry plants tend to develop fruit-deforming viruses with each
generation of runners (horizontal stems which propagate by
producing roots and shoots at their tips) that they produce after
fruiting. This is why it makes economic sense to plant runners from
certified stock. Apart from verifying the origin of the runners, check

that the plants you buy are growing vigorously and are free from leaf yellowing and distortion. If spring-sown healthy plants put out runners, these can be potted up in pots of moist compost embedded in the soil near the 'mother plant' for planting out in August to fruit the following June.

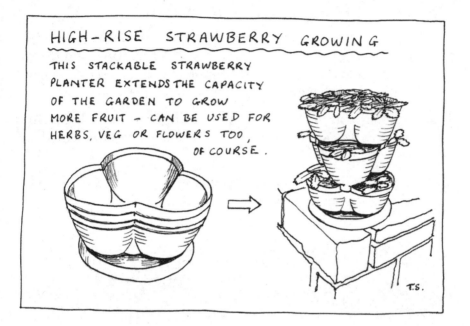

HIGH-RISE STRAWBERRY GROWING

THIS STACKABLE STRAWBERRY PLANTER EXTENDS THE CAPACITY OF THE GARDEN TO GROW MORE FRUIT – CAN BE USED FOR HERBS, VEG OR FLOWERS TOO, OF COURSE.

T.S.

WHEN AND HOW TO PLANT

Strawberries are happy to grow in a vertical or tiered planter (which suits a small garden where space is at a premium) or in an open plot or a greenhouse. However, the best time to put in new runners is in late summer (August to mid-September). All is not lost, however, if this is not possible. Strawberry runners can be planted now but it is normal practice to not expect fruit until next year. Any flowers appearing this spring should be removed to allow the plants to build up leaves and roots to store up energy. June of the following

43

year will reward this patience with a bumper crop. Many beginners rush to get a crop early and it can be disappointing if there is only a small yield.

Alternatively, if space is too tight in the garden, wait until August (see the First Week in August) and plant runners then.

OTHER JOBS FOR THE WEEK THAT IS IN IT:

🌿 Prepare ground for where runner bean seedlings are to be planted by digging a trench (1ft deep and 2ft wide) and filling it with 3 inches (7.5 cm) of compost and kitchen scraps. Then refill the trench with soil.

🌿 Trim herb bushes to check their spread. Overgrown herbs like chives and sage can be divided and each portion replanted as separate plants.

🌿 Finish pruning currant bushes and raspberry canes; this is your last chance before new growth appears.

The Bigger Picture:
The National War Garden campaign

During World War I, all farms in the embattled nations lost most of their male workers to the armed forces. National food security required all who were not engaged in fighting to roll up their sleeves and grow food in whatever space was available, urban and rural.

Charles Lathrop Pack (1857–1937) was one of the five wealthiest men in the USA. Born in Lexington, Michigan, he was educated at Brooks Military Academy, Cleveland, Ohio. He built on his family fortune through his forestry business. When World War I broke out, the USA was reluctant to get involved, but when it did the large-scale mobilisation of men left many farms unable to sow or harvest badly needed food. A co-ordinated plan was needed.

Charles Lathrop Pack was already a renowned philanthropist and he volunteered to set up a National War Garden Commission so as to 'put all idle land to work and to conserve by canning and drying all food that could not be used while fresh, and to co-ordinate an army of soldiers of the soil' (*The War Garden Victorious*, 1919).

In March 1917 the National War Garden Campaign was launched and the initiative was replicated in Britain, Germany, Italy and elsewhere. The need to grow food did not just apply to the folks back home. At the front the food supply problems were dire too. Bread could take up to eight days to reach the front. In the winter of 1916 flour became so scarce that bread was made from ground-up dried turnip. Some French soldiers at least had the benefit of fresh vegetables. The gardens of Versailles were sown with leeks – over twenty-five million in 1917. When the seedlings were large enough for transplanting, they were ferried by military trucks to the front and replanted close behind Allied army lines to continue growing and to be fed to the fighting troops. This was a more practical use for nutritious vegetables than the use associated with St David, who instructed his comrades to wear a leek when they went into battle against the Saxons.

One hundred years on, the energy of oil and gas for fertilising, mechanisation and transport has replaced a huge amount of human labour in farming. As peak oil prices rob farming of mechanical energy (just as World War I robbed it of human energy), we may need something equivalent to a 'National War Garden Campaign'. Perhaps it could be called a 'National Post-Oil Garden Campaign'?

❦ SECOND WEEK IN MARCH ❦

Planting up potatoes in bags or in a plot if you have space

'Those who have the will to win
Cook potatoes in their skin
Knowing that the sight of peelings
Deeply hurts Lord Woolton's feelings.'
(Jingle issued by UK Ministry of Food during World War II)

ABOUT 4,000 varieties of potato are grown in over 180 countries worldwide, making it the fourth most important crop after wheat, maize and rice. It is the best all-round source of nutrition we have, better than soya. Eggs would have a little more protein, but growing potatoes is the most efficient means of converting land, water and labour into wholesome food. A field of potatoes produces more food energy per acre than a field of any other crop.

The wild potato was first bred for eating at least 12,500 years ago over 3,845 feet above sea level on the shores of Lake Titicaca in the Andes. At this altitude, blight spores cannot survive. However, when cultivation reached lower altitudes in Europe, the scourge of blight in due course ruined crops in Ireland and elsewhere. Since then, the worldwide spraying to protect potato crops uses 2.5 million tonnes of chemicals and costs $20–$25 billion per annum.

Ireland has a reputation as a potato-producing country. Over 80 per cent of our potato crop is grown in Meath, Louth, Dublin, Wexford, Cork and Donegal. However, 20 per cent of the potatoes eaten in Ireland are imported. These include the so-called 'baby potatoes' which require conditions not common in Ireland. However, the home gardener can grow small, delicious early organic potatoes easily. The advantage of growing 'early' varieties is they are harvested by June at the latest, before the blight season takes hold, and there is therefore no need to spray for blight. If, by any chance, brown spots appear on the leaves, these leaves can be removed, thus removing blight symptoms and keeping the potatoes free from infection.

GET SEED POTATOES OFF TO A GOOD START BY CHITTING

I start chitting, or sprouting potatoes for planting, in mid-January. Seed potatoes, either bought or saved from the previous year's crop, are arranged, 'eyes' (immature sprouts) pointing upwards, in egg boxes and placed on a cool, bright windowsill indoors. After a couple of weeks, green sprouts can be seen growing. These are the start of the potato plant stems. Chitted seed potatoes give a week or two of a head start to the new plants, but if it is March and you have not chitted, plant them anyway and let nature do the rest.

GROWING POTATOES IN BAGS OR BUCKETS

So long as there is good drainage, any kind of sturdy bag or bucket will work as a potato planter. Depth of 30 cm (11.8 inches) or more should be adequate. The garden centres sell robust potato bags with handles which I have re-used over many years.

- Line the base with broken crockery or small flat stones to help drainage.

- If available, next place a layer of seaweed in the bottom of the container to ensure a good flavoursome crop.

- Fill to the half-way mark with compost (homemade or shop bought) mixed with soil (half and half).

- Bury the (chitted) potato seed 10–15 cm (4–6 inches) deep (use two or three seeds if the container is 50–60 cm (20–24 inches) in diameter).

- Place outside once the risk of frost has passed.

- Once the foliage is growing well, keep it watered and add feed. I use comfrey liquid feed (see the Third Week in February). Water the soil, not the leaves.

- Pile extra compost and soil mixture around plants as they grow to support stems, to stop light from spoiling the crop and to encourage more new potatoes to grow along the buried stems.

- Watch for flowers to appear; when these wither your crop is ready for harvesting.

- To harvest, gently tip the container contents out and rummage for your precious crop.

- I compost the potato foliage. (I used to burn blighted leaves but am advised now that the composting process renders the blighted leaves harmless.)

- The container soil remaining is excellent for vegetable growing or for pot plants.

Ag cur prátaí i málaí

3-STEPS TO POTATO HEAVEN :

1. 5cm SEAWEED LAYER FIRST, THEN 10cm SOIL + COMPOST MIX PLACE TUBER + 10 cm MORE MIX.

2. EARTH UP TO LEAVE TOP LEAVES EXPOSED, WATER.

3. WITH SACK ALMOST FULL WATER WELL WHEN IN FLOWER.

CHIT TUBERS TO PRODUCE STURDY SHOOTS. PLACE FULL 'EGG BOX' IN A COOL LIGHT PLACE.

1. 2. 3.

TS.

OTHER JOBS FOR THE WEEK THAT IS IN IT:

🍂 Remove the rhubarb forcer to give rhubarb a chance to build up stores of sunlight energy.

🍂 Protect brassicas with horticultural fleece to prevent the Cabbage White butterfly from laying caterpillar eggs. This butterfly lays now for a couple of weeks and again in September for a couple of weeks, so be vigilant.

The Bigger Picture:
St Patrick's Day and potato planting

I know farmers who plant potatoes during Christmas week in large glasshouses to get the earliest crop possible – and hence the best price – for Irish-grown early potatoes in the shops. This got me wondering about the longstanding tradition that St Patrick's Day is the best time for seed potato sowing.

Having done a little research into the history of the potato, I now have a theory of how this tradition came into being. On 27 December 1573, we have the first record of the potato being eaten in Europe as a health food in Hospital de la Sangre, in Seville, Spain. Sailors fed on potatoes were observed to be healthier and free of scurvy, a scourge on ships at that time.

The military rulers of Spain, followed by France and Prussia, knew a healthy high energy food when they saw it. To them the potato diet was a way to make soldiers march further and fight harder. However, the Roman Catholic and Protestant Church rulers were suspicious of this newcomer, of which there was no mention in the Bible. Not only had this tasty tuber voluptuous curves and suggestive shapes, but it multiplied and swelled when buried like a corpse, and was therefore clearly the work of Beelzebub!

Under pressure from the military rulers, the Roman Catholic

49

hierarchy softened its position and agreed to tolerate the vegetable provided it was ceremoniously planted on a holy day, like Good Friday, and liberally sprinkled with holy water to keep the Devil at bay. This tolerance was enough to drive Protestants apoplectic. Even as late as the eighteenth century, Presbyterian clergy in Scotland declared the potato unsafe to eat because it was not mentioned in the Bible. The vegetal battle lines were drawn in English politics as well in the elections of 1765. Whatever other policies the Protestant candidate in Lewes, Sussex, proclaimed, his posters simply read, 'No Potatoes, No Popery'!

Fortunately, these days the potato is recognised as the 'super food' it is, and we all owe a huge debt of gratitude to the pre-Inca Indians in the Andes of South America who ingeniously developed a healthy food out of what is, after all, a poisonous leafed plant. However, instead of the Church denigrating the potato these days, there are still some non-clerical people spreading rumours that the potato is not good, i.e. that it is fattening. The potato is, in fact, fat free; it is the added butter, cheese, mayonnaise, etc. which is fattening. Nonetheless, the tradition of planting the potato on St Patrick's Day, a holy day, is a poignant reminder that the potato has had to run the gauntlet of conspiracy theories and historic superstitions to emerge as the most under-rated healthy food one can grow or cook using any one of hundreds of recipes from all over the world.

✤ THIRD WEEK IN MARCH ✤

Learning to live with the 'hungry gap'

'In the depth of winter, I finally learned
that there was in me an invincible summer.'

(Albert Camus, French pacifist, philosopher and
winner of the 1957 Nobel Prize for Literature, 1913–1960)

THE tradition of fasting during the season of Lent is these days seen as a choice. Before freezers and food importation, fasting was a fact of life in the period between the previous autumn's stores of food running low and before the newly planted spring crops reaching maturity. Our predecessors coped well with this 'hungry gap' by ingenious means of storage: drying, bottling, preserving and, more recently, freezing.

The welcome renaissance of kitchen gardening has yet to be matched with a renaissance of the age-old techniques of preserving fresh surplus food from the garden. Even in my modest garden, there is annual surplus of garlic, onions, blackcurrants, apples, runner beans, chives and mint. The way things are going I will have a good courgette crop this year too for a change. As the GIY movement goes from strength to strength, I feel the absence of a 'Store It Yourself' movement. Immigrants to this country from Canada or Russia, where the soil is too frozen to dig for months on end, have much to teach us about coping with the 'hungry gap'. Let us practise bottling and preserving while we can, and be prepared for a time when importation may drive the cost of food too high.

BOTTLING OR FREEZING SOME FRESH FRUIT OR VEGETABLES

I am learning about food preservation techniques. To date, I have bottled my beetroot, juiced my apples for freezing and made a

51

quantity of soups from garden produce to freeze. General rules of thumb include:

- 🌿 Heat jars and equipment properly to prevent food spoilage.
- 🌿 Never use over-ripe fruit or vegetables.
- 🌿 Do not overfill jars.

An internet search engine will show a wide variety of video demonstrations under the key words 'preserving food'. The American 'Homestead Series' shows a video entitled 'How to Can Zucchini Relish'. I look forward to a courgette glut so I can experiment with that one.

STEP ONE IN PRESERVING SURPLUS VEGETABLES FROM THE GARDEN

If you have some space in your freezer, the easiest way to preserve surplus vegetables from the garden is to make a batch of soup and divide it into portions for freezing, using small lunch-box-like containers. Label these with the date of freezing and stack them in the freezer, to be thawed and re-heated when needed.

OTHER JOBS FOR THE WEEK THAT IS IN IT:

This is your last chance to plant raspberry canes or to cut down to the base the canes which bore fruit last year. Lightly fork in some wood ash as raspberries appreciate some potash.

The Bigger Picture:
Taking stock of water usage

World Water Day is marked on 22 March each year. It is an uncomfortable fact that over one billion people have to survive on just 4 litres of water per day. When I visited the Negev Desert in

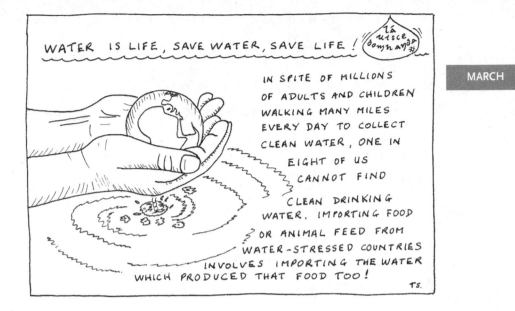

WATER IS LIFE, SAVE WATER, SAVE LIFE! (Tá uisce domhnap!)

IN SPITE OF MILLIONS OF ADULTS AND CHILDREN WALKING MANY MILES EVERY DAY TO COLLECT CLEAN WATER, ONE IN EIGHT OF US CANNOT FIND CLEAN DRINKING WATER. IMPORTING FOOD OR ANIMAL FEED FROM WATER-STRESSED COUNTRIES INVOLVES IMPORTING THE WATER WHICH PRODUCED THAT FOOD TOO!

TS.

Israel, I was told 5 litres is the minimum daily water ration for survival. The United Nations (UN) predicts that over three billion people may be suffering water shortages by 2025. Meanwhile, the average daily Irish domestic water use per capita is 160 litres (see L.M. McCumiskey, 'Water Resources and Management in the Republic of Ireland', July 2007).

Ironically, much of the food we buy out of season is imported from hot countries, which divert their water resources from local food production and human consumption to grow food for export. The amount of food we import generates debate on the energy used to produce and transport it. The debate often entails an evaluation of a 'carbon footprint'. But what about our 'water footprint'?

To put fruit and vegetables in context, a lot more water is required to produce some other goods people crave. According to the World Water Day 2011 (Siemens) website, it takes 148,000 litres of clean water to manufacture a car. For cattle that are slaughtered at three years old, about 15,550 litres of water are used to produce one kilogramme of beef.

Some other examples of 'embedded water' content in food:

- 5,000 litres of water go to make 1 kg of cheese.

- 2,400 litres go to make one hamburger.

- 3,900 litres of water go to produce 1 kg of non-free-range chicken meat.

- 200 litres of water go to produce a battery hen egg.

- 40 litres of water go to produce a slice of wheat bread.

- 50 litres of water go to produce one orange.

- 70 litres of water go to produce one apple.

- 190 litres of water go to produce a glass of apple juice (200 ml).

AQUIFER PROTECTION

Most freshwater in the world is contained in aquifers (underground layers of permeable rock, sand or gravel) and a quarter of the world's people depend on them for drinking. Yet all over the world aquifers are being depleted. A major aquifer in China has serious problems with agricultural nitrate contamination. Some aquifers in Britain are laced with benzene. Likewise, in Ireland, the debate about the measures needed to protect groundwater continues.

The prairie states of the USA are producing grain which goes a long way to feeding the world's human and livestock populations. This miracle of modern agriculture is made possible by tapping into the world's largest aquifer. This ancient water is a legacy of the melting glaciers at the end of the last Ice Age. Since it was seriously harnessed in the 1960s, 4–6 ft of water is now extracted each year and rainfall puts back only half an inch annually.

Eating less meat and dairy produce would take some pressure off the aquifers of the world. Every year, 760 million tonnes of grain are fed to livestock worldwide. This would be enough to solve global hunger fourteen times over. Eating locally produced seasonal food would also mean we would save water as well as energy consumed by long-distance food importation. However, until embedded water content becomes an integral part of food labelling, it is difficult to see Western public opinion getting behind aquifer protection.

❧ FOURTH WEEK IN MARCH ❧

The way to appreciate seasonal food is to grow it

'A thriving household depends on the use of seasonal produce
and the application of common sense.'

(Olivier de Serres, French soil scientist
and early advocate of crop rotation, 1539–1619)

A FARMING friend who grows lettuce for the supermarkets 365 days of the year illustrates very well the importance of buying food in season. Farmers do not like having to use sprays. Food grown in season as nature intended is generally stronger, faster growing and better able to naturally fight off attack from predators or disease. Most conventional or non-organic fresh produce sold in season has therefore little or no chemical residues. On the other hand, crops which are forced to grow outside their natural growing season inevitably struggle, either for adequate heat, daylight or pollination. Producing heads of lettuce commercially in November and December is an example of this challenge. As a result, the plants are weaker and prone to attack. The non-organic farmer must then resort to expensive sprays if the harvested crops are to be blemish free, as required by the supermarket.

Since I registered as an organic fruit and vegetable stallholder at Balbriggan Fish and Farmers' Market, I appreciate more the change in seasonal produce week by week. All the produce on my stall comes from Sonairte, the Ecology Centre at Laytown, Co. Meath, or from my own organically certified kitchen garden. In March, I would have rhubarb and leeks, but it would be too early to ask for peas and beans. Due to the 'hungry gap' in the kitchen gardens right now, most of my sales in March would be potted plants and trays of vegetable seedlings for grow-it-yourself enthusiasts. By May, the potted plant sales will be much reduced, but the autumn-sown vegetables and fruit will be coming on-stream. These seasonal crops will then form the bulk of my sales.

Eating in season keeps life interesting and the diet healthy. Some foods are famous for their seasonality, like strawberries, pumpkins and Brussels sprouts. My favourite food, when it is in season and locally grown, is asparagus. In a small garden it is a bit of a luxury, however, as it ties up a patch all year for maybe twenty or even forty years for the sake of a couple of weeks of asparagus spears around May or June. Nonetheless, having tried to grow asparagus, I now appreciate it needs light, easily worked and well-drained loam, and patience, as it must be allowed to develop for two or, better still, three years before spears are harvested – when they are 15–25 cm (6 to 10 inches) long.

The steps to be taken in establishing an asparagus bed:

1. Weed the chosen asparagus bed area well and add plenty of compost and horticultural sand if the soil is heavy, as mine was.

2. Buy asparagus crowns which display some greenery to indicate they are still alive.

3. Allow 40 cm (16 inches) between rows, if planting in rows.

4. For each crown, dig a round hole about 20 cm (8 inches) deep and wide enough so the roots can be spread like the legs of an octopus.

5. Make a small hillock, partially filling the centre of the hole so the crown head is just below the surface when the crown is buried.

6. Water well and keep the patch weed free. Avoid hoeing since this risks damaging new growth.

HOME-GROWN ASPARAGUS - A RARE PLEASURE!

1. TRENCH FOR ASPARAGUS GROWING, 30cm WIDE, 20cm DEEP, WITH A SLIGHTLY MOUNDED BOTTOM.

2. PLANT THE CROWNS ON THE MOUNDED BED 40cm APART AND COVER WITH SOIL. DO NOT ALLOW CROWNS TO DRY OUT.

3. HOE CAN DAMAGE NEW SPEARS SO HAND WEED. CUT THE SPEARS BELOW THE SURFACE WITH A SHARP KNIFE.

OTHER JOBS FOR THE WEEK THAT IS IN IT:

Prepare vegetable plots by weeding and cover any empty spaces with cardboard, carpet or old black plastic to warm the soil and prevent new weed seeds from germinating.

Put house plants which have become pot bound into larger pots with more fresh compost and soil mix. One good watering should give them a new start for the spring.

The Bigger Picture:
Unseasonal food is killing local supplies

It should be obvious that, from a nutritional point of view, eating food which is freshly grown in season is healthy. What may be less obvious is that the demand for the same foods all year round puts local growers of seasonal food out of business. Unwittingly, the Christmas party host who wants to show off his 'Rudolph red' strawberries is pushing his supermarket to depend more on foreign tropical strawberries than on the Irish grower.

Put yourself in the position of a supermarket buyer. If customers only bought fresh produce that is in season, then the Irish grower could supply all the fresh produce in that store. If, however, the customer wants carrots for fifty-two weeks of the year, then the wholesaler in Amsterdam is the easier person to deal with. I recall discussing this issue with Senator Feargal Quinn, who was at the time the boss of Superquinn, the supermarket chain. Feargal wanted to support Irish farmers, but was frustrated by avid cookery book readers, who seldom cooked, taking a fancy on a given weekend that they would cook and that they needed every ingredient in some recipe unrelated to that time in the farming calendar. Unless Feargal had everything such a customer needed, by importing if necessary, he was afraid he would lose his customer.

So the supermarket sees the Irish grower as supplying some of their requirements and the importer as supplying all of their requirements. Irish growers, therefore, struggle to extend their growing seasons to compete with importers.

Horticulture in Ireland has been whittled away as farmers are sidelined by supermarket buyers. While 60 per cent of the land in Ireland is agricultural, covering some 4,300,000 hectares, of that, horticulture uses just 5,140 hectares. The Central Statistics Office does not even give it a column in the 'Agricultural Land Use' graph. However, horticulture still involves 240 farms growing all manner of fruit and vegetables, some organically, and the sector employs18,500 people. Irish horticulture at this stage is under-supplying the Irish public, meeting 68 days of tomato demand, 53 days of onion demand, 211 days of cauliflower demand, 278 days of cabbage demand and 326 days of potato demand.

Although the horticulture area has remained static, the number of farmers growing fresh produce has decreased from 1,220 (1980) to 780 (1990), 540 (2000) and 280 (2010). Unless the Irish public gets really serious about buying Irish-grown produce in season, this decline will continue. The same trend occurred in England and, as a result, just three farms occupy the area of land required by the whole Irish horticulture sector. In other words, Lincolnshire Fresh Produce, Kettle Produce and David Marshall are between them farming 5,140 hectares.

All the evidence above suggests that supermarkets are too dominant, controlling over 80 per cent of the food trade in Ireland. Other models of food growing and distribution are seriously underdeveloped: farmers' markets, box schemes, local green-grocers, farm shops, community supported agriculture, farmer co-operatives, allotments, community gardens and out-of-our-back-yard (OOOBY) stalls. All these fresh produce enterprises are plentiful in the USA, France, Italy, Germany and Britain, and they keep supermarkets respectful of the needs of healthy food growing and the viability of farm enterprises.

Irish horticulture (and agriculture in general), like Nature herself, will be stronger for having greater diversity in terms of production and retailing. You and your kitchen garden are part of this greater diversity, as are farmers' markets, farm shops and the other new ways farmers and consumers are working together more and more.

Thoughts from other kitchen gardeners

MARY McALEESE

Former President of Ireland Mary McAleese secured organic status for the kitchen garden at Áras an Uachtaráin. Since leaving the Áras, her enthusiasm for empowering everyone to grow some of their own food is as warm-hearted and as infectious as ever.

Describe the location in which you grow your own food:

In a kitchen garden in three large raised beds right outside my kitchen's half door.

Which food do you look forward to harvesting most and why?

Potatoes. I can't fully explain it but it has something to do with the drama of digging, never knowing for certain what you will find and then the surprise of beautiful pink or white spuds.

Which garden tool do you value most and why?

The hoe. I hate weeds and weeding but the hoe makes it easier.

What motivates you to undertake the work involved in growing food?

The satisfaction and handiness of having fresh food from my own garden. The family always appreciates it more than shop-bought food and it ties me to my grandparents who ate virtually only what they grew. They lived on the hill that I can see from my front window.

What advice would you give to a person considering growing their own food?

Get started right away no matter how limited your space or experience. Herbs, tomatoes, even potatoes, can be grown easily in very small spaces and the return in terms of fun, interest, fulfilment and food is well worth the effort.

Have you an aspiration for the future in relation to food?

I have a hope that we will make time for growing our own food and that we will learn not just about food but about life, and at a more human pace.

ERNESTINE WOELGAR

Ernestine Woelgar is originally from Austria, and is now working and living, with her family, in North County Dublin. Ernestine not only has a natural flair for kitchen gardening, but also comes from a tradition of producing, cooking and preserving food in the context of freezing winters in Continental Europe. Ernestine is active in the Skerries Community Association and enthusiastically supported the initiative for local allotments in the town.

Describe the location in which you grow your own food:

I have grown my own food in my back garden in a housing estate in Skerries for twenty years and in an allotment in Skerries, which started in 2011.

Which food do you look forward to harvesting most and why?

I love harvesting the early crops, purple sprouting broccoli in particular. I try to grow it as a perennial and get really large plants that way. However, last winter's frosts killed them all and I have had to start over again. Such is life.

I also love harvesting my redcurrants (they remind me of my father) and my runner beans (they remind me of my mother).

Which garden tool do you value most and why?

I would really be lost without my garden trowel and, as it frequently gets forgotten among the plants, I often spend time searching and finding other plants I had overlooked. I use it to dispose of slugs and to deal with weeds. I like to weed close up and personal, as there are many welcome seedlings in the beds and I want to give them a chance. I think self-sown vegetable seeds in the vegetable patch are very valuable and do stand a better chance of survival.

Of course I use the trowel for planting and transplanting and also for digging up plants to give to friends, which I particularly enjoy.

What motivates you to undertake the work involved in growing food?

I am Austrian and grew up with food being grown in our garden and in all gardens around us. So it was a very natural thing for me to continue this. I think there is so much wasted potential in 'lawns'. Often, when I pass by houses surrounded by huge 'barren' green areas, I feel there is such a loss of potential, not only in terms of producing food, but also in terms of enjoyment, fulfilment and spiritual connection with nature.

I think this connection with nature – preparing the soil, sowing, nurturing, appreciating rain, being in tune with the weather, looking after all creatures (with the exception of the above mentioned villains) and then harvesting the fruits of my labour of love — is most important for me and what really motivates me.

What advice would you give to a person considering growing their own food?

Just do it! Start with easy crops and don't forget it is a natural process. So don't be too regimental; don't get too upset with failures. Once you start you will never look back. The connection with nature is a powerful force.

Have you an aspiration for the future in relation to food?

The bursting of the economic bubble has made growing your own food very popular. That is really great. I think we still import too much food. Growing your own also means cooking your own. Processed food is very poor value, both in terms of money and nutrition.

So more education in regard to food growing and cooking would be of huge benefit. The movement towards 'grow your own' will also increase the variety of fruit and vegetables grown. If such food is grown organically, it will make our gardens and allotments so much more biodiverse, which helps the planet and all on it in the long term.

Aibreán 🍂 *April*

The Month of Showers – Aibreán Bog Braonach

APRIL IS THE MONTH when I become most acquainted with the soil in the garden. Most preparation of new seed-beds is done and most seed sowing takes place in this month. It is a busy but satisfying month. I can identify with Charles A. Lindbergh (1902–1974), the American aviator, author and inventor, when he said, 'Man must feel the earth to know himself and recognise his values.'

The origin of Aibreán or April may be the Latin word *aperire*, meaning 'to open'. This could be a reference to buds and blossoms opening during spring. Others think the month is in honour of Aphrodite, the Greek goddess of fertility, and her Roman equivalent Venus, who the Romans held especially sacred during April.

.The Teutonic peoples like the Saxons also had a deity in mind when they named the month. They called it Eostre-monath after their goddess of the dawn, spring and fertility. They believed Eostre travelled around woods and field with her companion, a white rabbit, placing eggs under trees and shrubs to awaken them and make them blossom.

Before Pope Gregory decreed that January be the start of the year in the late sixteenth century, 1 April (for a while) was New Year's Day. With commu-nications much more basic than nowadays, news of the calendar change was slow to get out. Those who continued to celebrate the New Year on 1 April were taunted with jeers of 'April Fool', or in France 'Poissin d'avril' (April fish).

Fishing is traditionally quite good at this time of the year, so some locally caught fish and some fresh vegetables from the garden, or stored over winter in the garden shed, could be a good idea for dinner. In season are sea trout, mussels, cockles, turbot and sole. I must wait until the mackerel season from June to October before I can really enjoy my favourite fish!

Beannachtaí na Cásca - EASTER GREETINGS!

THE STORY OF THE TEUTONIC LUNAR GODDESS EOSTRE HAS GIVEN US THE SYMBOLS OF EGGS (FOR RE-BIRTH) AND RABBITS (FOR FERTILITY).

THE RE-AWAKENING OF SPRING IS CELEBRATED AS HER HOLIDAY 'EOSTARA' WHICH CHRISTIANS ALSO CELEBRATE AS THE DAY OF CHRIST'S RESURRECTION, EASTER SUNDAY - Domhnach Cásca.

TS.

An overview of the work ahead in the garden this month:

plant: potatoes, globe artichokes
sow out: carrots, beetroot, broccoli, kohlrabi, celeriac, radish, salsify, calabrese, cauliflower and peas. During spring, sow a few seeds of the following each fortnight to extend the harvest period of these crops: Brussels sprouts, cabbages, kale, lettuce and turnips.
sow under glass: French and runner beans, courgettes, marrows, sweetcorn, cucumber
Harvest: spring onions, sprouting broccoli, turnip tops, kale, cabbage, lettuce and spinach

🍂 FIRST WEEK IN APRIL 🍂

Look after your soil and your soil will look after you

> 'To be a successful farmer, one must first know the nature of the soil.'
>
> (Xenophon, from *Oeconomicus*, one of the earliest known works on economics, 400 BC)

SOME FACTS INVISIBLE TO THE NAKED HUMAN EYE

INTUITION alone would tell us the soil has a very special and precious life force. For example, it provides the wherewithal for a tiny acorn to become a mighty oak tree, especially as a tree or any plant has no digestive system as such. Aspects of soil activity are still a mystery to scientists today, but we do understand much more than Leonardo da Vinci did when he wrote in the early 1500s: 'We know more about the movement of celestial bodies than about the soil underfoot.'

WHAT LIVES BENEATH THE SURFACE?

There are four key players in the soil food web which are important for growing food:

🍂 **Bacteria**: these are mainly decomposers of simple carbon compounds, but they also hold nutrients in the root zone, improve soil structure, and filter and break down pollutants.

🍂 **Fungi**: these are multi-celled organisms that grow as long threads or strands call hyphae. They can range in length from a few cells to many metres. They physically bind soil particles into aggregates, thereby improving soil structure and controlling the availability of water for plants.

Protozoa: these are single-celled animals that feed primarily on bacteria, but also eat other protozoa, organic matter and fungi. When protozoa eat bacteria, nitrogen is released into the soil as a food for plants.

 Nematodes: these are non-segmented tiny worms. Some damage plants, but most are beneficial, eating bacteria, fungi and even other nematodes, which in turn releases nutrients which feed the plants.

HOW PLANTS THEMSELVES NURTURE SOIL-LIFE ACTIVITY

Plants, through their leaves, photosynthesise light into energy, but they do not have a digestive system and so they need the soil to 'pre-digest' their food. Amazingly, plants secrete 30 per cent of their photosynthesised energy (sugars and carbohydrates) out of the root system to feed the microbial workforce crowded around the root awaiting this daily feed. This symbiotic relationship between soil and plant is mirrored by the relationship between the garden and gardener. Whether the idea appeals or not, in reality humans and all animals have much in common with the earthworm and all valuable soil-borne creatures. We may walk instead of wriggle but if we analyse our common interdependencies, it is hard to disagree with the celebrated Native American head of the Duwamish tribe Chief Seattle (1780–1866) when he said: 'We are part of the earth and it is part of us…whatever befalls the earth befalls the sons of the earth.'

HOW THE GROWER CAN KEEP THE SOIL HEALTHY AND IMPROVE FERTILITY

Evidently, soil appreciates plants just as it appreciates moisture, air, warmth and organic matter. It does not appreciate being compacted by heavy feet or by machinery. Digging, especially if soil is wet, can be a setback for soil life as well. However, soil does recover once it is assisted in some basic ways. If in doubt about how to treat soil, look at what nature does and you will not go far wrong.

 Keep soil covered where possible. If a patch is vacant, either sow a 'green manure' crop (clover, alfalfa or whatever is in season at the time) or put an old piece of carpet, cardboard or old plastic over it to ensure rain does not leach away nutrients and to keep worms and other darkness-loving microbes active near the soil surface.

 Add bulky organic material in autumn or winter to improve soil structure and fertility, just as leaf fall does in a forest.

 Test the soil in the spring with a soil pH test kit which will indicate if the soil needs to be made more alkaline or acidic, depending on the vegetables and fruit you plan to grow.

I bought a Soil pH Testing Kit for less than €10 in a garden centre. It contains all I need to carry out numerous tests, but a couple of tests on soil samples from different plots in the garden indicate the suitability of the soil for the crops you are planning to grow.

 First, use a trowel to dig a soil sample from 15 cm (5.9 inches) or so below the surface.

 Crumble the damp sample and let it dry naturally.

 Spoon a small amount (as per instructions in kit) into the test tube provided.

 Add a smaller amount of soil testing powder (barium sulphate).

 Add some soil-testing solution as provided in the kit.

 Shake the test tube and allow it to settle for ten minutes.

 The liquid in the tube will show a colour which you match against the pH reading chart.

 The pH preference list in the kit should tell you which crops suit your soil.

🍂 You can then add lime, depending on whether you wish to make your soil more alkaline or not. Adding compost may make soil a little more acidic, as does rainfall. Most crops are quite tolerant of a pH range as long as it not too extreme one way or another.

SOIL TESTING IS SMART

TESTING THE pH OF YOUR SOIL HELPS IN CREATING OPTIMUM GROWING CONDITIONS.

THE COLOUR, ONCE THE SOIL IN THE SOLUTION SETTLES, TELLS THE TALE.

" ...and we can save a few Lira by not taking soil tests........."

Based on an image from 'Dave's garden' website owned by Internet Brands of Segundo, California, USA

OTHER JOBS FOR THE WEEK THAT IS IN IT:

🍂 Remove any flowers starting to form on rhubarb so as to channel energy into edible stems.

🍂 Plant spring onion sets.

🍂 Spread mulch around trees and on plots where vegetable seeds and seedlings are to be sown, except where carrots and parsnips are going as they require finer soil to avoid their roots forking.

The Bigger Picture:
A tribute to head gardeners of a past era

Imagine you are appointed as head gardener on an estate in the nineteenth century and you are in charge of a newly built walled garden. Your job would be to ensure that the family and staff in the Big House, maybe fifty or sixty people, had the best of fruit and vegetables, and indeed decorative flowers, 365 days a year, regardless of weather, soil or any other 'acts of God'.

The secret of a head gardener's success was his care of the soil. The average depth of topsoil in an agricultural field is about 20–25 cm (8–10 inches). Often there would be a hard pan below this and less fertile compact subsoil below that again, as a result of annual ploughing to this depth and no deeper. This depth of topsoil might suffice for field-scale tillage. However, the intensive cultivation of maybe twenty-five to thirty different crops of fruit and vegetables in a two- to three-acre walled garden required much deeper topsoil.

Measurements of topsoil depth in old walled gardens show that this fertile friable soil went down a metre or more. One could not buy topsoil then in the way this trade exists today. Instead, the plan was to use every available bucketful and cartload of organic matter to dig in directly or compost and then dig in, or to spread to build up the residual topsoil.

The complexity of soil needs time to incorporate organic matter, however. This natural order means that 2–3 cm (approx. 1 inch) would be the extent of the topsoil depth improvement one could strive for annually. This means the head gardener had a 25- to 30-year game plan to create the optimum growing environment to ensure a year-round supply of staple and exotic fruit and vegetables. Once the topsoil depth was adequate, the priority was to maintain the high level of fertility and resilient soil structure for the years ahead.

I am sure there was nothing romantic about the reality of a day's work as a head gardener, or a garden foreman, journey man or pot boy. However, I do feel a huge debt of gratitude to the gardeners who worked so hard and continue to work hard in any remaining walled gardens, especially in the 2.2-acre walled garden at Sonairte, the Ecology Centre at Laytown, Co. Meath, where I do some work as a volunteer. This eighteenth-century south-facing walled garden on the banks of the River Nanny continues to produce a range of organic fruit and vegetables for the Dublin Food Co-op, Balbriggan Fish and Farmers' Market and the Mustard Seed Café in Sonairte all year around (see www.sonairte.ie).

Tending plants is as important as sowing and harvesting

'It is women and small farmers working with biodiversity who are the primary food providers in the Third World, and, contrary to the dominant assumption, their biodiversity-based small farms are more productive than industrial monocultures.'

(Dr Vandana Shiva, physicist and advisor to the Government of Bhutan)

THE old motto 'A stitch in time saves nine' applies to gardening. A quick check on young seedlings and older plants can mean the difference between rescuing a plant, if it has been blown over, for example, and writing it off.

I regularly threw dirty dish water, once cooled, over raspberry canes growing in the shadow of the apple tree, which yielded much larger succulent and delicious raspberries last year compared to the raspberry canes in Sonairte, which were grown on a larger scale but were checked by drought.

The quote from Vandana Shiva above highlights the advantage of working a relatively small food-growing area and the higher yield per square metre which is possible in the hands of an attentive grower of food.

For ease of reference, here are some ways to ensure your hard work sowing and planting pays off.

TOP TEN TENDING TIPS

1. **Earth up potato plants.** This entails using a shovel or trowel and adding to the soil level around each potato plant, leaving most leaves showing to continue catching the sun, but burying as

much as possible of the stem. This stimulates the plant to grow more potatoes along the stem, giving a better crop return.

2. **Support any tall plants** which may be prone to blowing over, such as broad beans sown last autumn. I use garden canes, or thin lengths of rough wood, fixed firmly in the ground and tied to make a kind of 'boxing ring' around the beans or broccoli. This prevents wind damage and stops the plants encroaching on pathways.

3. **Coax peas and beans to climb** by guiding tendrils and growing tips towards the twigs, netting or twine that you've put in place to support these climbing vegetables.

4. **Blanche leeks.** When the plants are thicker than a finger, use a trowel or hoe to drag up soil around the stems. This both whitens the stem and anchors the plant to prevent it rocking about in strong winds.

5. **Inspect leafy vegetables** in particular, and remove caterpillars, slugs and snails before they eat their way through your crop. It helps to keep the soil as dry as you can to slow up mollusc mobility, and a fine mesh over brassicas stops butterflies landing and laying eggs.

6. **Remove tomato side shoots.** Removing shoots from the 'armpits' of the tomato plant, between the stem and side branches, channels the plant's energy towards more productive objectives, like growing tomatoes. The tomato plant aroma in the greenhouse is like the smell of summer.

7. **Tie back overhanging branches.** Good summer growth can result in branches and raspberry canes pushing out across footpaths. I tie these back out of harm's way. When the leaves fall next winter, these vigorous shoots can be pruned back – unless they are plums or other cherry family members, which only barely tolerate light pruning during summer and no pruning in winter.

8. **Carefully hoe around vegetables** to keep soil weed free. Hoeing does more than thwart weeds; it also keeps slugs at bay. Invisible to most human eyes are the slimy slug highways which generations of slugs and snails lay down to help the mollusc Diaspora to find and devour your crops. Every time you hoe, the slug equivalent of the National Roads Authority has to reconstruct those slug slip-roads. From a slug's point of view, life is too short, so with a bit of luck the slugs will go foraging in places undisturbed by hoes.

HOEING – A GOOD ORGANIC HABIT.

1. THE OSCILLATING HOE : WEEDS ARE UNDERCUT IN BOTH DIRECTIONS, AS THE BLADE SCUFFLES PARALLEL TO THE GROUND.

2. THE SWAN NECK HAND HOE : MOST FREQUENTLY USED TOOL IN SMALL GARDENS. KEEP BLADE SHARP.

3. THE DUTCH HOE : NOT AS EFFICIENT AS THE OTHER TWO, BUT USEFUL IF BLADE KEPT SHARP AND CLEAN.

TS.

9. **Water strategically.** Some people claim they can drink without getting their lips wet. In the garden it is helpful if one can water plants without getting the soil surface wet. This is possible if you place bottomless upturned plastic bottles in the soil near the plants which need regular watering. These can act like funnels. I have a bank of eight watering cans which I fill

with rainwater topped up with comfrey liquid plant feed. Each time I water by filling those upturned plastic funnels, I observe how fast the water level in each bottle goes down. This tells me how dry the soil in the region of the roots is. Again, dry soil surfaces hamper mollusc mobility.

10. **Keep pathways clear and dry** if possible, to deter slug and snail movements.

OTHER JOBS FOR THE WEEK THAT IS IN IT:

🌿 This is generally a good time to sow outdoor spinach, peas, radish, lettuce, carrots, turnips, salsify, chicory and onion sets.

🌿 Check to see if early-sown potatoes need earthing up.

The Bigger Picture:
Organic growing works with nature

Humanity has evolved as a result of the growth in biodiversity over millennia. The health of humans is dependent on a diverse diet.

Modern highly trained organic farmers take that reality check seriously, starting with the nurturing of healthy soil. Before Rachel Carson published her landmark *Silent Spring* (1962), in which she highlighted the way in which industrial societies were poisoning and extinguishing life, organic farmers were feeding the world without the use of poisons. Indeed, the farmers of forty centuries ago in China were articulating 'the Law of Return', in other words 'What goes around comes around', in their practise of organic farming. Organic farming measures success in terms of quality as well as quantity of food produced.

I hear non-organic farmers claim organic farming is less productive than cultivation using agri-chemicals. I would argue that organic farming optimises production without compromising the soil's capacity to go on producing. To push the soil beyond this optimum point of production is not farming; it is mining the soil – which is cold comfort to a growing world population. Many African governments and aid agencies realise the logic of this organic approach, which they generally call 'sustainable agriculture'. Proper training in modern organic agriculture has been shown to substantially increase production if it is taken up by small-scale food producers, which make up the majority of the world's farmers. According to Professor Ivette Perfecto and her team of researchers at the University of Michigan, USA, organic farming can yield up to three times as much food on individual farms in developing countries as low-intensive methods on the same land. Read more about this research at http://journals.cambridge.org. The Government of Bhutan is working on a plan to become a 100 per cent organic farming nation.

I genuinely believe it is in Ireland's interests to become incrementally 100 per cent organic. Given that much of our food production is already extensive, the conversion to organic methods would not be such a huge ordeal. It made good business sense for Irish salmon farmers to go 100 per cent organic. As a result, Irish salmon is now a big part of Irish food exports to Germany and elsewhere, outdoing much larger non-organic salmon producers in Norway and Chile. Ireland has not got the economies of scale to compete with beef production in Argentina or lamb production in New Zealand. What we can compete on is our clean, green landscape.

Having visited many farms around Ireland and seen a few others in England, Wales, Austria, Germany, Italy and Ethiopia, I can tell how organic and non-organic farmers have certain things in common, such as a wish to avoid problems, reduce overhead costs and get a fair price for the fruits of their labour.

Talking with non-organic farmers, we often agree on the merits of clover to fix, or harness, nitrogen from the atmosphere as a means to avoid the rising costs of artificial nitrogen bought in a bag. Overall, it costs a little more to run an organic holding. For a start, weed killers, pesticides, herbicides, fungicides and other agri-chemicals are not generally permitted on an organic holding. This often means direct labour is required to physically weed and erect pest barriers and netting, etc. to protect crops. A non-organic farmer with a weed problem could instead spray agri-chemicals. Meanwhile the organic farmer has to buy in (the proportionately) more expensive human labour to physically weed the field. However, the extra employment which organic farming generates is yet another reason to support organic production.

Another cost in commercial organic farming is certification. Customer confidence is key for all food producers. Organic farming, therefore, has a legal definition and regulatory requirements which guarantee that any food sold as organic has been produced to standards governing respect for the soil, use of organic seed, compassion for livestock, freedom from contamination by agri-chemicals and no genetically modified organisms. To help me appreciate the reality of converting a plot to become a certified organic plot, I undertook the two-year conversion process with the two main land-based Irish certification bodies, the Organic Trust (www.organic-trust.org) and the Irish Organic Farmers and Growers Association (www.iofga.org). My plot is just 0.0122 of a hectare so I do not expect to make a financial return on the annual fees I pay to be a legally organic holding, which are €200 and €159 respectively.

Personally, I decided to make my kitchen garden legally organic for three reasons: (1) The experience to help me relate to others undertaking or thinking of undertaking this organic conversion process; (2) To help Sonairte nearby in Laytown, Co. Meath, and other organic centres which could use or sell any surplus plants I raised; (3) The buzz of operating the smallest organically certified holding in Ireland, or maybe the smallest in the world – who knows?

Since I embarked on my mission to make my kitchen garden legally organic, the UK organisation Garden Organic have brought in voluntary organic gardening guidelines. These are an excellent way for the non-commercial kitchen gardener to appreciate the benefits and the challenges of growing food organically, without the requirement to pay a fee, keep a record book, make returns, be inspected annually and be subject to a spot check.

You can check out the organic gardening guidelines at www.gardenorganic.org.uk as they are quite comprehensive and helpful, especially for the beginner. All aspects of garden activities are rated in order of preference: (1) Best organic practice – the first choice; (2) Acceptable organic practice; (3) Acceptable, but not for regular use; (4) Never acceptable in an organic garden. Topics covered include:

- Organic soil care
- Plant raising and growing in containers
- Garden and plant health
- Weeds
- Water use
- Wood (timber) use in the garden
- Energy use in the garden

The Irish organic certification organisations are more concerned with commercial farmers and growers but have also mentored those running organic school gardens and encouraged amateur growers through various initiatives. The Irish organisations most relevant to organic horticulture can be contacted through their websites (see above). To read more about the bigger picture, a good start would be www.ifoam.org, which is the website of the International Federation of Organic Agriculture Movements.

🍂 THIRD WEEK IN APRIL 🍂

Tidy up the garden and build a compost heap

'My whole life has been waiting for an epiphany, a manifestation of God's presence, the kind of transcendent, magical experience that lets you see your place in the big picture. And that is what I had with my first compost heap.'

APRIL

(Bette Midler, actress, author and activist in providing environmental education programmes to students from New York high-poverty schools)

WHEN offered a brown bin by my Local Authority to take away all my biodegradable material from the kitchen and the garden, I declined. The compost heap needs all the grass, weeds, hedge clippings and kitchen scraps I can muster. Anyway, a third wheelie bin in this small garden would get in the way.

I have visited some gardens where the compost heap has been kept out of the way as if it was some kind of outdoor toilet or 'privy'. To me, the compost heap is the engine of the garden; the more efficient and fine-tuned it is, the happier everything in the garden will be.

WHY LOCATE THE COMPOSTER CENTRALLY IN THE GARDEN?

🍂 It is warmed by the sun which helps the breakdown of organic material.

🍂 There is sufficient space at the entrance to assemble 'ingredients' to create a compost heap.

🍂 The mature compost can be easily spread around the garden from a central location.

- The compost heap's contact with the soil benefits the adjacent crops of fruit and vegetables.
- The lid of the composter is a suntrap and a handy surface for seed trays and plant pots.

HOW OFTEN SHOULD I EMPTY AND FILL THE COMPOSTER?

Every spring I build a compost heap and it takes about six months for it to become useable compost, even though some partially decomposed twigs, etc. would still be visible. I dig out the composter contents in autumn and spread it as a mulch on plots and around trees and plants. Meanwhile, over the summer, the grass and hedge clippings are collected in old bins in readiness for the autumn compost-making session. Also, over the summer the kitchen scraps are thrown into a compost tumbler along with the newspaper lining from the kitchen compost receptacle which is kept handy under the kitchen sink. Each time the tumbler is 'fed' from the kitchen, it is turned to keep it aerated and to deter any possible visits from brave rats or mice. (They would find it difficult to get past the cat anyway!) In autumn, the empty composter is again filled in layers with the compost ingredients and closed up to 'cook' for another six months until it is opened and spread the following spring. During the winter, the old receptacles and bins are handy for collecting compost ingredients such as spent vegetable stalks and foliage, wilted flowers and prunings, as well as the usual kitchen scraps like banana skins and tea bags.

AS WITH COOKING, THE MAKING OF COMPOST GETS BETTER THE MORE OFTEN IT IS DONE

Compost should neither be too wet nor too dry. It should not smell any more than good soil does. The trick is to have a correct combination of dry organic material (woody, paper, carbon-rich material) with a wet or green mix (grass, vegetable peelings, weeds, old flowers, nitrogen-rich soft material).

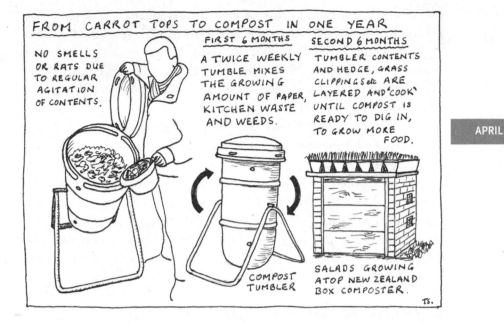

FROM CARROT TOPS TO COMPOST IN ONE YEAR

NO SMELLS OR RATS DUE TO REGULAR AGITATION OF CONTENTS.

FIRST 6 MONTHS
A TWICE WEEKLY TUMBLE MIXES THE GROWING AMOUNT OF PAPER, KITCHEN WASTE AND WEEDS.

SECOND 6 MONTHS
TUMBLER CONTENTS AND HEDGE, GRASS CLIPPINGS etc ARE LAYERED AND 'COOK' UNTIL COMPOST IS READY TO DIG IN, TO GROW MORE FOOD.

COMPOST TUMBLER

SALADS GROWING ATOP NEW ZEALAND BOX COMPOSTER.

A friend in the Welsh Centre for Alternative Technology, Peter Harper, likens building a compost heap to the making of a cheese sandwich. Too much cheese and the sandwich is too overpowering; too little and the sandwich is dry and lacks flavour. In composting terms the woody material is the 'bread' and the green material is the 'cheese'.

More woody material than green material is therefore the proportion to aim for. A 3:1 or 4:1 woody-to-green-material ratio ensures the compost has air pockets enough to help the microbe life in the heap to do its work. The green material provides the food and moisture to sustain the bugs and microbes, which transform these ingredients into 'brown gold' compost at no financial cost.

An hour or so building the compost heap on a spring or autumn weekend is like putting together a giant multi-decker sandwich. Begin with a woody material layer, then some green wilted weeds and grass clippings perhaps, and then add some semi-decomposed kitchen scraps, which I think of as mustard, or mayonnaise, in the multi-decker cheese sandwich. Add another layer of twigs and stalks and the order is repeated again. I have a sledge hammer handy to pound the cabbage and sunflower stalks a bit on the path first so the microbes can more easily get at them to turn this tough stuff into compost.

When the ingredients of this new compost heap are in place and the front or 'door' is put back on the composter, I do two things. First, I get a length of plastic piping, about 2–3 cm (approx. 1 inch) in diameter and long enough to be pushed in to reach the centre of the compost heap. This is an access point for air and any liquid activator. Second, I place old cardboard and carpet around the protruding pipe and cover the compost surface to insulate the heap. A lid of wood, tin, plastic or, in my case, slabs of limestone tops off the composter and keeps out heavy rain.

DOES MAKING COMPOST NEED THE ADDITION OF AN ACTIVATOR?

Compost will break down to become what looks just like soil, given enough time and without any human intervention. Just sprinkle some soil on the heap and you will be introducing millions of compost-transforming bacteria and other microbes. I tend not to use commercially made activators; they normally contain a high nitrogen ingredient like urea. As you might have guessed, there are several readily available free activators which have been used by gardeners down the years, such as:

- Urine is probably the cheapest and best. Some books recommend you dilute it with water 4:1, others say to use it neat. Along with other visitors, The Prince of Wales made an important contribution to the composting system of the UK Centre for Alternative Technology when he made a 'comfort stop' at this hugely popular Welsh tourist attraction. A plaque at the centre commemorates his contribution.

🌿 Seaweed, either freshly harvested, as liquid concentrate or as dried meal

🌿 Nettles compost extremely well, and are a valuable addition to any compost heap

🌿 Comfrey is as good as nettles, but with extra potassium. It is better to use 'Bocking 14' (see The Third Week in February), or another variety which does not spread as wild varieties tend to in a garden situation.

COMPOST AND SOIL GIVE NEW MEANING TO 'HAVING THE WORLD AT YOUR FEET'

A compost heap is even richer in life than soil. Early on in a compost heap, the measurement of vitality in the rough compost shows a hundred thousand million or so bacteria in a teaspoonful. These bacteria can double within an hour and keep on doubling. This frenetic activity gives rise to heat which provides an ideal habitat for the thermophilic (heat-loving) bacteria. This heat kills off weed seeds. As the heap cools, there is plenty of food for other important creatures like tiger worms, mites, springtails, spiders, ants, beetles, centipedes, millipedes, slugs, snails and woodlice. The compost heap is nature's version of 'Sin City'. Life forms prey on other life forms, creating waste which becomes food for others, and all are reproducing to their little hearts' content. All they need from their compost heap is:

🌿 **Air** – twigs keep airways open.

🌿 **Apartments** – scrunched up paper and egg cartons become 'microbe mansions'.

🌿 **Water** – some liquid activator or water is good if the heap becomes too dry.

🌿 **Food** – the green soft material and kitchen scraps become sustenance for all manner of creatures.

WHAT TO DO IF YOU SPOT A RAT NEAR YOUR COMPOST HEAP

In all the decades I have made compost, I have twice seen a rat in the vicinity of the compost heap. These were generally at times when I either did not have a cat or the cat was not well. Having a cat or two or perhaps a Jack Russell-type terrier is an effective rodent deterrent.

However, rats avoid places where there are regular disturbances. Therefore, I make a point of turning the compost tumbler each time I throw in some kitchen scraps. There is merit also (only if you have time) in turning with a garden fork the contents of the maturing compost heap, maybe mid-way through its six-month 'cooking period'. This normally means taking out the semi-ready compost and shovelling it back into the composter again to 'cook' for another while.

Aside from putting off any prospective rodent visitors, turning compost is good for livening up composting activity in the heap; a better, consistent compost generally results.

People advise not to put meat or cooked food in the compost as if rodents are only attracted to meat and ready meals. As it happens, I do not often add these items to my compost, but, in all honesty, rats are not that particular about their food. The key is to regularly disturb the compost. If that fails, copy nature and introduce a predator, in my case Arthur, my trusty cat.

> 'However small your garden, you must provide for two of the serious gardener's necessities: a tool shed and a compost heap.'
> (Anne Scott-James, gardening writer and publisher)

OTHER JOBS FOR THE WEEK THAT IS IN IT:

- Continue to hoe between crops.
- Dig, divide and replant clumps of chives, lovage, mint and marjoram.

Some parts of the world have a month of celebrations to focus on the planet which sustains all life as we know it. Other countries just mark the day itself. The concept of Earth Day is reported to have been first suggested by an Irish-American peace activist, John Mc Donnell, who made the suggestion at a UNESCO Conference on the Environment in San Francisco in 1969. It is fitting that the genesis of this initiative first came to light in the city named after St Francis of Assisi, the patron saint of ecology.

At the time, many American students were engaged in protests against the Vietnam War. Many US campuses had organised 'Vietnam War teach-ins' as a way to inform the protests and plan ways to encourage a military withdrawal from Vietnam. Senator Gaylord Nelson, an environmental activist from Wisconsin, came up with the idea to organise 'environmental teach-ins' in various university campuses, creating a political context which culminated in the declaration of 'Earth Day'.

Senator Nelson had an enlightened sense of urgency about the need for humans to repair environmental damage and to intelligently live within the life-carrying capacity of planet Earth. Given that the Vietnam War was raging at the time, I expect he would relate to Bette Midler who said more recently, 'Every day I have to remind myself that cleaning up the environment is like fighting a war.'

In the Woody Allen film *Annie Hall*, a surreal scene in a cinema queue sees Woody Allen's character calling on Marshall McLuhan, the Canadian philosopher and lecturer in culture and communications, to arbitrate in an argument. In the context of Earth Day, this is the same Marshall McLuhen who coined the expression 'the

APRIL

85

global village'. He is also renowned for having predicted the World Wide Web thirty years before it was invented.

Thinking of the Earth as a global village is now commonplace and helps us to get a better sense of our place in the world and the challenges we need to undertake to make it equitable and sustainable.

Imagine the world as a village of one hundred people. The following statistics are in proportion with the global situation, and certainly make interesting talking points:

🌿 33 are Christians, 28 are Muslims, 21 are from other religions and 28 have no religion.

🌿 The village has a yearly budget of $300,000. $18,000 is used for weapons and warfare, $16,000 for education and $13,000 for health care.

🌿 In 1960, the 20 richest villagers had 30 times more wealth than the poorest 20; now they have 82 times more and they generate 86 per cent of the garbage.

🌿 The village has quadrupled its carbon emissions in the past 50 years.

🌿 The village covers 600 acres of land, 70 of which are cropland, 140 are for pasture and 190 are woodland.

🌿 The average income in the village is $6,000 per year but 50 villagers live on less than $730 ($2 a day).

🌿 Only half the children in the village are immunised against preventable diseases.

🌿 17 villagers are without adequate shelter.

🌿 39 villagers are under 20 years old.

🌿 The life expectancy for the richer villagers is 78 years; for the poorest it is only 52 years.

🍂 78 villagers are in poverty.

🍂 27 villagers do not have access to clean drinking water.

🍂 One of the villagers is a doctor and one is infected with HIV.

🍂 39 villagers are of school age, but only 31 of them actually attend school.

🍂 7 villagers have a car.

🍂 15 villagers live in the richer areas of the village.

🍂 6 have a computer and 3 have access to the internet. 50 of the villagers have never made a phone call.

🍂 78 villagers are literate, 22 are not and only one has a college education.

🍂 Two babies will be born this year and one older person will die.

E.F. Schumacher, in *Small is Beautiful: Economics as if People Mattered*, wrote:

> We must do what we conceive to be the right thing and not bother our heads or burden our souls with whether we will be successful. Because if we do not do the right thing, we will be doing the wrong thing and we will just be part of the disease and not part of the cure.

In many ways Earth Day is a call to arms for every person to do anything at all to make this planet a more hopeful and happy place for all inhabitants. Not to make the greatest possible effort is, according to Schumacher, to be 'just part of the disease and not part of the cure'.

Marshall McLuhan was similarly forthright, but succinct, when he said: 'There are no passengers on Spaceship Earth. We are all crew.'

Springtime sowing

'To bury grief, plant a seed.'
(German proverb)

AT around this time in April, I set aside a couple of hours for a 'big sow'. Scattering seed on the ground is an option, but not the best one in a small garden. I tend to start seeds in pots or seed trays, either on a windowsill or in a small greenhouse.

Advantages of not sowing directly into the soil outdoors:

🍂 Seedlings grow big enough so they can better resist slug predation when planted outside.

🍂 The best seedlings can be selected for outdoor planting so the use of garden space is optimised.

🍂 The ground outside can continue to grow last year's plants for longer until new plants are started and established and ready for planting.

However, even in a small garden, outdoor sowing is better for certain crops. For example, carrots and other root crops, as well as potatoes, prefer to be sown in their ultimate location from the outset. The way to judge if it is the right time to sow outside in the spring is to look at weed growth. When weeds begin to grow well, the soil is then generally warm enough to start other plants from seed. The more tender vegetables like courgettes and tomatoes, whose ancestors originated in warmer climates, should not be planted outside until early June. Whereas kale is happy to grow with a temperature of 5°C outside, carrots, onion and leeks prefer 10°C, runner and French beans prefer 16°C, and tomatoes prefer a temperature of 21°C.

SOWING WITH A VIEW TO TRANSPLANTING THE SEEDLINGS WHEN OUTDOOR CONDITIONS ARE SUITABLE

Seed trays, which are roughly the size of an A4 sheet of paper, are the mainstay of my seed-sowing system. Each seed is sown into a module or block of seed compost. I bought a module-making hand tool which fits exactly twenty-four modules in each seed tray.

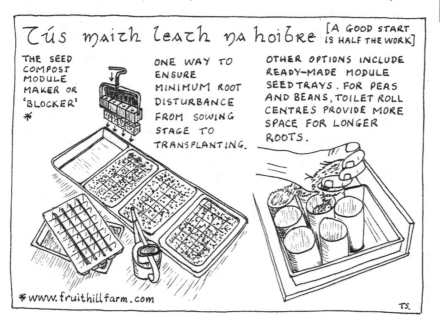

Tús maith leath na hoibre [A GOOD START IS HALF THE WORK]

THE SEED COMPOST MODULE MAKER OR 'BLOCKER' *

ONE WAY TO ENSURE MINIMUM ROOT DISTURBANCE FROM SOWING STAGE TO TRANSPLANTING.

OTHER OPTIONS INCLUDE READY-MADE MODULE SEED TRAYS. FOR PEAS AND BEANS, TOILET ROLL CENTRES PROVIDE MORE SPACE FOR LONGER ROOTS.

* www.fruithillfarm.com

T.S.

I use the compost module maker as follows:

🍂 Wet the required amount of seed compost to fit each seed tray in an old basin or bucket, just enough so that the compost is damp throughout.

🍂 Lightly press the damp compost into the mould in the module maker and force out the blocks line by line in the seed tray until it is full. If the compost is too compressed, the air will be forced out and the module will become too dense for the seed to grow properly.

🍃 The module maker leaves a small hollow in each module for the seed to go into. Bury each seed as deep as its own depth, e.g. lettuce seeds just under the surface but peas seed deeper.

🍃 Large seeds like peas and beans need more compost than the module provides, so I augment the module with a 'high-rise tube of compost' using cardboard toilet-roll centres, in which I sow the peas, beans and also courgettes. This allows the roots of these larger seeds to develop freely before transplantation.

🍃 Label each tray with the date of sowing and the variety of vegetable or flower.

HOW TO STORE THOSE PARTIALLY USED PACKETS OF SEEDS

I seldom use a full packet of seeds, unless I am planting courgettes, as they are sold in small quantities of a dozen seeds or so per packet and I tend to need all those courgette seeds. A packet of carrot seeds may have a couple of hundred seeds. Seeds have developed to remain dormant but alive over winter weather so the trick is to store them in a dry cool place, to trick them into thinking it is winter until they are needed again.

Small lunchboxes or re-useable transparent takeaway containers are handy for storing seed packets in the fridge. I categorise the re-sealed packets as brassicas, legumes, root crops, flowers, etc. Some seeds last longer than others. This is another good reason to sow in seed trays or pots first so any dud seeds are discovered before valuable garden space is used, and only successful seedlings are transplanted.

OTHER TIMES TO SOW SEEDS

Having the seed packets handy in the fridge encourages me to sow little and often throughout the summer and autumn.

🍃 **Summer sowing:** lettuce and radishes in particular grow faster than larger vegetables. I use any spare soil, window boxes and large pots to sow a couple of seeds as a 'catch crop' weekly, to get a salad harvest out before the larger plants grow and cut out the light.

🍂 **Autumn sowing:** the soil is warmer in the autumn than in the spring so germination happens faster. Autumn sowing is good for vegetables with a long-growing season like garlic. Broad beans or onion sets or flowers like candytuft, alyssum, limnanthes and love-in-the-mist are good to sow in the autumn so that next spring they are established enough to flower and crop earlier than spring-sown seeds.

🍂 **Winter planting:** bare-rooted dormant fruit trees and hedges, like beech and apple trees, and blackcurrants can be planted in the darkest days. This gives them time to establish themselves before the coming of summer.

WHICH COMPOST TO USE FOR SEED SOWING

It is possible to make seed sowing compost using leaf mould, comfrey, worm casts and domestic compost mixed with sharp sand, calcified seaweed, etc. However, in a small garden, the quantities required are relatively low. Therefore, I buy a bag of organic peat-free seed compost. I bought my most recent bag when visiting the Wexford Organic Centre at Cushinstown near New Ross. This will last me at least two, maybe three, years. I was glad to sign a pledge for the Irish Peatland Conservation Council not to use peat in the garden for two reasons: (1) to conserve important wildlife habitats in areas where peat may be extracted; and (2) to prove that gardening is possible if (or when!) all the remaining peat is exhausted.

OTHER JOBS FOR THE WEEK THAT IS IN IT:

🍂 Propogate thyme by 'layering', that is to say, pegging long stems from the parent plant into pots until the roots develop and the new plants can be cut loose from the parent plant.

🌿 Continue night patrols with a torch to counteract slug and snail predation on young crops.

The Bigger Picture: Where do we stand with our global ecological footprint?

Peat is just one of the many natural resources humans are consuming at a rate faster than nature can replace it. Given that peat is about 10,000 years in formation, we do not have the luxury of waiting 10,000 years to test the claim that peat is a renewable resource.

According to the 2010 report *The Living Planet*, commissioned by the World Wildlife Fund, humans on average are now living in a way which would require one and a half planets to sustain our current patterns of consumption.

According to the report, Ireland has partially reviewed its 'ecological footprint' account. However, much work still needs to be done. Ireland has the 10th most demanding consumption pattern amongst the 192 member states of the UN. We are not far behind ecological misfits like the United Arab Emirates and Qatar. Each person in Ireland inadvertently demands the equivalent of 6 hectares each to do all we want to do. This is more than double the per-person ecological footprint of other EU member states like Hungary and Romania.

The land area of the island of Ireland is almost 8,193,174 hectares. There are about 6.2 million people resident on the island. Evenly divided, each person would receive about 1.32 hectares or just over 3¼ acres. Not all of this figure is arable land or even open country. About 10 per cent is forestry. However, given the large amount of land now covered in concrete, it makes sense to cultivate any under-utilised areas of soil if we are to be resilient in the face of worldwide competition between arable farming, meat production and energy crops. All I have available to me is my kitchen garden and it is my passion to get as much food from this 0.0122 hectares as nature and organic ingenuity will allow.

The Living Planet report proposes a solution to the global ecological footprint in the form of increasing the biocapacity of the planet. It goes on to state: 'Increasing the yield of crops per unit area can also increase biocapacity.'

Any food grown in Ireland is reducing the need to import food from far away. Instead of tramping our ecological footprint beyond our shores, let us cultivate seriously and seasonally our own island home.

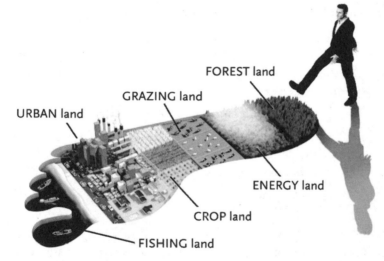

FOREST land

GRAZING land

URBAN land

ENERGY land

CROP land

FISHING land

Thoughts from other kitchen gardeners

LILY CHAMP

Lily Champ is a farmer well known to readers of the *Irish Farmers' Journal,* for which she writes a weekly column about her own kitchen garden near Portarlington, Co. Laois. I look forward to seeing these columns of horticultural wisdom being issued as a book some day. Meanwhile, here is an overview of Lily's kitchen garden.

Describe the location in which you grow your own food:

The kitchen garden is only a few metres from our front door so vegetables do not have to travel far. It is only a small plot and we grow all of our own vegetables there that supply the house all year round.

Which food do you look forward to harvesting most and why?

The new potatoes and luscious peas, which are usually starting to come into use at the end of June, as well as our Royal Sovereign strawberries. These are the first fruits and vegetables of our labour.

Which garden tool do you value most and why?

The hoe is a very valuable tool and we have a couple. One is long handled; the other is a small hand-held swan-neck. This is very handy for negotiating onion ridges and small seedlings, where the seedling weeds seem to thrive.

What motivates you to undertake the work involved in growing food?

I was reared on an almost self-sufficient farm where all our vegetables and poultry came from the farm. I acquired a taste for fresh fruit and vegetables and that never changed through the years.

What advice would you give to a person considering growing their own food?

First of all, you have to be really interested in setting up a garden. Small is the best way to start. Enjoy what you are doing and do not make a chore out of it. Enjoy the fulfilment of seeing a small seed mature into a gorgeous vegetable full of goodness and flavour.

Have you an aspiration for the future in relation to food?

I think we should go organic as much as we can and keep away from the temptation of spraying with insecticides and pesticides, and we should use farmyard manure or compost, not artificial fertiliser

BRUCE DARRELL

Originally from Canada and a qualified architect, Bruce has extensively researched how communities can feed themselves sustainably. He has worked with FEASTA, the Foundation for the Economics of Sustainability (www.feasta.org). Now married with a family, he lives and works at Ireland's first eco-village in Co. Tipperary. Having grown up where no harvesting can take place during the frozen winters, his interests extend beyond growing food and include storage techniques and preserving.

Describe the location in which you grow your own food:

I am a resident of the Cloughjordan Eco-village in North Tipperary, and have had an allotment on the site of the eco-village for five seasons. For the past year I have also been growing vegetables for the Cloughjordan Community Farm, a Community Supported Agriculture project that provides food to about sixty households within the eco-village and surrounding community. Although I have been growing a few vegetables on a field scale, my main focus is on year-round protected cropping within a few polytunnels on the eco-village site.

Which food do you look forward to harvesting most and why?

The foods I look forward to harvesting the most are peas. One of life's simple pleasures is sitting in the garden eating raw peas straight from the plant. I also eagerly anticipate the first new growth of kale in the early spring. I can't understand why most people eat the tough old kale leaves in the autumn and winter. I prefer to leave the plants alone to overwinter and then eat the tender growth of young leaves when other fresh vegetables are scarce. Better still are the immature flower shoots later in the spring, which are very similar to sprouting broccoli, and are one of the true delicacies available during the hunger gap.

Which garden tool do you value most and why?

My most valuable tool is the hoe. I used to prefer a gooseneck or

Dutch hoe, but now I am more likely to use an oscillating hoe with a double-edged blade for managing larger areas. A hoe is the ideal tool for weeding, but I always make sure that it is kept very sharp, so that it cuts the weeds at the soil surface, rather than dragging and transplanting them to a new location. Regular shallow cultivation of the soil also breaks the capillary action by creating a 'dust mulch', which prevents soil moisture from being drawn to the surface and evaporated. This is essential in a polytunnel or greenhouse.

What motivates you to undertake the work involved in growing food?

My primary motivation for becoming involved in growing is food security. As we enter the era of collapsing economies, declining energy availability and climate chaos, developing resilient food systems is an essential task. Although community gardens are a fantastic way to build community and introduce people to food growing, we need to also develop much more productive food systems in a very short time span. This is currently my focus.

What advice would you give to a person considering growing their own food?

For many years I have been advising people to focus on the small and simple. Starting with a few vegetables in the first season, and adding more area and types of vegetables in subsequent years, prevents novice gardeners from becoming overwhelmed before the first season is halfway through. Lately, though, I have been suggesting that people need to produce as much as they can, but to be very focused, especially at the beginning of the year.

Have you an aspiration for the future in relation to food?

My aspiration for the future is to gain the skills, experience and knowledge that are needed to produce the healthiest food possible. What I currently grow is fresh and tasty, but I have come to accept that it is only mediocre in nutritional quality. I believe that understanding how to balance nutrient availability and correct deficiencies in the soil is an essential first step to producing an abundance of highly nutritious food.

Bealtaine 🍃 *May*

Bal's Fire – The First Month of Summer

I N MAY, the penetrating rays of the sun, while not yet at their warmest, shake off the hold of the winter period on the earth. To hasten the coming of fine weather, the Celtic solar deity Bal or Balor was honoured by lighting Bal's Fire, or, in Irish, Bealtaine. At one time, archaeological evidence in Ireland suggests animals were sacrificed as burnt offerings. Other accounts of Lá Bealtaine (May Day) say that two large bonfires were lit. With great incantations, the druids would drive cattle and other livestock between the fires, so the animals would be protected as they were herded to their summer grazing grounds.

Lá bealtaine - MAY DAY

IN GAELIC FOLKLORE, CATTLE AND
PEOPLE PASSED BETWEEN TWO FIRES
TO PURIFY THEMSELVES, TO HONOUR
BAL, THE SUN GOD, AND TO BRING LUCK.
Théidís idir dhá thine na bealtaine.

Bealtaine was the month when the shepherds and herders would head for the hills with the livestock to find fresh lush grazing, while the rest of the family stayed behind to carry out the rest of the farm work and housework. Bealtaine was therefore a festival of farewells. It was also the last festival for a while when all the villagers could let their hair down. This may explain why so many babies were conceived at this time, with birthdays taking place at the festival of Imbolc, in early February, the following year.

The healing and power of growth suggested by Bealtaine is also reflected in the English word 'May' or, in classical traditions, 'Maia'. *Maia* means 'midwife' in Greek. In both Roman and Greek mythology, Maia was the goddess of growth. Christianity capitalised on the goddess Maia tradition and now the month is associated with Mary, the mother of Jesus Christ. Christians also mark 1 May as the Feast day of St Philip and St James, the patron saints of workers. In many places, May Day is a rest day from farm work if the main seed sowing has been completed. In other places, mainly near Government buildings, it is associated with street protest.

In the kitchen garden there is still plenty to be done. If you have marked Lá Bealtaine well, hopefully the work during the rest of the month will, at least some of the time, see the sun on your back.

An overview of the work ahead in the garden this month:
Plant: transplant brassicas from seedbeds.
Sow out: winter cabbages and cauliflower, sprouting broccoli, lettuce; successional sowings – lettuce, radishes, turnips, beetroot, carrots, peas, parsnips, onions, spinach, Japanese brassicas, Oriental salads
Harvest: spring cabbage, spinach and radishes; plus, from now onwards, continual thinnings to be eaten from successively sown crops – lettuce, Japanese brassicas, radishes, turnips, beetroot, carrots, parsnips, onions and spinach, and broad bean tops and kale tops for salads. Thinnings are any crowded seedlings removed to create space for remaining young plants to fully develop.

🍂 FIRST WEEK IN MAY 🍂

Rotation once again as leeks are cleared to make way for the planting of runner beans

'I had four green fields,
Each one was a jewel.'

(Tommy Makem, Irish story teller, poet and artist, 1967)

THE old rebel song 'Four Green Fields', which I have associated since my youth with Tommy Makem, recalls an old woman's fixation with four green fields. As a vegetable gardener, I can relate to that fixation. Every garden should have at least four green 'fields', so that the different families of vegetables can be rotated from field to field each year.

Of course, one man's field is another man's window box. In my case, I have four square plots of four square metres each. The size and shape of the plots naturally vary according to one's balcony, garden, allotment or farm, but the principles across the board are all the same.

Factors in locating your four green fields:

🍂 Try to have each plot as large as possible, but not too wide so you can avoid having to stand on the soil. Compacted soil is less productive. It helps to not walk on the soil, so have all parts of the plot reachable from the pathway.

🍂 Position the plots in as sunny a location as your growing area will allow.

🍂 Keep the soil in each plot either growing a crop or, if the soil is bare, cover it with mulch-like grass clippings, or carpet, cardboard or a purpose-made black porous material from the garden centre.

Two reasons for rotation:

1. To ensure plots are fully used and crops get all the food and growth they need. Each crop family draws on various nutrients in the soil. Legumes (peas and beans), on the other hand, generously take nitrogen from the air and leave it behind for the brassicas to use the following year when cabbages are planted in the same plot, in which the peas and beans have left their fertilising roots.

2. To thwart any diseases and pests. For example, if clubroot, which attacks brassicas, took hold, this would mean that it would not be possible to grow brassicas in the garden for at least twenty years. Similarly, no gardener would want white rot, which attacks onions, or eelworm-infested potatoes. Disciplined rotation denies these soil-borne diseases and pests a source of food or a host, except once every four years. We live in hope that potential pests and diseases starve and expire in the intervening three years of a rotation.

WHAT GOES WHERE IN THE ROTATION?

The St Valentine's message in the Second Week in February 'People Love Bunches Of Roses' is a useful *aide-mémoire* to the traditional ordering of crop families in a five-year rotation, making it easy to recall potatoes–legumes–brassicas–onions–roots.

However, I have had to change this to 'Organic People Love Bunches of Roses', to suit my personal tastes and the limited space in my own garden. As a result, my four plots are growing, in rotation:

- Onions and potatoes
- Legumes
- Brassicas
- Roots

The rotation works in a greenhouse as well as outdoors. The space in my new greenhouse is tight. I got the biggest structure I could to fit the small garden. Nonetheless, the rotation is worth doing under glass, which in effect mirrors the same rotation outdoors.

🌿 **Plot A.** In the 'Organic People' plot outdoors (Plot A), I fill potato bags to plant up potatoes, setting aside some Plot A soil for earthing up the potatoes as they grow in the bags. Onion family crops go in the outdoor plot. Plot A in the greenhouse grows tomatoes and peppers.

🌿 **Plot B.** In the 'Love' plot outdoors (Plot B), I grow legumes – the peas and runner beans. In the greenhouse Plot B, I grow French beans.

🌿 **Plot C.** In the 'Bunches' plot outdoors (Plot C), I grow brassicas such as cabbage, kale, turnip, kohlrabi and radish, which are all related. Plot C in the greenhouse grows lettuce, pakchoi and radish for winter use.

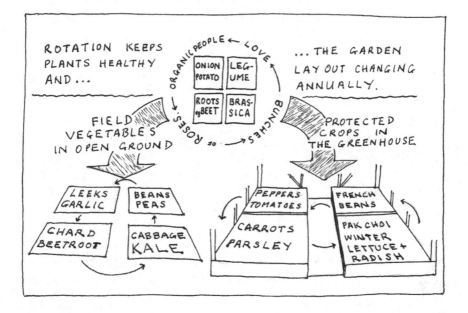

🌿 **Plot D.** I put the beetroot family and carrot family together in the outdoor 'Roses' plot, Plot D, as I do not have space for a fifth plot. As with the potatoes, I fill a large terracotta pot with soil from Plot D in which to sow the carrots. This leaves me space outdoors to grow my favourite vegetables – beetroot, chard, spinach and leaf beet. In the greenhouse Plot D, I grow carrots and parsley as well.

WHICH PLOT GETS THE MATURE COMPOST EACH YEAR?

🍃 Plot A gets the bulk of the spring compost. After the winter, the compost is good but not very fine. Both potatoes and the onion family are happy to grow in this rich but somewhat rough mixture of soil and compost.

🍃 Plot B gets no compost as the fertility is still high enough from last year's potato and onion crops. Anyway, the legumes can supplement their nutrient needs by fixing nitrogen from the air into the soil.

🍃 Plot C gets the bulk of the autumn compost mulched around the brassicas already growing there. This is a finer compost than the compost dug out in the spring, as it has had the heat of the summer to help it decompose more fully.

🍃 Plot D gets no compost as it is fertile enough from the composting of cabbages which grew there last year. Anyway, to grow carrots and beetroot, the finer the tilth, the better. If fresh compost is put where carrots are to be grown shortly afterwards, the roots tend to fork.

AUTUMN AND SPRING PLANTINGS ALL FOLLOW THE ROTATION ROLLER COASTER

The discipline of commercial farming tends to see fields cleared fully before the next crop is planted. In a kitchen garden, the ebb and flow of planting happens on a more staggered basis to ensure as continuous as possible an availability of fresh produce day by day, all year around.

For example, the broad bean plants will be ready for planting out in the autumn. These will go into the space from where I harvested the garlic. The leeks, which grow alongside this space, will remain as I need them over the winter. In spring, when the runner bean plants are ready to go in, I clear away any remaining leeks and then the plot will become fully a legume patch. That is the job I have been doing this week.

OTHER JOBS FOR THE WEEK THAT IS IN IT:

🌿 Sow peppers for greenhouse growing.

🌿 Sow courgettes indoors for greenhouse growing, or, if space is tight, transplant later outdoors.

The Bigger Picture:
Weed identification and usefulness

Weeds (or self-sown plants, if you prefer) are first and foremost indicators of soil fertility and growing conditions. For example, if the stinging nettle is growing well, the soil is both fertile and warm enough to germinate a whole range of vegetable seeds.

VEGETABLE	GERMINATION TEMP. (°C)	VEGETABLE	GERMINATION TEMP. (°C)
Lettuce	2	Radish	6
Broad bean	5	Peas	6
Broccoli, sprouting	5	Beetroot/leaf beet	7
Brussels sprout	5	Spinach/chard	7
Calabrese	5	Carrot	7
Cabbage	5	Leek	7
Cauliflower	5	Onion	7
Kale	5	Parsnip	7

Other vegetables whose wild ancestors hail from warmer climates must wait for higher outdoor temperatures before sowing and planting out.

VEGETABLE	GERMINATION TEMP (°C)
Celery/celeriac	10
French and runner bean	12
Sweet corn	12
Cucurbit	13
Tomato	13
Courgette	13
Pepper	13

Weeds which indicate problems:

🌿 If Creeping Buttercup (*Ranunculus repens*) dominates, this indicates a soil with deficiencies, which needs compost. This weed also uses up potassium in the soil and so needs to be taken out and kept out of where vegetables are growing.

🌿 Groundsel (*Senecio vulgaris*) indicates a moist heavy soil, and, again, the addition of compost and perhaps some horticultural sand would improve drainage and lighten the soil. Groundsel is a plant which harbours rust, however, so it is not compatible with my garlic, for example, which is showing the blotchy leaves associated with rust. However, rust does not affect the garlic bulbs, so it could be worse.

🌿 Chickweed (*Stellaria media*) is edible and so can be useful. However it is also a host plant for whitefly, red spider mite and cucumber mosaic virus. As such, it makes sense to keep on top of it with the hoe around vegetable plots. It procreates very fast, producing seed in as little as five weeks. Regular hoeing in all areas that need to be weed free is good practice.

The case for keeping some weeds as food for humans and wildlife alike:

PLANT	EDIBLE PART	PREPARATION	WARNING
Borage (*Borago officinalis*)	Leaves and flowers	Flowers in salads. Cook leaves with cabbage or soups.	
Chickweed (*Stellaria media*)	Foliage	In salads or sautéed in a little oil with a splash of soy sauce.	
Cleavers (*Galium aparine*)	Seeds, leaves and stems	Cook young shoots as a 'spinach'. Seeds can be roasted and ground for a coffee.	
Common Sorrel (*Rumex acetosa*)	Leaves	In salads	Oxalic acid can be toxic in large quantities, so use sparingly.
Dandelion (*Taraxacum officinale*)	All parts	Young leaves in salads. Flowers to make wine. Roots for coffee	
Fat Hen (*Chenopodium album*)	Leaves and seeds	Cook leaves as 'spinach'. Eat seeds as a whole grain or grind into flour.	Can be toxic in large amounts. Cooking reduces the potency.
Ground Elder (*Aegopodium podagraria*)	All parts	Young leaves in salads or cooked as 'spinach'. Roots dried and ground into flour	
Hairy Bittercress (*Cardamine hirsuta*)	Leaves have a rocket-like flavour.	In salads	
Stinging Nettle (*Urtica dioica*)	Young shoots and leaves	Cook as 'spinach' and in soup. Infused as a herbal tea	Do not eat mature flowering plants as at this stage they can cause kidney damage.
Sheep's Sorrel (*Rumex acetosella*)	Leaves have a sharp flavour; best eaten young.	In salads	
Smooth Sow Thistle (*Sonchus oleraceus*)	Leaves are not prickly.	In salads	
Spear thistle (*Cirsium vulgare*)	Flower heads	Strip out base of flower heads and steam lightly or eat raw.	
Thale Cress (*Arabidopsis thaliana*)	Leaves have a mustard flavour.	In salads	
Wild Garlic (*Allium ursinum*)	All parts	Leaves in salads or cooked as 'spinach'; use bulbs as for cultivated garlic.	
Wood Sorrel (*Oxalis acetosella*)	Leaves have a tangy flavour.	Leaves in salads or cooked as 'spinach'.	Contains oxalic acid so should not be consumed in large quantities.

(Information based on www.dgsgardening.btinternet.co.uk/weeds.htm).

ADDING TO THE WILD LARDER BY LETTING CULTIVATED PLANTS GO TO SEED

The above 'weeds' and many others are all interesting, mainly because they are edible or they are important food plants for butterflies like stinging nettles and Buddleja. Over the years, I have purposely allowed some specimen vegetables go to seed as an experiment. As a result, I now have the pleasure of self-seeded fennel, lamb's lettuce, nasturtiums, white and blue-flowered borage, sunflowers, cosmos, cabbage, kale and chard – all conveniently popping up year after year in various corners of the garden with no effort on my part.

THE GARDEN AS A 'MEDICINE CHEST'

Seán Boylan, the very successful former Meath football manager, is one famous herbalist I know. Some years ago I invited him to speak to parents at the school where I was principal teacher in Balbriggan. He shone a light on the potential of many wild or naturalised plants which are familiar. If you think you have a plant in your garden which can cure an ailment, consult a qualified herbalist about it or become more qualified in herbal medicine yourself. Meanwhile, the Latin names of plants can be a clue to their past uses. Many plants which have a medicinal or culinary use have the species name officinale or officinalis.

🍃 SECOND WEEK IN MAY 🍃

Air wars and ground wars
– the challenges of slug and caterpillar predation

'You don't have a slug excess, you've got a duck deficit.'
(Bill Mollison, permaculture teacher and 'Alternative Nobel Prize' winner)

WHEN it comes to slugs and snails, I have changed my attitude and actions over the years. I used to think that killing them was the only effective way to control their prolific numbers and voracious appetite for my vegetables. After all, a garden slug can lay 400 eggs in a year. Like conveyor belts, replacement rows of slug teeth move up to replace the row which has worn out. A small slug can eat twice its body weight in one night. Only 5 per cent of the slug population appears above ground at any one time. However, believe it or not, experience and some research have taught me to be less into killing and more into cunning.

GETTING INSIDE THE MIND OF A MOLLUSC

Slugs need moisture to travel efficiently. Also, if it is dry, slug eggs do not hatch well. To compensate for the nuisance of dry days, slugs and snails excrete slime to create pathways along which they travel back and forth, similar to the way humans travel along paved roads and paths. Like humans, too, slugs hate rush hour, so they stagger their feeding times; however, they prefer night time since they can avoid the dryness of sunshine and wind. Slugs are territorial and mark their territory and favourite feeding areas with their own scent. So throwing the slug over a fence is not very clever, unless your plan is to breed fitter marathon-running slugs. Slugs

107

attack (small) intruders in their patch such as caterpillars, but their defence against humans is stealth and strength in numbers. They also figure humans will not bother to study the form and understand the ways of the slug. In this regard, slugs are generally on the ball.

PLAN YOUR GARDEN TO BE AN UNATTRACTIVE PLACE FOR SLUGS AND SNAILS

Slugs and snails are not comfortable in an open tidy garden and find it difficult to move around on dry rough surfaces. Having a couple of ducks or hens would certainly put off the most stubborn slug. My garden is too small for poultry, so I am one of the many who swap tips and stories about the latest gadgets, potions and 'cute hoor' tricks to protect the garden produce from the mollusc menace.

Top ten strategies to keep slug and snail numbers at a low level:

1. Pray for a very cold spell to kill off the overwintering slug eggs in the soil.

2. Put comfrey leaves or a damp plank of wood on a seedbed before sowing for a few nights to lure slugs to hide underneath it – then remove them in the morning.

3. Bury glass jars with just rims showing between slug haunts and the vegetable-growing areas. Fill them with beer and water, half and half, and add a little sugar. When full of slug bodies, empty the jar and refill it with the same mixture. Glass jars are best as the slug finds them too slippery to climb out of.

4. Hoe in the morning to expose slug eggs for the birds and to wreck the slimy slip-roads made by molluscs the night before.

5. Before going to bed, search by torchlight and, as humanely as possible, put a halt to the gallop of any slug or snail you encounter gnawing at your plants.

6. Place a few physical mollusc barriers around vegetable patches and vulnerable plants, such as wood ash or sand or old ground coffee. Dry material like ash or even cat fur is a desiccant and dries the slug slime, stopping them in their tracks. Crushed egg shells roasted in the oven are dry and also sharp to a slug or snail. These tricks are better in a greenhouse than outdoors. Once rain falls, the 'dry factor' disappears and all bets are off once again!

7. Water plants without wetting the soil surface. As mentioned in the Second Week in April, upturned plastic bottle 'funnels' stuck in the soil near the plants needing water are filled from the watering can, thus keeping dry the soil around each watering point.

8. Copperband barriers are sold as rolls of sticky-backed copper tape. These can be stuck to the rims of pots. The copper gives a small electric shock to any moist mollusc touching it. I used a garden riddle with copper stuck around it as a slug deterrent when I placed it over radish seedlings in the soil. It seemed to work.

9. Encourage mollusc predators like frogs, toads and hedgehogs to frequent the garden. A pond is a bonus in this regard but a shallow basin of water or a bird bath is good too. Blackbirds sometimes go for snails but I have yet to see them devour slugs. Can't say I blame them!

10. Commercial organic slug pellets like Fertosan or nematode slug parasites sold at Nemasys (www.nemasysinfo.com), and other such products, are used by my grower colleagues, including large-scale organic farmers. Commercial garlic-spray products, now on the market, may deter vampires, whatever about slugs and snails. I regard these as products of last resort, but their time may come yet.

How to get slug slime off your hands:

Pour a little white vinegar on your hands and wash it off with lukewarm water. Repeat if necessary. Better still, wear gloves and avoid getting slime on your hands in the first place.

PROTECT YOUR BRASSICAS WITH FLEECE OR FINE NETTING TO GUARD AGAINST THE 'CABBAGE WHITE'

There are three species of caterpillar which can damage brassicas: (1) the Large Cabbage White butterfly; (2) the Small White butterfly; and (3) the Cabbage Moth. If you have just a few plants, an inspection every couple of days to check the underside of brassica leaves for clusters of yellow eggs will be necessary. Once you find eggs or caterpillars, rub them off with your thumb.

The eggs start to appear during April and May. If allowed to hatch, these caterpillars return to your brassica patch during August and September to lay more eggs with a view to feeding their young on your plants. Therefore, remember to inspect in the autumn too.

If you have no time to check each leaf underside, then a fine mesh or fleece draped over a frame of sticks can protect your crop. I put upturned cartons or bottles on each stick or bamboo cane to prevent the net or fleece from tearing. Then be sure to seal the edges where the fleece or net meets the ground. Also, ensure no brassica leaves are touching the edges as the butterfly can lay eggs if in contact with a leaf.

Even with the netting, keep an eye on the patch. It is incredible how determined these butterflies are to find brassica leaves. The slightest gap in your defences will be found and it is quite frustrating to find a butterfly merrily flying and laying on the *inside* of the defences you have worked long and hard to construct, believe me!

OTHER JOBS FOR THE WEEK THAT IS IN IT:

Sow French and runner beans indoors for greenhouse growing or, if space is tight, for transplanting later outdoors.

🍃 De-blossom spring-sown strawberry plants to help them develop for a good crop next year.

The Bigger Picture:
Benefits of compost and compost tea for a productive garden

As mentioned before, the making and spreading of compost is critical for good soil health and a sustainably productive garden.

The curriculum vitae of compost is impressive:

🍃 Provides food for plants slowly over time, which is the best way.

🍃 Improves the soil structure.

🍃 Makes heavy soils more workable.

🍃 Increases the amount of water a soil can hold.

🍃 Promotes the biological activity in the soil, which keeps it healthy and vibrant for plants.

🍃 Cushions extreme changes in pH.

🍃 Reduces erosion and nutrient leaching.

🍃 May help suppress plant diseases.

WHAT IS A GOOD RATE AT WHICH TO APPLY COMPOST?

Generally, one wheelbarrow load for every 5 sq. m of soil (16 sq. ft) is a good guide to how much compost should be applied. This equates to a layer of compost about 1 cm (0.5 inches) deep over the growing area. Apply compost annually to plants that like rich soil – for instance, soft fruit and roses – and every second or third year to plants that are less hungry, such as top fruit, for example, apples, most shrubs and herbaceous perennials like hedges.

As mentioned above, give compost to the plants which make the most use of it – potatoes and the cabbage families. On poorer soils, squash, chard, onions and beetroot will also benefit. Carrots, peas, beans and parsnips will generally thrive on the leftovers from a previously composted cropping area.

WHAT DOES COMPOST CONTAIN – IN THE MAIN?

Good quality compost is bountiful with a diverse and thriving community of billions upon billions of beneficial microorganisms, for example, bacteria, fungal feeders and predatory nematodes, which introduce a microbial workforce into the soil environment. It also contains plant foods like potassium and trace elements, and offers a reasonable supply of phosphate. It also contains some nitrogen, but, as this is released very slowly, compost is not regarded as a high-nitrogen source.

HOW TO MAKE 'COMPOST TEA'

'Compost tea' is a good nitrogen tonic to use when watering crops. Because compost is not a high-nitrogen feed, it makes sense to add nitrogen in liquid form when watering the crop to assist plant growth. I use two forms of compost tea as liquid feeds.

🌿 Nettle compost tea: stinging nettles are rich in nitrogen. In spring, I collect enough to fill a barrel with a tap to the base. This is topped up with rain or tap water. After 'stewing' for a fortnight or more, I drain off the liquid into two-litre empty plastic milk containers and seal the screw-tops. It is now ready for use.

🌿 Comfrey compost tea: 'Bocking 14', the variety of comfrey I have growing, is fast growing and rich in potassium as well as nitrogen. I make this compost tea in the usual way when the nettle compost tea is finished. The extra potassium in this compost tea help plants when they are fruiting, like tomatoes, peas, beans and potatoes.

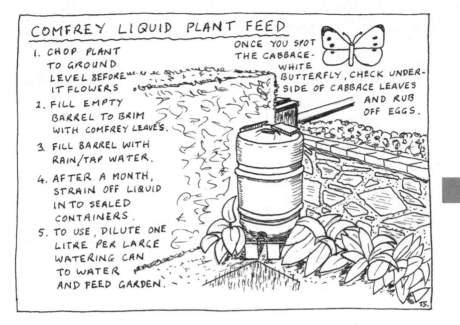

COMFREY LIQUID PLANT FEED

1. CHOP PLANT TO GROUND LEVEL BEFORE IT FLOWERS

2. FILL EMPTY BARREL TO BRIM WITH COMFREY LEAVES.

3. FILL BARREL WITH RAIN/TAP WATER.

4. AFTER A MONTH, STRAIN OFF LIQUID INTO SEALED CONTAINERS.

5. TO USE, DILUTE ONE LITRE PER LARGE WATERING CAN TO WATER AND FEED GARDEN.

ONCE YOU SPOT THE CABBAGE-WHITE BUTTERFLY, CHECK UNDER-SIDE OF CABBAGE LEAVES AND RUB OFF EGGS.

USING COMPOST TEA IN THE GARDEN

One must be careful not to water, or indeed liquid feed, plants too often. To know if watering is required, remove a few centimetres from a patch of soil. If the soil below is dry then it is time to water.

I have eight watering cans. I fill each almost to the top but leave space to pour a litre of nettle or comfrey compost tea in each one and mix it with a stick to aerate the solution. I leave this overnight, so that the microbes can multiply in the liquid compost, fed by the oxygen in the agitated watering can.

The next day, with a watering can in each hand, I head for each vegetable plot. The healthy size of the cabbage leaves, sunflowers, peas and all the vegetables and fruit convinces me that compost tea is a worthwhile addition to those watering cans.

Planting window boxes and containers with radishes

'What do I know of man's destiny?
I could tell you more about radishes.'

(Samuel Beckett, 1906–1989)

GROWING radishes whetted my interest in container growing. The shop-bought, imported radish was never satisfactory, tasting of chemicals and always softer than the ones picked and eaten fresh from the garden. However, radishes grow to the beat of a different drum compared to other vegetables. Radish seed can be sown in any month of the year, under a cloche or in a greenhouse in the winter. The time it takes to grow is between three and five weeks, depending on daylight hours. Radishes can be grown in between slower growing vegetables as a 'catch crop'. I do this, but for a continuous supply of this peppery crunchy brassica, I have devised a successional sowing system using window boxes.

ASSEMBLING WINDOW BOXES TO KEEP ME IN RADISHES FROM SPRING TO AUTUMN

Seven window boxes at chest height atop the composter in the garden has that 'Gulliver in Lilliput' feel to it, as I treat each container as a tiny plot or 'field' in a successional planting system. I sow a fresh window box each week with a couple of dozen radish seeds. By the time the third box is sown, the first box has seedlings growing away. By the time the seventh box is sown, it is time to harvest the first box, leaving a cleared box to sow another few seeds the following Sunday. From then on, there will be a continuous new supply of radishes each week if the following straightforward steps are followed:

QUICK RADISH — SOW SOME SEED EVERY SATURDAY
(AND HARVEST AT THE SAME TIME!)

—KEEP SEED PACKET IN SEALED JAR IN FRIDGE.
— SOW SOME SEED EVERY WEEK.
— KEEP SEEDBED WEEDED AND WATER AS REQUIRED.
— AS RADISHES ARE EATEN, PREPARE SEEDBED
AND SOW AGAIN.

WK. WK WK WK WK WK WK
1 2 3 4 5 6 7

SOW SPARINGLY. RADISHES NEED THEIR SPACE TOO.

'FRENCH BREAKFAST' MY FAVOURITE RADISH TO GROW — AND EAT.

1. Clear a surface such as an outdoor table, a corner of a balcony, or, in my case, the flat top of the composter. Check the surface will take the weight of a few window boxes full of damp soil.

2. Assemble a few containers. I re-use my window boxes each year as they fit the space well.

3. Number the containers one to seven, or six, or five, depending on your situation.

4. Fill the containers with the most fertile soil you have. Water the first container of soil where the first sowing is to take place. If you are planning a rotation, then you can take some soil from where the brassica (cabbage) family are to grow. Even though we generally only eat the root, the radish is in fact a brassica.

5. Buy a packet of radish seed and, once opened, keep the packet of remaining seeds in a sealed glass jar in the fridge.

6. Pour a dozen or more seeds into the palm of your dry hand.

Reseal the packet in the glass jar. Space the seeds evenly on the container's soil surface.

7. With a trowel, barely cover the seeds with a thin covering of soil. Pat down the new seedbed to ensure the seeds are firmly in contact with the damp soil.

8. A week later, perform the same routine with the second window box of damp soil, and so on, week by week.

9. Water this mini-patch of containers as necessary and pick out any weeds which are competing with your radish seedlings.

A lettuce plant can be grown at the end of each window box. Having chest-high radish and lettuce leaves ready for picking at any time gives the term 'raised bed' a whole new meaning!

SOME FRAGRANT FLOWERS

Are there any fragrances more enticing and memorable than Night-scented Stock, Nicotiana or Honeysuckle? Maybe there are, but these are the ones I enjoy on a sunny evening when their perfume is strongest. As darkness falls, those fragrances get stronger. It is well worth having a couple of containers of these flowers and a window box or two near the house, to remind one and all that there is so much more to a kitchen garden than the production of food. Once the seedlings of annual flowers grow big enough to withstand slug attacks, they take very little looking after. Watering is important as containers dry out quicker than the open ground. Removing flowers once they wilt is a neat trick which encourages more flowers to form. I find 'deadheading', as this is called, quite therapeutic, but perhaps that is just me!

OTHER JOBS FOR THE WEEK THAT IS IN IT:

This is your last chance to sow seed potatoes.

Transplant any young rhubarb plants grown indoors from seed.

The Bigger Picture:
'Eat food. Not too much. Mostly plants'

Kitchen gardening for me went from being a hobby to being a crusade after a conversation I had over breakfast with the Vice-President of the American Diabetes Association while we were both guests at Ballymaloe House, near Midleton in Co. Cork. Apart from the pain, inconvenience, personal cost and expenditure incurred by each patient and their families, the diabetic was costing the US taxpayer about ten times the cost of health care for a relatively healthy citizen. If ever there was an argument for prevention being better than a cure, then the potential collective cost – more of us getting sick – is it.

I then had the good fortune to read a brilliant, witty and intelligent book by the US writer Michael Pollan, called *In Defence of Food – The Myth of Nutrition and the Pleasures of Eating*. Pollan's manifesto is 'Eat food. Not too much. Mostly plants.' His research is worth noting.

The paradox of the food business is that it is more profitable to sell us processed food than it is to sell us fresh unprocessed food. Yet the processed food is less nutritious. Food with a long shelf life takes longer to go off. It is not attacked by fungi or bacteria because these microbes do not rate it as nutritious and desirable either – so why should we?

Michael Pollan reminds us that in France and Italy people eat all sorts of food, including chocolate, meat and dairy, as well as fresh vegetables and fruit, yet they have nothing like the obesity problem of the USA. He contends that, in the USA, food is seen mainly as a delivery system for nutrients, whereas in the Mediterranean countries, food is first and foremost about pleasure, sociality and identity. One salient difference is that, Stateside, over half of all meals are now eaten outside of the home and most of the ingredients are therefore unknown to the consumer. I hear from friends who are coeliac that this is a hassle when on holidays in the USA as it is difficult to know *exactly* what is being offered in a meal or snack.

The perennial debate about whether Ireland is closer to Berlin or Boston is now dated, as, in truth, Ireland is tied economically to Berlin. However, in health terms, we could do worse than learn from the food cultures of people who are healthier than we are, such as those of Continental Europe. In culinary terms, are we closer to Naples or New York, Turin or Texas, Bordeaux or Buffalo? The signs are not encouraging, if health is the yardstick.

Let us take a look at the countries eating the most processed breakfast cereals in the world. The average consumption of dehydrated cereals in Mediterranean countries is 1 kg per person per annum. Our neighbours in the UK like their processed cereals, eating 6.7 kg per person. Before we presume the USA has the highest per capita consumption, think twice. The highest per capita consumer of processed cereals in the world is Ireland, where we munch through 8.4 kg per person every year, according to Felicity Lawrence in her book *Eat Your Heart Out*: *Why the Food Business is Bad for the Planet and Your Health*.

During a recession, there are many people who cannot afford to get sick. As a country, we cannot afford to ignore dietary trends and habits which make us unhealthy, overweight and, all too often, sick. During my time as Minister for Food, I was like a broken record urging anyone who would listen to eat at least five and, better still, ten portions a day of fresh fruit and vegetables, particularly leafy green vegetables. There is evidence that more people are eating a greater percentage of fresh food in their diet now, thankfully. However, on average, Irish people still eat less than five portions of fresh fruit and vegetables a day.

Even so, the growing of fresh produce in Ireland does not meet the demand (see the Fourth Week in March). While some crops are seasonal, like tomatoes, cauliflower and cabbage, the technology is now there to store onions, potatoes and apples all year round if necessary.

If Irish people were eating a healthy diet containing enough fresh fruit and vegetables, then these production levels would look even more inadequate. The challenge for our economic as well as our personal health is twofold. First, more of us need to include more fresh unprocessed seasonal food into our dietary habits. Second, our farmers and growers, especially those growing organically, need to be able to make a living supplying their wider communities with sustainably produced healthy food.

In terms of the first challenge, I have seen with my own eyes how children will eat lettuce they have grown themselves, whereas before they shunned lettuce bought in a shop. One answer to eating more fresh food is to grow some food yourself.

In terms of the second challenge, I have seen people grow cabbage and then be more open to buying it when they have no more in the garden, while appreciating the farmer's efforts all the more. One answer to instilling loyalty to local farmers is to grow some food yourself.

There is a further challenge which is looming as well, of course. Who is going to make up the shortfall in fresh produce production if, and I predict when, those ubiquitous imports are not available to buy? Then we will not be so much digging for victory as sowing for survival!

Beetroot, the easiest to grow and tastiest crop (in my opinion)

'When I was a childcare and gardening volunteer at an orphanage in Mexico, the head gardener often lamented to me that he was never able to raise a crop of beetroots to maturity. The kids loved them so much that they would sneak into the garden in the evening, uproot those beets, and eat them raw!'

(John Peterson, *Farmer John's Cookbook*, www.angelicorganics.com)

The fact that beetroot is my favourite vegetable has nothing to do with Sergeant Beetroot, the character played by the British comedy actor and vegetarian Bill Maynard, who I remember from *The Trial of Worzel Gummidge*. Such are the childhood memories of this kitchen gardener.

However, like many people, my childhood memories of beetroot are of cold round slices from a jar, tasting more of vinegar than vegetable. The first time I ate hot freshly cooked beetroot dug fresh from the garden, my respect for *Beta vulgaris* was assured for life. I became another of a long line of beetroot fans going back over 4,000 years, when there are records of beetroot growing in the Nile and Indus region. Such a useful, nutritious and flavoursome vegetable was bound to be popular.

Both the leaves and root are edible. The Ancient Greeks ate the leaf of the beet, while the Romans mainly enjoyed its swollen red root. This may explain why English records refer to 'Roman beet' in Tudor times. In 1597, gardening writer John Gerard of London, England, wrote of the 'great red beete': 'the beautiful roote which is to be preferred before the leaves, as well in beauty as in goodnesse.' By 1656 the beetroot, now being grown by the English gardener and plant hunter John Tradescant the Younger, was referred to as the 'beet-rave' or beet radish, from the French 'betterave' (see *Spade, Skirret and Parsnip: The Curious History of Vegetables* by Bill Laws).

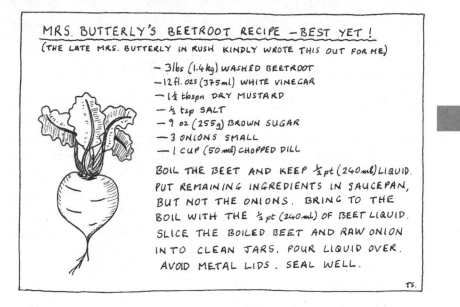

MRS. BUTTERLY'S BEETROOT RECIPE — BEST YET!

(THE LATE MRS. BUTTERLY IN RUSH KINDLY WROTE THIS OUT FOR ME)

- 3 lbs (1.4 kg) WASHED BEETROOT
- 12 fl. ozs (375 ml) WHITE VINEGAR
- 1½ tbspn DRY MUSTARD
- ½ tsp SALT
- 9 oz (255 g) BROWN SUGAR
- 3 ONIONS SMALL
- 1 CUP (50 ml) CHOPPED DILL

BOIL THE BEET AND KEEP ½ pt (240 ml) LIQUID. PUT REMAINING INGREDIENTS IN SAUCEPAN, BUT NOT THE ONIONS. BRING TO THE BOIL WITH THE ½ pt (240 ml) OF BEET LIQUID. SLICE THE BOILED BEET AND RAW ONION INTO CLEAN JARS. POUR LIQUID OVER. AVOID METAL LIDS. SEAL WELL.

TS.

SOIL AND LOCATION REQUIREMENTS FOR GROWING BEETROOT

Beetroot is not a direct relative of the carrot or parsnip, but it does behave like a root crop. In other words, it is prone to deformity if grown in soil containing fresh compost or manure. It makes sense to grow beetroot in a patch which was composted the previous year, perhaps to feed soil growing a hungry brassica crop. The ancestor of today's beetroot was a coastal leafy plant called sea beet. This wild species was bred to accentuate various characteristics, which led to the commercialisation of beetroot, leafbeet, chard, perpetual spinach, sugar beet and mangle, as well as many different colours and shapes of beetroot also. Location wise, therefore, the beet family has a traditional tolerance for salty air conditions. It is not a fussy vegetable and is generally free of pests and diseases.

If you sow beetroot directly into the garden, sparrows may swipe a couple of seeds. If the patch has been home to large families of slugs, then slug patrols and deterrents will be needed (see the Second Week in May). I have heard gardeners say that sprinkling rock salt around young plants is an option as the beet family are not averse to salty coastal conditions.

WHEN AND HOW TO SOW BEETROOT SEEDS

April and May are the normal times to sow beetroot in Europe. However, sowing later in Ireland is sometimes better to ensure vigorous growth. Beetroot does not like a 'start–stop' growing season, which can happen if the seeds go in too early in changeable weather.

I have sown beetroot directly into the ground but now I prefer to sow a seed in each module of seed compost in a seed tray. To sow directly, I scooped out a line with a trowel about 2 cm (1 inch) deep. The seeds were spaced about 5 cm (2 inches) apart. In the seed tray, it is best to wet the compost first, press a seed in and press down each module of compost gently. Avoid letting the seeds and compost dry out but do not over-water either.

CARE AFTER GERMINATION

In about fourteen days, the beetroot seeds germinate. If the day is fine, leave the seed tray outdoors in the sun. Watch out for pigeons which can pick at the leaves. When the seedlings are a couple of inches tall, thin those in the ground or plant out the modules from the seed tray, leaving 9 cm (4 inches) or so between each plant. If predation by slugs or birds is a problem, then a mini-cloche can be a help, i.e. a clear plastic 1l or 2l bottle, with the base cut off and the bottle cap removed, placed over the seedling. Do not forget to water the plants if the soil is dry.

HARVESTING BEETROOT

After about nine weeks, attention turns to harvesting. Beetroots with a diameter of 2–6 cm (between 1 and 3 inches) are worth digging up. The smaller they are when they are picked, the sweeter they are. Others may be afraid the roots will go woody if the plants are left too long in the ground. However, I have let my crop sit until Christmas and they tasted wonderful.

STORAGE OF BEETROOT

I have pickled beetroot on a number of occasions and may do so again. The beetroot from my patch, both bottled and stored, and cooked fresh, lasted me the whole year. The space this patch took up is exactly the rectangular outline of an average internal house door. If bottling is not your thing, then store the beetroot in damp sand in a cool dark place. Before placing the roots in the sand, twist off the leaves about 5 cm (2 inches) above the globe root. I normally make a lovely side dish with the leaves, cooking them as I would spinach. They're not as tasty as spinach, but are good in small quantities.

OTHER JOBS FOR THE WEEK THAT IS IN IT:

- Take advantage of any dry warm days to hoe weeds.
- Re-pot into larger containers any pot-bound plants, unless you are ready to transplant them in open soil.

The Bigger Picture: Rachel Carson's birthday

Rachel Carson was born on 27 May 1907 and grew up on a small farm in Pennsylvania where she later became a marine biologist. She worked for the US Fish and Wildlife Service and lectured in zoology at the University of Maryland. At a time when female scientists were rare, this shy but determined woman recognised that the growing use of pesticides was having a devastating effect on far more than the target pests for which the chemicals had been designed.

Since 1947, Rachel had been collecting disquieting evidence of the ecologically disruptive effects of organochlorine pesticides, especially dichlorodiphenyltrichloroethane, later to be known as DDT, which had been used to prevent epidemics of insect and acarine-borne diseases such a malaria and typhus during the latter years of World War II. New markets for these chemicals were sought after the war and agri-chemicals became the new growth area for chemical companies.

While living in Southport, Maine, Rachel received a letter to say that after an agri-chemical sprayer aeroplane had flown over the letter writer's home area, all the birds had died. Rachel, who was fighting breast cancer at the time, felt she had to investigate what was going on.

DDT was the chemical of choice for farmers as it was deadly against insects but had a low toxicity for warm-blooded animals, with the exception of cats. Fish also found DDT very toxic. Unlike pre-war chemicals, which contained arsenic, or plant substances such as derris or pyrethrum, the new organochlorine (as above) compounds were persistent and did not quickly break down in the environment.

Rachel found that insects were developing immunity to the insecticide that had been designed to kill them. As a result, stronger and stronger varieties had to be developed. Her conclusion was that the human battle to subdue nature is unwinnable, as natural pests will always adapt to the latest poison. This reality continues to be ignored by developers of genetically modified crops today, who design their product to contain pesticide. The knock-on effect remains the same – the creation of highly resistant super bugs, requiring more and more toxic chemicals to control them.

Further research by Rachel revealed that these persistent poisons were accumulating in the insect-eating birds, making these sick birds easier prey for the predators which fed on them. As a result, in the 1950s and 1960s, there was a 'crash' in the population of the Peregrine falcon *(Falco peregrinus)* worldwide. Coverage of this ecological disaster awoke in me a life-long interest in ornithology.

The rapid decline of Peregrine falcons showed a clear link to pesticides, with post-mortem examinations showing high levels of DDT, dieldrin, DDE, BHC and other such chemical compounds. Those birds of prey that were still alive had difficulties raising a family. Closer examination of eyries or nests revealed that the eggs were being laid with shells so thin that they could not be incubated, and so they broke before hatching.

In 1962 Rachel Carson published her findings in her book *Silent Spring*, which unleashed a wave of hostility towards her from the pharmaceutical and political establishment. Ironically, the ferocity of these verbal attacks on Rachel played a significant part in making *Silent Spring* a best seller. The American biochemist Robert White-Stevens labelled her 'a fanatic defender of the cult of the balance of nature'. The former US Secretary of Agriculture Ezra Taft Benson reportedly concluded in a letter to Dwight D. Eisenhower that Rachel 'was unmarried despite being physically attractive' and that she was 'probably a communist'.

Of course, Rachel was ahead of her time. The social and green movements of the 1960s were only starting and in many ways came about as a result of her pioneering work. Sadly she did not live long enough to see the many effects of her legacy for science, ecology, health care, food production and politics. She died on 14 April 1964 before the ban on DDT was brought in. By 1970, the US Environmental Protection Agency was established. Amongst the many posthumous awards she received was the Presidential Medal of Freedom from President Jimmy Carter. There is also now a Rachel Carson bridge in Pittsburgh.

However, the most visible tribute to Rachel Carson for me is the majestic sight of Peregrine falcons flying over the estuaries and cliffs and quarries of my home area of North County Dublin. From near extinction, these elite athletes of the air, the fastest creatures on the planet, are breeding again and their numbers are healthy. It may be no more than a coincidence, but the patron saint of people with cancer, the disease that led to Rachel's death, is St Peregrine.

Thoughts from other kitchen gardeners

JOHN HOLLAND

John shares an allotment area and the care of beehives with his near neighbour, Milo Doyle, in North County Dublin. I am indebted to both John and Milo for their time and advice in helping me to look after my own bees.

Describe the location in which you grow your own food:

It is a part of a friend's large – c. 1 acre – back garden in Rush, Co. Dublin. It is a sand-based area and requires a lot of seaweed or farmyard manure each year.

Which food do you look forward to harvesting most and why?

I like potatoes and onions as they are relatively easy to store and provide a home-grown supply and flavour for six to eight months.

Which garden tool do you value most and why?

The fork. It doubles as a digging and harvesting tool. It is less likely to damage the crop when harvesting.

What motivates you to undertake the work involved in growing food?

Odd though it may sound, I actually like digging and preparing the patch. The satisfaction of watching the crop mature and finally the real genuine flavour of the crop motivates me.

What advice would you give to a person considering growing their own food?

Get a good book and start with the basics – potatoes, onions, carrots, etc. Also, remember that the seeds or plants are as keen to grow as you are to grow them. They survive and prosper if given half a chance.

   Raised beds make weeding and general care of the crop so much easier.

Have you an aspiration for the future in relation to food?

To continue doing what I am doing. I will probably stick to the old reliables and try to improve the yield and quality.

I would like to recommend the Teagasc Advisory Service for assistance regarding questions you may have or problems you may encounter. I have found them to be very approachable and helpful to a far-from-expert gardener.

CÁIT CURRAN

Cáit Curran is the editor of *Organic Matters*, the magazine produced by the Irish Organic Farmers and Growers Association (IOFGA). Cáit makes time to be, not just an organic, but a biodynamic grower. Biodynamic farming goes beyond organic methods and uses homeopathic preparations and phases of the moon to guide sowing and harvesting times, etc. (see the Fourth Week in January). Selling her own produce weekly at Galway City Farmers' Market, Cáit also helps communities, through IOFGA, to grow more of their own food as well as helping farmers to get a fair price for the fruits of their labours.

Describe the location in which you grow your own food:

I'm a biodynamic grower based in Connemara, Co. Galway, on a fairly windswept but beautiful mountainside. I'm not blessed with great soil so I put a lot of work into raising fertility levels by adding compost, farmyard manure, seaweed and biodynamic preparations.

Which food do you look forward to harvesting most and why?

It doesn't matter which crop – it's always the first of the season. There is nothing like pulling the first carrot of the season or digging an early potato in May. The first totally organic dinner of the year from my own garden is always an event to celebrate.

Which garden tool do you value most and why?

The fork – the most versatile of all garden tools! Once your garden is up and running, all you ever need to do is to dig it over, and a digging fork is always the best tool. It's great for breaking up the ground, rooting out stones and digging in manure. After that, the tool I use most is a shovel – mainly to construct ridges.

What inspires you to undertake the work involved in growing food?

All my formative years were spent in an environment of self-sufficiency where producing your own food was the norm. The garden work I undertook reluctantly as a child became a pleasure later in life when I acquired my own land to grow on. Mostly, I was motivated by the need for self-reliance, by health concerns about the quality of food I was consuming and by love for an agricultural lifestyle. A lifetime of growing food has given me a connection to nature that I will appreciate and value forever, and the longer I garden, the more it feels like a spiritual experience.

What advice would you give to a person considering growing their own food?

Try it. Even if you are clueless to begin with, you will still have some success. Start small and add a little each year as you grow in confidence. There is no feeling like the satisfaction of harvesting and eating something you have grown yourself. Remember, it's not rocket science; things will grow – and you will enjoy it.

Have you an aspiration for the future in relation to food?

Food security is a serious issue for the country. Even though Ireland is still an agricultural country, a whole generation has lost the skills to grow food and we need to reverse that trend. Everyone should have the opportunity to learn how to produce food and the basics should form part of the school curriculum.

Meitheamh ❧ *June*

The Month of the Longest Day

EITHEAMH MEANS THE 'middle month' and nowadays it refers to the mid-summer month of June. In old Irish, *meitheamh* was a generic word which also referred to September as mid-autumn, December as mid-winter and March as mid-Spring. Nowadays, Meitheamh is the month of June and the summer solstice occurs around the twenty-first of the month in the Northern Hemisphere. (In the Southern Hemisphere, the summer solstice is around 21 December.) At this time of the year, the sun is at its highest in the sky in the Northern Hemisphere (or at its lowest in the Southern Hemisphere). Although such a phenomenon is vital in terms of food growing, it is not one of the most important Celtic festivals. Perhaps the fact that July is often warmer than June watered down the significance of the summer solstice in Ancient Ireland.

In Ancient Rome, however, the term 'solstice', from two Latin words *sol* (sun) and *sistere* (to stand still), indicates that the longest day was big news for the Romans. They named the month Junius after their goddess of married life and the well-being of women, Juno. There is a tradition that June was the month of younger people or *juvenis* in Latin, while May was the month of older people.

The Saxon word for summer is Litha. Litha is also the pagan feast of midsummer, when it is believed the Holly King dethrones the Oak King, causing the sun to wane until Yuletide in December. Litha was Christianised as St John's Day, normally celebrated on 24 June, and it often features bonfires. Garlands of flowers are also worn, among them St John's Wort, a protective herb. These and other herbs were collected early in the day and blessed in the church. Some were hung for drying to make herbal treatments for the household; others made garlands for those attending the bonfire. The old dried herbs from the previous year were thrown into the bonfire and the cycle of herbal remedies continued, and continues, on.

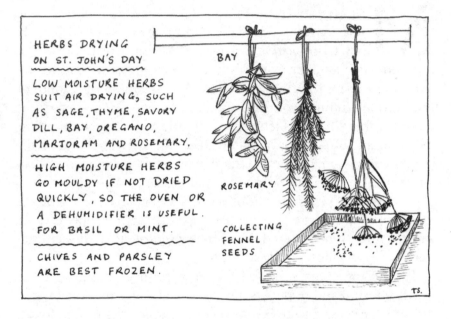

HERBS DRYING
ON ST. JOHN'S DAY

LOW MOISTURE HERBS
SUIT AIR DRYING, SUCH
AS SAGE, THYME, SAVORY
DILL, BAY, OREGANO,
MARJORAM AND ROSEMARY.

HIGH MOISTURE HERBS
GO MOULDY IF NOT DRIED
QUICKLY, SO THE OVEN OR
A DEHUMIDIFIER IS USEFUL.
FOR BASIL OR MINT.

CHIVES AND PARSLEY
ARE BEST FROZEN.

BAY

ROSEMARY

COLLECTING
FENNEL
SEEDS

TS.

An overview of the work ahead in the garden this month:
Plant: transplant celeriac, leeks, celery, brassicas.
Sow out: swedes, endive, parsley; successional sowings – beans, lettuce, radish, beetroot.
Harvest: peas, broad beans, potatoes, spinach, turnips, kohlrabi; plus successional pickings and thinnings.

🍃 FIRST WEEK IN JUNE 🍃

Care of broad beans, sunflowers and tomato plants

'I will arise and go now, and go to Inisfree,
And a small cabin build there, of clay and wattles made;
Nine bean rows will I have there, a hive for the honey bee,
And live alone in the bee-loud glade…'
(William Butler Yeats, 'The Lake Isle of Inisfree', 1893)

THE broad bean is as revered in the vegetable hall of fame as W.B. Yeats is in the world of literature. The broad bean, however, has greater antiquity on its side. Broad bean seeds have been found going back some 8,500 years, although it was the Romans, we believe, who brought this favoured food to Northern Europe. Any army worth its salt in the ancient world brought with it the most nutritious food and seeds, when marching long distances.

Nowadays, and specifically at the start of June, I am concerned that the broad beans I planted last October are under attack from a horde of aphids call 'black fly'. These aphids are after the sap in the stems, rather than the beans. However, as sap is the lifeblood of the plant, the bean crop will be less than expected unless I destroy these aphids which are sucking on the tender growing tips of each plant. During the Middle Ages, not only aphids suffered at the hands of bean growers, but any human caught stealing another person's broad beans could be punished by death! Today I would be happy enough to sentence the culprit to community service – the thief could prepare the ground for a community garden.

THREE STEPS TO STOP BLACK FLY ATTACKING BROAD BEANS:

1. Encourage black fly predators such as hoverfly, ladybirds and lacewings, and insectivore birds like blue tits, by growing calendula, poached egg plant, morning glory and stinging nettle in the garden.

131

2. Rub off the black fly with fingers or, if they are too numerous, use a hand-held mist sprayer. Fill with water, add a drop of washing-up liquid and shake. Turn the nozzle to create a strong single jet of water. Use the sprayer like a mini-water cannon to dislodge black flies from the broad bean plant. Soapy water clogs the pores through which they breathe.

3. If bean pods are well formed, pinch off the affected growing tips and cremate the aphids in a solid fuel stove or fireplace. (Bonfires are illegal nowadays – another change from the Middle Ages!)

SUNFLOWERS AND TOMATO PLANTS WILL GROW TALL IF SUPPORTED BY TALL STAKES

For years I have been staking sunflowers, tomatoes and other such tall plants, but whenever a big wind got up, the plant would act like a sail and would fall over, stake and all. So when all else fails, try

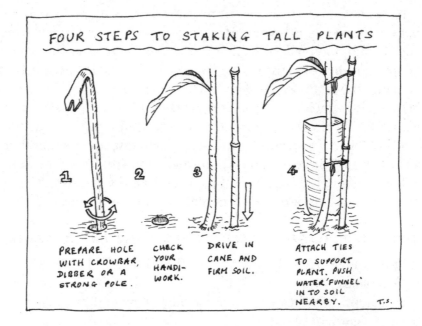

FOUR STEPS TO STAKING TALL PLANTS

1. PREPARE HOLE WITH CROWBAR, DIBBER OR A STRONG POLE.

2. CHECK YOUR HANDI-WORK.

3. DRIVE IN CANE AND FIRM SOIL.

4. ATTACH TIES TO SUPPORT PLANT. PUSH WATER 'FUNNEL' IN TO SOIL NEARBY.

T.S.

some common sense. It is clearly not sufficient to ram sturdy bamboo canes into the ground. First a dibber, crowbar or some class of metal bar is required to prepare a hole in which to put the lighter bamboo. This allows you to shove the cane down the pre-moulded hole to a decent depth. Once the cane is firmed in, it should hold fast in any normal wind. All that remains then is to tie garden string to the cane first and tie the plant close to the cane afterwards, but leave space for the stem to thicken as it grows. Extra ties are often needed as the plant continues to grow.

OTHER JOBS FOR THE WEEK THAT IS IN IT:

🌿 Check autumn-sown onions; if any are running to seed, snap off the flower head. The bulb will be fine but will not store well, so use early on after harvest.

🌿 This is your last chance to sow peas and mangetout for harvesting in late September.

The Bigger Picture:
Celebrate World Environment Day on 5 June

The UN urges us to celebrate positive environmental action all year round but especially on 5 June, World Environment Day. One way to do this, according to the UN Environment Programme website www.unep.org, is to 'eat organic and locally grown foods, and thereby help reduce the clearing of forests for agricultural lands.'

Listening to the news as I write this, I cannot but be moved and alarmed by the scale of suffering and starvation affecting East Africa due to drought. It is notable, however, that there is now certainty in the voices of the reporters and the former President of Ireland Mary Robinson as to the connection between this food shortage and the devastating effects of climate change (or 'climate chaos', as I think it is better described). At last the message is getting through. After countless other horrific droughts and forest fires in Australia as well as ruined harvests in the grain belts of Russia and the Ukraine, and other extreme climatic events, the realisation is dawning for many that failure to stop burning fossil fuels will hand a death sentence to millions around the world, many already on the brink of starvation.

In spite of this, food security and climate chaos are still small side shows in the media, compared to other urgent campaigns to reduce road deaths and hospital waiting lists, for example. However, if food security is to be considered seriously, now is the time to ensure the food sector itself is not needlessly adding to environmental degradation and starvation, instead of alleviating it. Back in the year 2000, Dr Caroline Lucas, then an MEP and now a Green Party MP for Brighton, produced a timely report called 'Stopping the Great Food Swap – Relocalising Europe's Food Supply' (March 2001).

Countries swapping exactly the same type of food seems about as useful as the swapping of conkers I engaged in as a child in the schoolyard. Nonetheless, *food swapping*, which is a major part of the international food trade, has increased the worldwide vegetable trade alone from 8.7 million tonnes in 1968 to 38.1 million tonnes in 1998. That is an increase of over 337.9 per cent. Meanwhile, trade in offal has gone up 533.3 per cent and trade in starchy roots has increased by 250.6 per cent. Overall, international trade in food on average went up almost 300 per cent over a thirty-year period. In the same period, the world's population rose by 91 per cent. See www.carolinelucasmep.org.uk/stopping the great food swap.

With an extra 84 million humans needing to be fed each year, we require an extra 5 million hectares of agriculturally productive land per annum. Unfortunately, due to climate chaos as well as soil erosion and competition for other land uses, we are losing 10 million hectares a year (see *Eating Fossil Fuels: Oil, Food and the Coming Crisis in Agriculture* by Dale Allen Pfeiffer.) Global food production increased fourfold from 1945 to 1994 as a result of the input of fossil fuels. However, food output in this period grew just threefold. Since 1994, the growth in energy use in farming has had a diminishing impact on food production growth levels, but it has compensated for soil erosion by the use of fossil-fuel derived fertilisers. In other words, harvests are not as large as one should expect, given the huge inputs of energy and fertilisers being used.

Likewise, water is essential to maintain levels of food production. The American prairies are productive due to the vast ancient aquifers which underpin their irrigation needs (see the Third Week in March). Less than 1 per cent of this well water is replaced by rainfall (see *Eating Fossil Fuels* by Pfeiffer). Essentially the groundwater is also being mined as if it was oil or gas. As well as 'peak oil', our global food production policies must also prepare for 'peak water', and there is not the time to come up with a long-term solution.

This 'perfect storm' is on course to seriously disrupt global food production. Whatever the merits of global trade in computers, chemicals or cars, the treatment of food and animals as 'things' to auction around the world is what has us staring in to the abyss of famine and a collapse of civil society. Remember the food riots about rising food prices in Rome and Mexico City and thirty other cities in 2008? It is worth remembering that food supplies had not become the central issue at that time.

It would be a start if food and agriculture could be taken out of trade liberalisation rules. Food and water provision are part of what sustains all life, like the air we breathe and move in. Their provision must firstly meet the needs of local communities, regional ecosystems and sustainable food economies.

Nothing short of a revolution to sustain life is needed. It is a big deal but it can't succeed unless it begins with what we put into our mouths. Eat seasonally; grow organically; use unprocessed food; buy locally – these four cornerstones spell out the word s-o-u-l. Life without soul is a poor life. Indeed, I believe life without soul, in this context, is unsustainable. Let's hope more and more people (who can choose) choose a sustainable life. *Sláinte agus saol!*

Planting out young leeks in modules

'Give us nothing but vegetables to eat and water to drink. Then compare our appearance with that of the young men who eat the royal food, and treat your servants in accordance with what you see." So he agreed to this and tested them for ten days. At the end of the ten days they looked healthier and better nourished than any of the young men who ate the royal food.'

(Daniel 1:12–15)

This reference to vegetables in the Old Testament could well include leeks, as this venerable vegetable has been a staple food of many civilisations since about 2,000 BC. It is one thing to say vegetables are good for you. It is a different matter entirely to bet your life on proving it in ten days. Yet the quote above relates the extraordinary scene where a lowly Daniel dismisses the king's rich food and requests vegetables and water instead. I would be interested to read any advice Daniel might have on growing leeks, but I have not come across this yet. Instead I have been out in my garden planting out my own leek seedlings in the allium, or onion family, patch, in the hope that they grow on to maturity. Some funny traditions have developed around planting out leek seedlings and all I can say is 'each to their own'! The Roman Emperor Nero believed eating leeks improved his singing voice, earning him the nickname *Porrophagus* (leek eater).

TRADITIONS AROUND PLANTING OUT LEEK SEEDLINGS

🍂 People used to trim some roots and the tips of leaves – this was pointless and possibly counterproductive.

🍂 Make holes with a dibber, 20 cm (8 inches) deep. Drop a

seedling into each hole. Using a watering can, fill the hole with water and allow it to soak away. This will draw enough soil over the plant to cover the roots. I have done this and it works.

🌿 Leeks are planted in a trench 30 cm (1ft) deep and as they grow the stems are gradually buried so they are denied light and 'blanched' to give whiter, sweeter and more tender stems.

PLANTING OUT LEEKS TO SUIT A SMALL GARDEN

Logic tells me to disturb the roots of growing plants as little as possible. Therefore, last March, I sowed a leek seed in each module or cell of compost in one of those plastic subdivided seed trays. Each subdivision fits enough compost to grow a leek to the size of a very thin pencil. All I need to do then is ease out the module of potting compost, damp from a watering, and gently place it in a small hole dug in a level, moist, weed-free part of the allium patch, without disturbing the roots at all. Leeks particularly suit a small garden and a low budget. They grow quite close together and vertically. Also, to buy, they are more expensive than onions in the shops.

WHAT ABOUT 'BLANCHING' THE STEMS LIKE IN THE OLDEN DAYS?

I read on modern organic seed packets that there is no longer a need for 'blanching'. However, making a ridge to cover the stems of leeks can look decorative, so the choice is yours. For my part, I squeeze in two dozen seedlings in the space recommended (about 20 cm or 8 inches) for only one dozen leeks. Again and again, I experiment by growing plants closer together than the seed packets recommend. I have never been disappointed yet. Could it be that the seed packet information is designed for large gardens and field-scale production?

WHEN WILL MY LEEKS BE READY FOR HARVEST?

Leeks like a well-composted soil and this also retains moisture. I give my plants a diluted nettle or comfrey liquid feed in the watering can each time I water. The water and feed are poured into plastic bottle 'funnels' stuck in the soil amongst the growing leeks. Once October comes, I start to sample the leeks as I need them. There is no hurry to harvest, however. Leeks are hardy and will grow as long as it is mild; and they stay fresh in the ground even in snow and frost. I look forward to preparing a 'leek bake' for the oven next winter.

OTHER JOBS FOR THE WEEK THAT IS IN IT:

- Take cuttings of sage to pot up as gifts or to sell at a local market.
- Remove raspberry suckers which can appear far from the parent and tend to sap energy from the fruiting canes.

The Bigger Picture:
A history of walled kitchen gardens

An Irish monk, St Gall, is well remembered as risking everything to bring Christianity and learning to the people of Continental Europe in the Dark Ages. Nowadays, the Abbey of St Gall in St Gallen, a canton in eastern Switzerland, crops up in any research one does on the origins of walled gardens. Around 820 AD, almost two hundred years after St Gall's death, a plan of a monastic walled kitchen garden was first produced for the abbey and described as a hortus (garden) with the words 'Hic plantata holerum pulchre nascentia vernant' (Here planted vegetables flourish in beauty). This plan was an inspiration for many others, including the monks who founded the Cistercian order in 1098, to follow closely the

Rule of St Benedict. St Benedict put a huge emphasis on humility, charity and self-sustenance. From then on, the walled garden developed widely to provide food, medical herbs and a place of tranquil beauty 365 days of the year.

While the garden was a central aspect of the Rule of St Benedict, the location of a walled garden in the secular world was sometimes seen as an afterthought. Walled gardens are now most closely associated with present or former large country houses. The location of the country house nearly always took priority in terms of the view and the surrounding landscape. The walled garden, even though it had to keep everyone in the Big House fed, was generally out of view and located on soil of an indifferent quality.

TO CREATE A WALLED GARDEN, AT TIMES IT IS NECESSARY TO CLEAR SOME LAND!

THIS DRAWING IS BASED ON AN OLD ENGRAVING AT TULLY CASTLE ON THE WESTERN SHORE OF LOWER LOUGH ERNE, COUNTY FERMANAGH, WHICH DATES FROM 1617.

T.S.

However, in spite of these inauspicious out-of-sight-out-of-mind origins, it is not uncommon to find a mature kitchen garden with nearly 76 cm (30 inches) of top soil, while the adjacent agricultural field might have just 20 cm (8 inches) of topsoil. What this means

139

is that, with hard work and assiduous attention to the health of the soil, and the addition of compost and other organic matter, one could increase topsoil depth by 2.5 cm (1 inch) per annum. This implies that there were about twenty-two years of carting large amounts of organic matter to augment the soil over a typical two-acre walled growing area, before the garden was considered to have reached optimum levels of fertility and production.

The walls were as vital as the quality of the soil in these gardens. The temperature from a sunny wall after sunset could be ten degrees centigrade higher than the temperature from a north-facing wall. This meant certain fruit and vegetables could be brought to harvest point quicker or slower, depending on their growing location in relation to warmer or cooler walls. When Northern Europeans got a taste for Mediterranean or even tropical fruits, those with wealth went to extreme measures to recreate a warm growing environment. Fireplaces were built into the garden walls so that tropical fruit could be grown, as transport was then too slow and expensive for fruit importation.

Brick was favoured over stone as a wall-building material, because it stored the heat from the sun better and gave it out over a longer period after nightfall. It is no surprise, then, that the introduction of a tax on bricks during the reign of King George III of England in 1784 had a profound effect on some walled garden designs. How could a wall be built with fewer bricks and not fall down? One way was to build in a zig-zag line or a *Klagemuren* (snake wall), as it was called in the Netherlands. Another way to avoid the tax was to build a cob wall, made of mud and straw. It was said the way to ensure a cob wall lasted was to give it 'a good hat and a good pair of shoes'. The Brick Tax was repealed in 1850.

With the repeal of the Window Tax in 1845, the development of glass lean-to hothouses heralded a major expansion of the range of food and ornamental plants which a Northern European garden could produce. Many glass structures in Ireland, from the Palm

House in the Botanic Gardens, Dublin and the Victorian Conservatory at Ardgillan Castle between Balbriggan and Skerries, to the Melon House at Strokestown House, Co. Roscommon, are all a legacy of year-round production of wholesome and exotic food.

Queen Victoria had an influence on the growth of walled gardens and had her thirteen-acre kitchen garden at Windsor Castle constructed in 1844. There she had 150 men working on her 'quarters' or plots. Even wealthy folk had to adhere to the laws of nature and follow a rotation of their crops.

During World War I, many of the pot boys, journeymen and gardeners were killed and so many of the gardens could not be staffed as they had been before. The pre-war heyday of the walled garden had given rise to thousands of varieties of vegetables and fruits, all developed to suit various soil types and microclimates. Apple names today can remind us of the gardens and orchards where they originated: Blenheim Orange, Allington Pippin, Beauty of Bath, Chivers Delight, Ribston Pippin and Howgate Wonder, amongst many more.

Many varieties of plants have been lost over the years, along with the skills of the gardeners who nurtured these year-round food producing gardens. Thankfully there are records and books which record many 'tricks of the trade'.

The two-acre walled garden where I work at Sonairte, the National Ecology Centre at Laytown, Co. Meath, is worth a visit. Dating back to the eighteenth century, it is both historically and horticulturally interesting. Yet today it produces organic vegetables, fruit and bouquets of garden and common wild flowers to sell on site as well as at a number of markets in Dublin and Balbriggan. I know the gardeners are always keen to hear from volunteers who want to experience life in a present-day walled kitchen garden, so take a look at the website: www.sonairte.ie. For a list of walled gardens in Ireland, see the Third Week in August.

❧ THIRD WEEK IN JUNE ❧

Harvesting early potatoes and re-using the soil for newly planted courgettes

With a small space for food growing, it becomes clear quite quickly that there are certain crops which take up an inordinate amount of space or are just too awkward for you to grow. For me, these include artichokes, gooseberries, asparagus, cauliflower, Brussels sprouts and main crop potatoes. Mind you, never say never. I have grown Brussels sprouts and asparagus, and I may eat my words and try others too as the mood takes me.

In the shops and markets main crop potatoes are plentiful and relatively cheap to buy. I often wonder how commercial potato farmers make any money from them! From June on, potato blight would become a problem and, even though there are sprays permitted for an organic grower to use, the hassle of spraying in my small garden is something I can live without.

However, early potatoes are well worth growing as they are ready for harvest before the blight spores turn up, and so no sprays are required. I have grown potatoes in the open ground, in plastic black bags and in a stack of old car tyres. At this stage, my favourite way to grow potatoes is in purpose-made potato bags which have two strong handles for careful lifting. The back muscles appreciate the word 'careful'.

HOW MANY SEED POTATOES GO INTO A POTATO GROWING BAG?

The instructions on the box in which the potato bag is sold boasts how five seed potatoes can be sown in each bag. True, but what the box does not say is that you will get tiny potatoes if the bag is overcrowded with five potato plants. This year, I demonstrated huge restraint and used just one potato seed in each bag. The result was twelve medium to large new potatoes from that one seed. The variety was Orla. I had done the same for Charlotte, Colleen, Queens, Sharpes Express and Pink Fir Apple – one seed to each bag. Next year I might try three seeds to a bag, but five seeds per bag is excessive in my view.

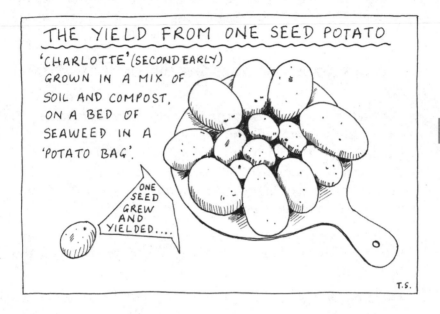

THE YIELD FROM ONE SEED POTATO

'CHARLOTTE' (SECOND EARLY) GROWN IN A MIX OF SOIL AND COMPOST, ON A BED OF SEAWEED IN A 'POTATO BAG'.

ONE SEED GREW AND YIELDED....

T.S.

THE ADVANTAGES OF GROWING IN POTATO BAGS IN A SMALL GARDEN:

🍃 The seed is sown in a bag only half full of soil, to allow space for earthing up with more soil as the stems grow. Being only half full, the bag can be lifted and started off indoors in January or February while frosts are a risk outdoors. Once frosts are over, at around April time, the bag can be lifted outside for the potatoes to grow to maturity.

🍃 The harvesting of the crop is much easier from a potato bag. The contents are just emptied on soil, lawn or pavement, and

143

the potatoes picked out. No tools of any sort are needed.

🍃 The potato bags yield not only potatoes but also rich soil with a good structure. This 'bag soil' is returned to the open garden where it helps to grow other later sown crops, such as courgettes or autumn-sown garlic. The pavement where the potato bags sat in spring is meanwhile restored to the 'sunbathers' for July and August, as by that stage the bags are packed away for use again the following February.

TIPS TO GET GOOD FLAVOURSOME YIELDS FROM POTATO BAGS:

🍃 Put a layer of seaweed or farmyard manure (6–10 cm/2.4–3.9 inches) at the bottom of the bag before half filling it with soil that has good organic matter in it, for example, compost added the previous autumn. In the absence of seaweed or manure, an upturned sod of grass at the bottom of the bag would also rot down to provide organic matter and nutrients.

🍃 The more earthworm and tiger worm activity in the soil, the better, as the potatoes thrive on the by-products of this biological activity.

🍃 Water potato bags more often than you would water the garden normally. The soil in the bags dries out quicker than open soil. Also, moisture helps the new potatoes to swell and helps the microbes to be more active, which in turn keeps feeding the potatoes.

THE SOIL IN WHICH POTATOES GREW IS VERY FERTILE AND SUITS HUNGRY YOUNG COURGETTES

At the beginning of May, I sowed a courgette seed per plant pot in the greenhouse. I used disposable paper coffee cups actually! I see courgette plants for sale in garden centres and at farmers' markets now, to facilitate all those kitchen gardeners who do not drink coffee-to-go! Now is the time to plant out the young courgette plants which are getting too big for their coffee cups. If there is no planting space left in the garden, I fill larger patio pots with the soil from the used potato bags and plant up the courgette plants in a sunny location where I can easily keep an eye on their progress, dispensing water with liquid feed and removing the odd slug. There is a quiet satisfaction in getting two crops from the same soil in the one growing season – early potatoes and courgettes, grown in the same soil and enjoyed together in a frittata special, perhaps.

OTHER JOBS FOR THE WEEK THAT IS IN IT:

🍃 Thin ripening fruit. In other words, pick out any damaged or over-crowded immature apples or pears so the ripening fruit is spaced about 5 to 8 inches (13–20 cm) apart.

🍃 Check all brassica leaves for Cabbage White caterpillar eggs and rub them off once spotted.

The Bigger Picture:
Memories from attending the World Organic Congress in Modena, Italy

Alas, there was no time for opera while I attended the sixteenth Organic World Congress in Modena, the birthplace of Pavarotti, in the Emilia–Romagna region of northern Italy on 17–19 June 2008. As the Irish minister with responsibility for the development of the organic farming sector at the time, it made sense to see what other governments, farmers, food entrepreneurs and consumers around the world were doing organically.

Organic agriculture is defined by the US Department of Agriculture's National Organic Standards Board as '…an ecological production management system that promotes and enhances biodiversity, biological cycles and soil biological activity. It is based on minimal use of off-farm inputs and on management practices that restore, maintain and enhance ecological harmony' (www.nal. usda.gov). We heard that there was a 21 per cent growth in sales of organic products in the USA in 2006, amounting to just under $18 billion annually. This growth is based on the growing interest among consumers in healthy and more sustainably produced food.

Organic farming systems use, on average, 30–50 per cent less fossil fuels than their conventional agricultural counterparts. Energy from fossil fuels is largely replaced by human labour and generally there are 35 per cent more labour costs on an organic farm than on a conventional farm. This means organic farms provide a good way of tackling rural unemployment. However, the cost of human labour is more expensive than the current cost of fossil fuels. Looking ahead, with the rising cost of fossil fuel energy, we could see organic food being priced lower than conventional food in time, but currently organic food sometimes costs more, as additional labour costs have to be factored into production.

This price differential is the main reason why organic food has to be legally certified. The consumer must be re-assured that organic farms have been audited and that the food grown is in accordance with high standards and using only permitted inputs, for example, no genetically modified organisms are permitted in feeding organic livestock.

The University of Michigan in the USA put a spring in the step of all delegates in Modena with their concluding research which found that organic farming can feed the growing human population. As mentioned before, the research by Professor Ivette Perfecto and research scientist Catherine Badgley found that organic farming can yield up to three times as much food on individual farms in developing countries as low-intensive methods on the same land.

Professor Perfecto said the idea that people would go hungry if farming went organic is 'ridiculous', and she went on to say, 'Corporate interest in agriculture and the way agriculture research has been conducted in land grant institutions, with a lot of influence by the chemical companies and pesticide companies as well as fertilizer companies – all have been playing an important role in convincing the public that you need to have these inputs to produce food.' With the greater employment potential per hectare for organic farming in these recessionary times, it makes sense to shop around for good value organic produce. At my stall in Balbriggan Fish and Farmers' Market, I try to ensure the organic price is the same or lower than the conventional alternative. People ought to have access to the healthiest food at affordable prices.

According to the organisers of the World Organic Conference, IFOAM (International Federation of Organic Agriculture Movements), in the year 2000 close to 8 million hectares were dedicated to organic farming worldwide. By 2006 this had risen to 51.2 million hectares. This figure, divided among continents, had Australia with 39 per cent organic production, Europe 21 per cent, Latin America 20 per cent, North America 4 per cent, Asia 13 per cent and Africa 3 per cent. Before we wonder why Africa is only officially at 3 per cent, the figure for Ireland is less than that! Ireland's organic farming percentage has more than doubled, however, since I inherited a paltry 0.9 per cent figure at the start of my two-and-a-half-year term as Minister for Food and Horticulture.

My good friend Dr Vandana Shiva was at the World Organic Congress in Italy, having travelled all the way from her home in India. She told us that fertilizer prices in her country had tripled in the last year. She described genetic modification not as a high yield technology but a technology which increases toxicity in the soil, due to the way it is designed to be used with a specific herbicide. The claim that GM can feed the world she describes as 'the biggest lie in agriculture'. She also forecast problems from feeding cattle too much soya and grain, as cattle had evolved to be grass fed. She would describe Irish cattle as luckier than most in this regard. Dr Shiva is currently working as advisor to the Government of Bhutan to make that country 100 per cent organic.

I met with the Bolivian Minister of Production and Small Enterprise Javier Hurtado Mercado, who is also working at making his country 100 per cent organic. Even though only 3 per cent of the land area in Bolivia is agricultural, the country has four distinct ecosystems: the Andes, the tropics, the valleys and the Amazon basin. Afterwards, Minister Mercado wrote to me to 'appreciate your interest to collaborate in the Bolivian development process towards an ecological community and I hope to work on related projects in the future'.

Apart from officials, there were many farmers there also. One who had travelled from Illinois in the USA was John Peterson, who was a sort of 'agricultural St Paul'. Having tried conventional agriculture and run up massive debts, he turned to biodynamic organic farming and now he was a very happy man (see the First Week in February).

Naturally enough, the Italian Ministry of Agricultural, Food and Forestry Policies was prominent wherever one went. However, the most passionate Italian contribution to proceedings came from the founding father of the International Slow Food Movement Carlo Petrini, who told us with much gesticulation, 'Play the game of food by the rules of nature, not by the rules of agro-industry', a term he described as an oxymoron.

🍁 FOURTH WEEK IN JUNE 🍁

Watering with minimal use of tap water and no hose pipe

'Water is more valuable than gold –
you can't drink gold.'

WHEN you see people walking miles in Africa for water of a lower quality than most people in Ireland take for granted, it makes me think of ways to avoid wasting water, especially in the garden where irrigation does not require pristine drinking water quality. Water consumption has been growing at twice the rate of population growth in Ireland. Globally, consumption of fresh water is doubling every twenty years; 65 per cent of that is used by industrial agriculture, 10 per cent is used directly in domestic consumption and 25 per cent is used by industry (see the Third Week in March). Can our gardens buck the trend and use less water?

First rules of watering the garden:

1. Check the soil below the surface to see if it is damp already.

2. Only water when necessary, unless you are trying to encourage slugs who like damp soil!

3. A thorough dose of water once a week is better than a little bit every day.

TIPS FOR EFFECTIVE WATERING

I used to have the garden hose pipe on stand by for watering duty. No doubt the slugs appreciated the moist conditions I was creating. However, to liquid feed my plants, I still needed to dilute nettle or comfrey feed in a watering can. In effect, I was watering twice needlessly. This is when I decided to retire the hose and develop a watering-can based system instead.

149

My liquid engineering involves a bank of eight watering cans and two water butts, as barrels for holding water are called. The down-pipe from the gutter at the front keeps one water butt topped up with rainwater running off the house roof and the down-pipe at the back does likewise for the second butt. I constructed a handy wooden bench with a front but no back to conceal a row of eight large plastic watering cans. The bench also shades the watering cans and prevents sunlight deteriorating the plastic.

To prime the watering cans for action to feed and irrigate the garden, fill each watering can, leaving space to add a litre of diluted feed to each can. I often do this job in the late evening and the cans are left full and ready for watering in the early morning. The biological life in the diluted liquid feed has a chance over night to become active and hit the ground running, so to speak, when it enters the soil.

Watering the soil surface is inefficient and the water does not get directly to the plant roots. Much of it runs off and evaporates. To save time and water, upturned bottomless plastic mineral bottles are filled with water and in their own time the water seeps directly into the vicinity of the plant roots (see the Second Week in April).

Cover the soil with a mulch to save water loss through evaporation. Think forest floor! It is rare to see bare soil in nature, except perhaps in the event of a landslide. The beauty of a mulch is that it copies this tendency in nature to cover bare soil. Some people put down paper weighed down with stones, some use comfrey leaves or big rhubarb leaves, some use old carpet or black plastic. If you require 'retail therapy', garden centres sell porous black membrane to cover soil, letting rain through but excluding light. For the bee's knees in mulch, collect damp leaves in the autumn in a corner separate from the compost heap or in old black plastic bags. Put air holes in the bags with a garden fork and leave for one or, preferably, two years. The resulting leaf mould is a replica forest floor and excellent mulch. Use leaf mould as a mulch and earthworms and soil life in general will thank you. You will be happier, too, as you will help to suppress weeds by covering the soil.

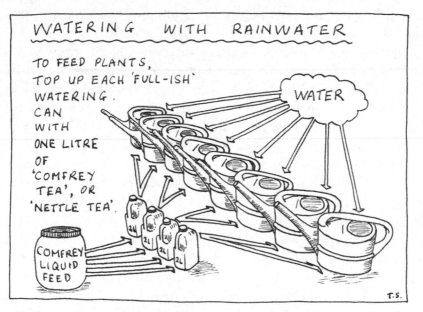

OTHER JOBS FOR THE WEEK THAT IS IN IT:

🌿 Sow a few more beetroot seeds to extend the beetroot harvest in the autumn.

🌿 Prune plum trees lightly, as stone fruit trees need only minimal pruning, which should only be done in the summer.

The Bigger Picture:
The UN Food and Agriculture Organisation grapples with over a billion people starving

A World Food Summit was convened by the UN Food and Agriculture Organisation (FAO) in Rome to agree an international strategy to reverse the growing problem of hunger affecting over one billion people, that is, about one in seven of the human population. I was asked by the Government to represent Ireland at this gathering on 20–21 November 2008 and I was not the only one who came away frustrated.

The summer of 2008 had seen a doubling of grain prices worldwide on the back of unprecedented rises in the price of a barrel of oil to $147 in July. In the Sudan, the refugee camps of Darfur were bulging with over two million starving refugees. During the first three months of 2008, fifty-six grain-laden lorries bound for Darfur were hijacked and some twenty-four drivers are still unaccounted for.

In 2008, this was far more widespread than a Sudanese crisis. Food riots due to food shortages and high food prices were commonplace in Egypt, Yemen, Cameroon, Ethiopia, Haiti, Indonesia, Mexico, the Philippines, Senegal, Japan and in Rome itself.

I had half expected demonstrations during my stay in Rome and there were. However, the demonstrations were about access to land to grow food, not about the price of food per se. The demonstrators were mainly small farmers from South America and they were part of the global La Via Campesina. This is an international movement of small farmers and landless farm workers who are defending small-scale sustainable agriculture. Understandably, they feel very let down by the world's governments whose policies have allowed large food and agriculture corporations' interests to be prioritised in the World Trade Organisation and in international law, resulting in many farmers being forced out of farming.

This *laissez-faire* 'free trade' approach to food security is not working. Tensions are currently rising as China, with 9 per cent of the world's farmland but 40 per cent of the world's farmers, is buying up arable land in Africa, South America and elsewhere, with a view to repatriating the food produced to China.

The FAO has the stated objective of 'global food security', which is a technical concept arising from the 1948 UN Universal Declaration of Human Rights. This Declaration contains the line 'to do no harm to an individual's access to food'. If the food is not available in the first place, then having access to an empty warehouse is cold comfort. Likewise, the UN often refers to a person's 'right to food' – a legal concept, which again implies that somebody is in possession of the food which another person needs.

The La Via Campesina farmers' movement in 1996 launched the concept of 'food sovereignty'. This is ultimately a political concept and challenges the existing mandates of international law and institutions that govern food law. Ireland has a proud record in trying to help eradicate hunger with the Hunger Task Force and Irish Aid, etc. However, getting involved in access to land for growing food has been seen, at Government level, as too hot a platform to be standing on.

Unless we address the issue of access to land for growing food worldwide, then social unrest and political instability will spread, I fear. As things stand, food aid will be worth less and less, as the price of food, especially grain, increases. Future scarcities of transport fuel will increase pressure to use farmland to grow energy crops. There is already emerging a direct competition between the priorities of the 800 million people who own automobiles and the world's 2 billion hungriest people about whether to turn a significant amount of that grain into bio fuel or to eat it.

However, the proponents of food sovereignty need to demonstrate more clearly how greater access for more people to arable land will deliver the food security which eludes so many at present. After all, growing food takes certain skills, the right conditions, access to market and a fair price – conditions that have to be put in place and maintained.

For the duration of the World Food Summit, I happened to be sitting beside the Bangladeshi Minister of Food and Disaster Management Dr Muhammad Abdur Razzaque MP. His title alone puts into context the urgency of growing food and accessing markets in which to sell food at a fair price. Unless we develop sustainable ways to grow more food in local food economies without fossil fuels, then sadly the work of that ministry and others like it will become more and more difficult. The hope is that the more locally sustainable food we grow, the less need there'll be for disaster management.

Thoughts from other kitchen gardeners

NEVEN MAGUIRE

Award-winning chef Neven Maguire is the owner of the famous MacNean House and Restaurant, Blacklion, Co. Cavan. Neven is very 'hands on' in sourcing locally grown seasonal produce for the restaurant. The Organic Centre nearby in Rossinver, Co. Leitrim grows organic fruit and vegetables for Neven, but he also has a kitchen garden behind the restaurant which he tends himself. At the same time, Neven is an ambassador with Bord Bia for Irish food, apart from being a TV and radio chef, and a top-selling author.

Describe the location in which you grow your own food:

A few metres from the kitchen door, I have enough space for two polytunnels. There I cultivate the fresh salad leaves and herbs used in the restaurant. The range of crops varies with the seasons. At different times, the menu would reflect the availability of beetroot, ruby chard, courgettes, etc. Due to lack of space, I would buy in other produce such as carrots or potatoes from the Organic Centre nearby, or strawberries from Pat and Mary Clarke of Clarke's Soft Fruits in Stamullen, Co. Meath.

Which food do you look forward to harvesting most and why?

Every year I look forward to the courgette flowers which keep me supplied in the restaurant from May to September. They are so delicate and delicious; I enjoy picking them in the polytunnel, and stuffing them to make a range of very special dishes. As well as that, nothing beats the flavour of fresh Irish strawberries.

Which garden tool do you value most and why?

The watering can is the tool I use most in the polytunnel. It does more than water the plants, however. Watering is part of my routine which gets me out in the garden. In a way, it helps me to know what is coming on and what is ready for harvest, so I can plan the menus for the kitchen in advance.

What motivates you to undertake the work involved in growing food?

There is nothing nicer than enjoying fresh home-grown food. I also enjoy being able to tell customers in the restaurant the origin of each ingredient that makes up any meal. The fact that all home-grown food, by its nature, has to be seasonal also helps me appreciate what other food is in season when I go to buy in additional produce to meet the restaurant's requirements.

What advice would you give to a person considering growing their own food?

I would tell them to go and do a course on growing food, in the Organic Centre near us in Co. Leitrim or in any of the other organic centres around the country: Sonairte in Co. Meath, the Wexford Organic Centre, Irish Seed Savers in Co. Clare, etc. Learning from an experienced grower is the most enjoyable way to become an experienced grower yourself.

Have you an aspiration for the future in relation to food?

I would love to see more people growing, and indeed cooking, their own home-grown food. Apart from the health benefits and social side of growing and cooking at home, this pastime will also save money for the household. It will also save the country money as fewer imports of fruit and vegetables would be needed. Irish farmers can supply us with the food we may have no space to grow, but we must eat food which is in season.

JOE BARRY

Joe Barry is a farmer, forester and journalist with the *Farming Independent*. Joe has a natural flair for writing about biodiversity and the interdependence of food growing and the well-being of the wider environment. The thinnings from his well-managed woodland are now also the basis for his son, Peter's, wood delivery business, which keeps my wood store well stocked (www.logonfirewood.ie).

Describe the location in which you grow your own food:

I live on a farm on the Meath–Kildare border where the main enterprises are grazing cattle and sheep and, more recently, growing trees. My farm was originally an old and well-wooded estate laid out in the early 1700s, but few of the original trees remain. Seventeen years ago, I planted 40 hectares in different sections and corners and the new trees are now well established; many are over 12 m tall. This has produced the multiple benefits of sheltering our south-facing home and garden from the prevailing winds, providing fuel for home heating, enhancing bio-diversity, and providing food and habitat for a multitude of wildlife species. At the last count there were over seventy-one species of birds around the farm and garden and many of these are proving remarkably efficient at pest control.

Which food do you look forward to harvesting most and why?

This has to be the potato. There is simply nothing to compare with the taste of freshly dug new spuds, boiled and eaten with a large dollop of butter and a pinch of salt. I grow the earlies in a polytunnel in drills fertilised with compost and well-rotted farmyard manure. The main crop is grown outdoors, again in drills, and earthed up as required. Spuds are wonderful for cleaning up ground and suppressing weeds and, following their normal manuring, create a fertile environment for follow-on crops such as brassicas.

Which garden tool do you value most and why?

This may seem an odd answer, but, as the soil in my area of Meath is mostly heavy clay, good garden compost is undoubtedly the finest tool I have for creating a friable, easily worked and fertile loam. My garden used to be extremely difficult to cultivate when wet and, in dry spells, the soil would turn hard and unyielding. By digging in large amounts of compost over the years, the fertility has increased, with lots of organic matter providing a natural growing medium. Earthworms are now plentiful and the crops are healthier and, as a result, more resistant to disease. As a soil improver, good compost has to be the most important tool available for producing food naturally. Feed the soil, not the plant.

What motivates you to undertake the work involved in growing food?

When I was growing up it was considered extravagant and wasteful to purchase anything that could be made or grown at home and the habit has stuck. Possibly the most powerful motivation is to have fresh food available for most of the year that I know has not been treated with either fungicides, pesticides or other chemicals to prolong shelf life, improve appearance, or whatever. Wandering through the garden on a summer's evening, nibbling on raw carrots, radishes, peas or broccoli spears is hard to beat. Fresh food tastes better.

What advice would you give to a person considering growing their own food?

Getting your soil in the right condition is the first and most important task. If, like many people, you have a back garden with a few shrubs, flowers and a lawn, and you wish to convert part of it to producing food, just grow spuds in the chosen area for the first year. By digging in lots of compost and/or farmyard manure you will raise the fertility, improve the organic content and the spuds will suppress weeds. Following harvest, your garden is ready for more ambitious and varied crops. You can even grow salads and herbs in a window box if space is limited.

Have you an aspiration for the future in relation to food?

My aim is to have fresh, home-grown fruit from May until the following January. I have fenced off an additional small area for use as an orchard and have purchased twenty trees from English's Fruit Nursery in Wexford, a mix of apple, pear, plum, cherry and damson. Paddy English tells me that, with the correct choice of varieties, this is now possible to achieve. The early ripening apples will be ready in August and, with the aid of modern rootstocks, the later varieties can hold the apples on the trees longer, are relatively frost resistant and some can be picked as late as January. I plan to have strawberries ready in May (in the polytunnel) followed by other soft fruits until the first apples are ripe, and hopefully I will be able to enjoy both for the remainder of the summer and the early part of winter. This will avoid the traditional autumn glut of fruit with its consequent wasted windfalls.

Júil 🍃 *July*

The Month of the Man who gave us Onions

NO DOUBT Julius Caesar would have preferred to be remembered for 'I came, I saw, I conquered' or 'Veni, vidi, vici', as he said himself. However, his campaign to extend the Roman Empire has left a legacy for all who work in a kitchen garden. That legacy is the range of Roman-grown vegetables which are today the staple vegetables of temperate climates all over the world: radish, onion, garlic, cucumber, parsnip, carrot, etc.

AN IMAGE BASED ON AN ANCIENT WALL PAINTING IN OSTIA, A MAJOR PORT OF THE ROMAN EMPIRE NEAR ROME, WHICH APPEARS TO BE OF A CARROT WITH OLIVES AND A CUP.

T.S.

All these vegetables, hopefully growing bigger week by week in the patch you are cultivating, are, in their own way, a memorial to the Roman emperor. The Roman Senate decided to call the month after the same Julius Caesar as a birthday present, given that this emperor, the original 'Prince of Parsnips', was born on 12 July.

July is my favourite month: the growth is good and, wet or dry, it is generally warm enough to work outside in the bright evenings. Before the potato was introduced to Europe in the 1500s, there was a need for ordinary people to depend on stored vegetables and cured meat until the main harvest the following month. July was the last month before the big harvest and, therefore, supplies of food were sometimes quite scarce. As a result, we can find references to 'Iúil an Ghorta' (July of the Famine) or 'Iúil an Chabáiste' (July of the Cabbage) in Irish literature. Today, we have a greater range of fruit and vegetables and if we are organised to sow seed in succession, we need not go hungry in July.

Beyond Ireland, the same seasonal lack of food and the associated family crisis can be understood better in a children's rhyme:

> Please remember the Grotto, Father's gone to sea,
> Mother's gone to bring him back, so please remember me.

The 'Grotto' was made from shells by children for St James' Day on 25 July. One can imagine the crops being nearly ripe enough to harvest and Mother being distraught that Father has not returned from herding, fishing, warring or otherwise wandering to harvest the crops on which the family would depend for the months ahead. The rhyme suggests the children were left to fend for themselves while Mother was gone to bring him back. The Welsh word for July, Gorffennaf (end of summer), seems to anticipate the autumn harvest starting in August also.

An overview of the work ahead in the garden this month:
Sow out: successional sowings – spinach, beetroot, turnips, lettuce, carrots, kohlrabi, endive, leeks, broccoli, cabbage, Japanese brassicas
Harvest: broad and French beans, potatoes, carrots, celeriac, spinach and runner beans

🍁 FIRST WEEK IN JULY 🍁

Harvesting blackcurrants, a favourite summer pastime

'Don't deprive them of any blackcurrant juice you can get…'

('Wise Eating in Wartime', British Ministry of Food booklet, 1943)

MY father grew blackcurrants and the family tradition continues in Trevor's Kitchen Garden. Even before taking into account the health benefits of this flavoursome soft fruit, the best reason to grow blackcurrants is that it seems to suit the growing conditions in my small garden.

Blackcurrants are renowned for their high content of vitamin C, a powerful antioxidant. They also contain GLA (gamma-linolenic acid), a rare Omega-6 essential fatty acid, as well as potassium. To put their worth in context, they are reported to have twice the potassium of bananas, four times the vitamin C of oranges and twice the antioxidants of blueberries. So the kitchen gardener gets all the health benefits, and more, of imported fresh fruit, with none of the unhealthy air miles associated with fruit imports.

Blackcurrants are a relatively new plant in kitchen gardens. Given the soft spot I have for this soft fruit, I was surprised to hear that it was the whitecurrant like 'White Dutch' which was more prized in Victorian kitchen gardens for fresh desserts. Next most popular was the redcurrant, which was used for pie jelly. Redcurrants are still popular with jam makers as they have high levels of pectin, which helps strawberry jam especially to set. In the nineteenth century, the blackcurrant was viewed mainly as a medicinal fruit. In the twentieth century, sweeter varieties were bred. Since the Middle Ages the blackcurrant has had a reputation in the treatment of bladder stones and liver disorders. To alleviate coughs, blackcurrants have been blended into medicinal syrups for years.

FACTORS WHICH MAKE BLACKCURRANTS A GOOD SOFT FRUIT TO GROW

So why blackcurrants over red or white currants, I hear you ask. I know kitchen gardeners who prefer red or white currants, but we agree to differ. Blackcurrants are the new black for me! Is there any more interesting addition to piping hot organic porridge than a freshly picked handful of blackcurrants on top with some brown sugar and milk? This is my favourite breakfast. Is there any more exotic or simple dish than blackcurrants topped with a spoonful of organic natural yoghurt and a spoonful of local honey? I confess that this is my favourite dessert. Other reasons to grow blackcurrants are:

- It has no thorns so children especially can pick the fruit safely.

- Fruiting stems can be removed by secateurs and the blackcurrants on them picked in the comfort of the kitchen. This clears space for new wood to grow where next year's fruit will develop.

- Birds seem less attracted to black than other colours of currant, leaving more fruit for you.

- I have had the same bushes for over fifteen years and I have seen no disease or poor crops in that time.

- Blackcurrant bushes suit a small garden as they do not grow too high or too wide, and they can be pruned to fit the space.

ARE SOME VARIETIES BETTER TO PLANT THAN OTHERS?

As the blackcurrant is an important crop for some commercial growers, especially in Co. Wexford, the breeding of bigger, sweeter and more disease-resistant varieties continues apace. The two bushes I planted are both called 'Ben Lomond', a variety developed in 1975. It was good then and it still is. However, others have been bred since to be even more dependable and disease resistant. The flavour of the month (so to speak!) now seems to be 'Ben Hope', bred in 1998.

GROWING BLACKCURRANTS – A NOTE TO LOOK BACK AT IN THE AUTUMN

If you have no blackcurrants growing in your garden, you can either buy them at a farm shop or a farmers' market. Lucky you if your local shops sell locally grown blackcurrants; I have never seen them for sale in shops near where I live anyway. The Sonairte walled garden ecology centre stall in the Dublin Food Co-op sells them on a Saturday in July, as do I at Balbriggan Fish and Farmers' Market. The other option is, of course, to grow them yourself.

I would plant blackcurrant bushes in October or November, but there is no harm in preparing your site and digging in compost and leaf mould in July. Keep removing any weeds which germinate, so, come the time to plant, the site will be as weed free as possible. Some books recommend a space of 1.25 m between bushes. I have mine planted closer as I do not have much space for the blackcurrants which have served me so well. My two bushes are both in a 1 m x 2 m plot. They are planted on the bank of the garden pond so they are well irrigated.

- On planting day, have to hand the blackcurrant bush, well watered and in its pot from the garden centre, a spade, a garden fork, leaf mould or compost, and a full watering can.

- Using the spade, dig a hole twice the diameter of the pot.

- Fork the edge of the hole to loosen soil.

- Place the potted bush in the hole to ensure the soil top in the pot is level with the surrounding ground.

- Add compost and/or leaf mould to the hole depending on how rich the soil is.

- Remove the bush from the pot and position it correctly in the hole.

- Hold the bush upright while refilling the hole with soil.

- Water the newly planted blackcurrant bush.

- Mulch the soil around the bush with grass clippings, cardboard or even carpet or black plastic to retain moisture and suppress competition from weeds.

- Look forward to next year's harvest in early to mid-summer.

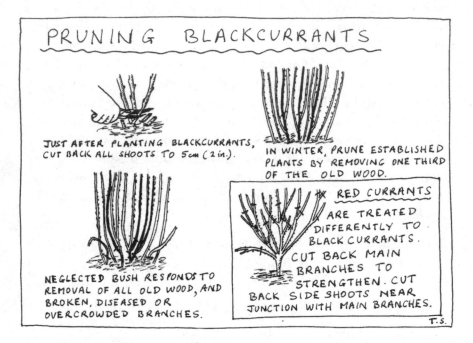

PRUNING BLACKCURRANTS

JUST AFTER PLANTING BLACKCURRANTS, CUT BACK ALL SHOOTS TO 5cm (2in.).

IN WINTER, PRUNE ESTABLISHED PLANTS BY REMOVING ONE THIRD OF THE OLD WOOD.

NEGLECTED BUSH RESPONDS TO REMOVAL OF ALL OLD WOOD, AND BROKEN, DISEASED OR OVERCROWDED BRANCHES.

RED CURRANTS ARE TREATED DIFFERENTLY TO BLACK CURRANTS. CUT BACK MAIN BRANCHES TO STRENGTHEN. CUT BACK SIDE SHOOTS NEAR JUNCTION WITH MAIN BRANCHES.

T.S.

OTHER JOBS FOR THE WEEK THAT IS IN IT:

- To preserve lavender for use in the house during winter, cut lavender stalks before the flowers are fully open. Tie them in small loose bundles and hang them in the greenhouse, a warm shed or a wardrobe to dry.

- Weeds will be growing vigorously so keep hoeing and hoping that big-leafed vegetables like courgettes cover the soil enough to block the light and halt the growth of overshadowed weeds.

The Bigger Picture:
Hats off to Michelle Obama for digging up the White House lawn to organically grow food

Less than three months after the inauguration of Barack Obama as the forty-fourth President of the USA, First Lady Michelle Obama showed true leadership in the campaign to solve the epidemic of childhood obesity and to improve food security and quality of life for everyone. With the help of local school children, Michelle Obama prepared part of the pristine White House lawn for an organic kitchen garden.

I was Minister for Food and Horticulture at the time and this initiative was one I was determined to emulate in Ireland, starting with the Bloom Festival that year in the Phoenix Park. With the help of Bord Bia and the American Embassy in Ireland, the first 'White House kitchen garden' outside the USA was opened jointly by the acting ambassador, US Chargé d'Affaires Robert J. Faucher, and myself on behalf of the Irish people. There were minor differences between the American and Irish kitchen gardens. In the USA, pumpkins took pride of place, whereas potatoes, courgettes and cabbage featured more in Ireland. Had there been more musicians present, we might have tried a verse of the song 'You say tomato, I say tom-ah-to'. On second thoughts, this may not have been a good one to sing. Although written in 1937 by George and Ira Gershwin, the title of the song is 'Let's Call the Whole Thing Off', which is far from the message the governments of both nations wished to convey!

However, not everyone was happy with Michelle Obama and her organic kitchen garden. On 22 April 2009, *The Times* in the UK published a report about a letter of protest against the fact that the White House vegetables were to be grown organically. The letter came from the Mid-America Croplife Association (MACA), which (surprise, surprise) represents agri-chemical companies producing pesticides and fertilisers.

The letter was addressed to 'Mrs Barack Obama'. It tried not to be provocative and instead encouraged Mrs Obama to recognise the role played by conventional agriculture in feeding America's growing population. To quote Ms Bonnie McCarvel, the MACA executive director: 'We live in a very different world than that of our grandparents. Americans are juggling jobs with the needs of children and ageing parents. The time needed to tend a garden is not there for the majority of our citizens, certainly not a garden of sufficient productivity to supply much of a family's year round food needs.'

Unfortunately for MACA, the real motivation for the letter came out in an internal email to MACA members and supporters which said, 'While a garden is a great idea, the thought of it being organic made [us] shudder.'

Thankfully Michelle Obama has been hugely supported in America and worldwide for her initiative to organically cultivate an iconic kitchen garden. One wonders if the MACA executive director would relish the prospect of children gardening with pesticides. The US Environmental Protection Agency lists pesticides in the top three causes of cancer in the USA.

The Times story has a happy ending, however. It reports that more than 100,000 people have signed an online petition supporting Michelle Obama and asking MACA to stop its 'propaganda about pesticides'. 'Stop asserting that the First Lady is somehow disserving our nation's citizens by encouraging them to grow their own food locally, sustainably and without your industry's chemicals,' the petition says. 'We know better and you should too.'

Meanwhile, the 'White House kitchen garden' grows, as does the global movement to encourage every person to grow as much as possible of their own food, and to do so as healthily as possible. Happy growing this 4 July!

❦ SECOND WEEK IN JULY ❦

Strawberries can put a smile on any gardener's face

'Doubtless God could have made a better berry [than a
strawberry], but doubtless God never did.'
(William Butler, physician, 1535–1618)

THIS week, the strawberry plants are sending out runners, and
if these touch soil they root to form new plants. It is time to pay
attention to ensure another strawberry crop next year.

It seems odd to be describing this most popular fruit by the name
we use. Botanically, the strawberry is neither a berry, nor does the
name come from straw. This name is said to come from Anglo-
Saxon. Mind you, straw has become useful mulch which keeps the
fruit clean before it can be picked. One way or another, it is a
member of the Rosaceae or rose family, genus Fragaria, which
means 'a pleasing aroma'. This I can certainly relate to.

One might think that the wild strawberry, Fragaria vesca, is an
ancestor of the larger strawberry we mainly eat today, but
apparently not. The modern cultivar resulted from crossing two
American species, which were then brought to Europe. Apart from
the legendary flavour of strawberries in so many dishes, the fruit
itself is very healthy, with higher levels of vitamin C than citrus
fruits and high levels of folic acid.

GIVING YOUR STRAWBERRY PLANTS THE CONDITIONS
THEY NEED

Strawberries grow best in soil which is rich in compost or manure
and which warms early in spring, so pick a patch which gets the
sun for most of the day, or position your strawberry-growing

container in such a sunny location. As the flowers are susceptible to frost, a growing area which retains some heat at night is important. Some people cover the plants with horticultural fleece at night if frost is forecast.

WHEN TO PLANT STRAWBERRY PLANTS

In the next couple of weeks, strawberry plants can be planted to develop before winter sets in. If you wait until springtime to plant, then you should remove the new flowers over the following months and allow the plant to build up its energy levels over a winter first before allowing it to fruit the following spring (twelve months).

START WITH HEALTHY RUNNERS

A runner is a young strawberry plant. Small plants form at the end of what could be described as an umbilical cord still attached to the parent strawberry plant. These strawberry plants can be separated from the parent once the young runner roots have become established in the soil. Strawberries are prone to a number of viral diseases, mostly spread by aphids. The main effect of these viruses is that they distort the shape of the fruit and leaves. Research stations have devised ways of removing the viruses and so they can supply virus-free runners. This is why it is recommended to buy 'clean runners' from a reputable garden centre to begin your 'strawberry fields'.

After fruiting, remove unwanted runners as they sap energy from the parent plant. If, however, you wish to propagate some new generation plants, check that the chosen runners are healthy to use first. It makes sense and saves money to propagate from runners if the parent plant is healthy. Health-check factors are:

🌿 The plant is growing vigorously.

🌿 The leaves are healthy with no yellowing or distortion.

🌿 The plant has yielded an ample crop.

168

TURNING A RUNNER INTO A NEW STRAWBERRY PLANT:

🌿 Embed a 9–12 cm (3.5–4.7 inch) pot filled with good soil or potting compost in the soil where a runner is growing (probably suspended in mid-air, attached to parent plant).

🌿 Using a u-shaped piece of wire (a large straightened and bent paper clip will do), plant the runner in the pot and pin it in place so it does not lift out by accident.

🌿 Water judiciously.

🌿 The young plant should be growing well by the end of August and the cord to the parent can be cut. The pot can be taken out of the ground, ready to be transplanted into the final growing location.

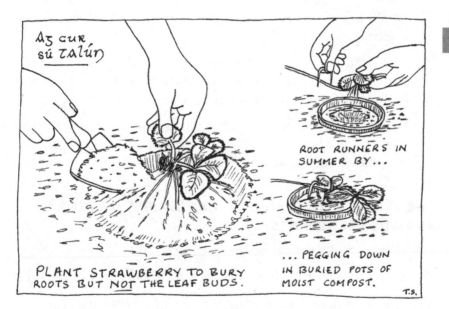

Ag cur, sú talún

ROOT RUNNERS IN SUMMER BY...

PLANT STRAWBERRY TO BURY ROOTS BUT NOT THE LEAF BUDS.

... PEGGING DOWN IN BURIED POTS OF MOIST COMPOST.

T.S.

PLANTING UP THE NEW STRAWBERRY PLANTS

🌿 Sprinkle and lightly fork in some wood ash if the soil is not rich in potash.

- Plan to have the plants 40 cm (approx. 6 inches) apart as they fill out and cover the soil with a mat of vegetation.

- Be careful not to bury the crown of the plant as it rots if submerged.

- There is no need to provide liquid feed of nitrogen, for example, nettle tea, as this encourages leaf growth at the expense of fruit.

- Good compost in the soil should retain enough moisture for a while, so only water if the soil is very dry. The upturned bottles (homemade funnels) allow watering without wetting the leaves.

USING CONTAINERS TO GROW STRAWBERRIES

- Small containers dry out too quickly so choose the biggest your available space allows.

- The health of the soil and compost mix, along with keeping the roots from drying out, will be key factors in the success you have growing strawberries in a container.

- Having an upturned bottomless plastic bottle stuck in the soil is handy as a watering funnel to avoid water spilling over the side and washing away nutrients from the soil.

THE AVERAGE LIFESPAN OF STRAWBERRIES BOUGHT IN AS VIRUS-FREE PLANTS

- Year 1 – the largest strawberries produced.

- Year 2 – may be the biggest crop, with a variety of berry sizes.

- Year 3 – smaller berries, often used for jam making.

- After three years, most growers replace their plants with virus-free new plants.

PROTECTING YOUR STRAWBERRY HARVEST FROM BIRDS

🍃 The most expensive bird excluder is a greenhouse or polytunnel. Lucky you if you have one.

🍃 Netting the strawberry bed by hanging the net above the plants on a framework of sticks works well.

🍃 A fruit cage is a fancier, more permanent version of netting, but is also more expensive.

🍃 The Victorian kitchen gardeners used to encourage a kitten to play in the strawberry bed to scare away birds. If you are a cat person, this may be an option.

🍃 Other endless options include hanging old CDs or streamers from strings suspended over the strawberry bed or container.

OTHER JOBS FOR THE WEEK THAT IS IN IT:

🍃 Dry out harvested onions and garlic on a sunny day on a warm, dry path. The dryer these alliums are, the longer they will store over the winter.

🍃 Pinch out the tops of climbing beans, especially runner beans. Some growers recommend spraying the bean flowers with water using a hand-held mister, to encourage pods to form.

The Bigger Picture:
Napoleon Bonaparte and the farmers' market

Much has been written about the French Revolution, especially in reference to Bastille Day, which is marked by French people worldwide on 14 July each year. A lesser known aspect of the history of this eighteenth-century period is the role food, or, more correctly, the lack of food, played in the upheaval and the lessons which were learned as a result.

Before the French revolution, bad weather, a number of years of poor harvests and poor distribution of food caused hardship and resentment amongst the majority in France. The poor response and lack of empathy from the aristocracy incensed the starving people even more. With poorer people, especially children, dying of starvation, mothers and fathers of France could see no alternative but to overthrow the obscenely rich ascendancy. Then perhaps people could get their hands on whatever food the rich were eating.

Much of the rioting was sparked by lack of food and a young French army officer called Napoleon Bonaparte was ordered to restore order in response to a number of these riots. When Bonaparte rose to become First Consul of France at the start of the nineteenth century, he was sensitive to the importance of food. He also believed that military victory would depend on finding a way to preserve food for the marching soldiers to carry with them.

In 1800 he offered 12,000 francs to anyone who could invent what we call 'canning' today. A confectioner called Nicolas François Appert won the prize, which Napoleon personally presented to him.

Napoleon wanted to avoid any repeat of the food riots he had to quell as a young officer and which led to such social unrest during the French Revolution. Therefore, he brought in the requirement that the mayor of each town in France would organise a farmers' market in their own town to ensure food was grown locally and could be sold directly to local people as freshly and as cheaply as possible. This would also give the farmers a way to sell their produce directly to customers without the requirement of a 'middle man'.

To this day, the tradition of farmers' markets in France is strong and a big attraction for local producers, local shoppers and visitors alike. All too often it is forgotten that these outdoor markets selling local produce were established to firstly prevent starvation and social disorder.

Over two hundred years later, there is a real risk that history could repeat itself again, unless the growing and distribution of food are assisted by local direct routes to market like farmers' markets and farm shops. In a tangible way, supporting genuine local producers at your local farmers' market, for example, and growing some food to sell at the market are real contributions to future food security.

Green roof on the garden shed needs a 'haircut'

'No plot so narrow, be but Nature there,
No waste so vacant, but may well employ
Each faculty of sense, and keep the heart
Awake to Love and Beauty!'
(Samuel Taylor Coleridge, 1772–1834)

WHEN I bought my home in 1987, it was as much to have a south-facing garden I could cultivate as a home to live in. I had a garden shed but it was too big for the small garden so I sold it. I thought I could manage without a garden shed and have a more productive garden using all the space for growing. I leaned my spades, rakes and garden forks against walls, as neatly as possible in the kitchen and in a corner near the back door. It was hardly a surprise that this was not a long-term solution!

Both front and back gardens had been roughly grassed when the builders left. The growing of fruit, vegetables and herbs, and having a wood-store and a patio area would need some comprehensive planning. With this in mind, I sat down at the kitchen table with a measuring tape, pencil, ruler and paper. I incorporated a plan for a garden shed into this garden plan – but not the type of garden shed I had seen at garden centres. This one would be a lean-to and have a living green roof. The field behind the house had recently been built on and I wanted to create a space where the natural flora of the former field could continue to grow, even on a small scale.

Reasons for having a living green roof on a garden shed:

❧ The green roof soaks up water and decreases the quantity of rain run-off from the shed roof.

- The weight of the roof, aided by the grasses and plants, gives the shed stability to withstand high winds.

- Insulation provided by the roof keeps the shed temperature cool in summer and warmer than outdoor temperatures in winter.

- Over the past fifteen years, the shed, roof and all, has been maintenance free, apart from the need for a coat of water-based, non-toxic wood preservative every one or two years and some cutting back of green growth.

- The green roof is aesthetically pleasing.

WHAT ARE THE FUNDAMENTALS OF DESIGNING A GARDEN SHED WITH A GREEN ROOF?

- Provide strong upright supports to bear the weight of a rain-sodden heavy earth roof.

- Cement upright bolts into the single course of foundation brick, which keeps the damp course and wooden foot board off the ground and as dry as possible during rainfall.

- Thread damp course through bolts and then thread a drilled 4 ft x 2 ft plank through the bolts down on top of the damp course. Secure all to create a timber base upon which to fix upright roof support timbers.

- Build a roof of timber with a 1ft high plank all around the roof perimeter to create what looks like a shallow wooden box.

- Leave a gap at the eave of the roof box to allow rain water to drain away and drop to the path.

- Use corrugated plastic and waterproof membrane and durable tape to keep the wooden shed roof surface separate from the damp soil and rainwater.

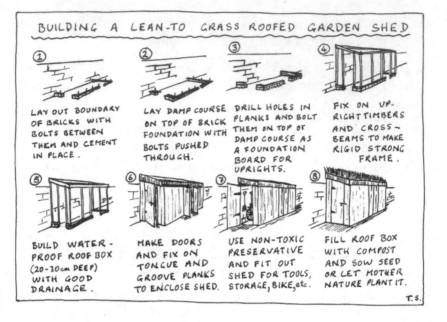

BUILDING A LEAN-TO GRASS ROOFED GARDEN SHED

① LAY OUT BOUNDARY OF BRICKS WITH BOLTS BETWEEN THEM AND CEMENT IN PLACE.

② LAY DAMP COURSE ON TOP OF BRICK FOUNDATION WITH BOLTS PUSHED THROUGH.

③ DRILL HOLES IN PLANKS AND BOLT THEM ON TOP OF DAMP COURSE AS A FOUNDATION BOARD FOR UPRIGHTS.

④ FIX ON UP-RIGHT TIMBERS AND CROSS-BEAMS TO MAKE RIGID STRONG FRAME.

⑤ BUILD WATER-PROOF ROOF BOX (20-30cm DEEP) WITH GOOD DRAINAGE.

⑥ MAKE DOORS AND FIX ON TONGUE AND GROOVE PLANKS TO ENCLOSE SHED.

⑦ USE NON-TOXIC PRESERVATIVE AND FIT OUT SHED FOR TOOLS, STORAGE, BIKE, etc.

⑧ FILL ROOF BOX WITH COMPOST AND SOW SEED OR LET MOTHER NATURE PLANT IT.

T.S.

PLANTING UP A GREEN ROOF

Personal preferences play a big part in planting this new growing space. From my point of view, I simply emptied the contents of my soil-like compost onto the ground and shovelled all this up into the retained box-like area where the green roof was to grow in due course. Having read a bit about planting up green roof space, I was all set to plant sedum. This shallow-rooted and drought-tolerant plant is a favourite amongst green roof gardeners, as well as being attractive to butterflies and bees. Other recommended plants were rosemary, thyme and sage. However, I could not see myself climbing up on this roof to snip herb leaves whenever there was a sandwich to make or a dinner to cook, so I decided to grow herbs only on *terra firma*.

In the meantime, the roof began to grow of its own accord. Composted radishes which had gone to seed last year germinated and grew into the biggest radishes I have ever seen before or since.

Seeds similar to the flora of the field which had been built upon also germinated until the roof began to look like the former field in miniature. At that point, I decide to allow nature to take its course and landscape the roof for me.

A WORD OF WARNING ABOUT LETTING NATURE TAKE ITS COURSE

Having taken my eye off the roof as it grew naturally, I now find ivy has taken hold. Although I like the look of ivy and it is a rich habitat for birds, bees and biodiversity in general, the strong and determined roots of ivy can demolish a stone building, not to mention a wooden one. At present, I am curtailing the ivy as best I can, preventing it from entering gaps and cutting back its growth where I can reach it. There have been no leaks from the roof so far (fingers crossed!). However, if I had my chance again, I would keep ivy off a green roof.

OTHER JOBS FOR THE WEEK THAT IS IN IT:

- Pinch out side shoots of tomatoes which sprout in what looks like the 'armpits' of the tomato plant, as these sap energy which would otherwise go to make better fruit.

- Earth up leeks, any cabbage family plants which have developed wobbly stems and main crop potatoes, in order to bury more of the stems but have leaves exposed to catch the sun's energy.

The Bigger Picture:
Is it legal to sell your own garden or allotment produce?

Unless you are a super-organised grower with a sage-like ability to predict the weather over a growing season, inevitably there will be

177

a glut of one crop or another which cannot be predicted at the time of sowing. Most people turn their gluts into acts of generosity. You can sometimes get a name for being a supplier of free courgettes or tomato plants, or, in my case, a distributor of free apple juice, cabbage plants or night-scented stock plants, depending on the time of the year. But there can be a limit to the number of relatives and friends who will want these gifts – and what about people you do not know who might love one of your courgettes?

Thoughts such as these prompted me to officially facilitate back garden and allotment growers who wanted to sell some of their surplus produce at their local farmers' market. As Minister for Food and Horticulture, I set about drawing up a 'Voluntary Code of Good Practice for Farmers' Markets', in 2008. The Code was launched by me at the Bloom Garden Festival in the Phoenix Park in 2009. It included the following requirements for good practice for markets which wanted Bord Bia recognition:

> Each market shall have a written policy/charter. This policy must provide for (amongst a number of requirements)...a communal site/stall (when a demand exists) for the sale of local garden/allotment produce and seasonal foods.

Local authorities sometimes stipulate the criteria upon which allotments are rented to members of the public. These criteria often make an obvious point that allotments are not 'mini-farms'. They are intended primarily for home consumption and to feed a family or a number of friends who share the cultivation work.

In the absence of any clearer legislation in Ireland, the UK Allotments Act 1922 states that an allotment garden must 'be wholly or mainly cultivated for...consumption by the occupier or his family'. So there is no restriction on the distribution, by sale or otherwise, of a certain proportion of the crop.

When a group of us came together a few years ago to establish Balbriggan Fish and Farmers' Market, we resolved to encourage as much availability as possible of locally grown, cooked, baked, pickled, caught and cured food. To this end, every week, during the market opening hours, a stall table is provided on which sits a number of empty wicker baskets. Clearly displayed underneath is a notice which reads:

GARDEN PRODUCE STALL
SELL YOUR OWN HOMEGROWN FRUIT + VEG
RENT A BASKET: €2

To date, we have had home-grown gooseberries, cabbage, runner beans and apples for sale at the garden produce stall. The varieties for sale were generally not available commercially, which has added a welcome diversity to the produce for sale at the market. There is a more profound aspect to the garden produce stall, however. As the price of transportation rises, so will the cost of the food system we often take for granted. Kitchen gardeners will become more and more important, as will garden produce stalls. Other routes to market like out-of-our-own-back-yard shops, known in New Zealand, the USA and elsewhere as OOOOBY stores, are popular and I know of one OOOOBY store in Glenealy, Co. Wicklow. I look forward to hearing about other similar initiatives.

Gardeners need bees and bees need gardeners

'Bees are required to pollinate 77 per cent of the world's most valuable crops.'
(Federation of Irish Beekeepers' Associations, www.irishbeekeeping.ie)

THE link in people's minds between bees and honey is an old one and goes back some 10,000 years to a time when we raided hives for honey. For the last 3,000 years, beekeeping techniques have developed towards 'farming' the bees with a view to abstracting the honey and maintaining the hive. This method has varying degrees of success.

As Minister for Food and Horticulture, I was also responsible for the craft of beekeeping and the honey sector of the Irish economy. Less than 4 per cent of the honey consumed in Ireland is produced in Ireland. Clearly there is a need for more beekeepers. So I became a novice beekeeper, initially through Jim O'Donohue of the Midlands Beekeepers Association, who has been a very supportive teacher. Workshops are held there by Jim and his colleagues on a Sunday in the grounds of Belvedere House, near Mullingar, Co. Westmeath (see www.mbka.ie).

Back in my own kitchen garden, I had a new incentive to make my garden as attractive as possible for bees. This plan is the ultimate win-win strategy. The bees benefit and hopefully make more honey due to the diversity of flowering plants. A hive of bees visits on average 2 million flowers, and flies over 200,000 km, to make just 1 kg of honey. Also, the garden benefits as honey bees, bumble bees, butterflies and many insects are vital for healthy plant life. Crops such as apples, pears and berries are entirely dependent on pollinators such as bees for fruit production.

The greater the diversity of flowering plants the better. It is better still if those plants flower in succession so there are always flowers in season for bees and other pollinators from early spring to late autumn.

Spring flowering plants which bees forage include: snowdrop, yellow crocus, gorse, yew, willow, poplar, box, plum, wild cherry, pear, apple, laurel, wallflower, dandelion, cabbage and berberis.

Spring–summer flowering plants include: common beech, lilac, copper beech, broom, wild bluebell, plantain, sycamore, ash, white horse chestnut, red horse chestnut, hawthorn, oak, buttercup, mustard, oil seed rape, holly, mountain ash, elder, lupin, broad bean, raspberry, red and white clover, blackberry, dogwood and wild honeysuckle.

Summer–autumn flowering plants include: rosebay willow herb, bell heather, privet, common lime, borage, hogweed, Californian poppy, onion, meadowsweet, field thistle, evening primrose, sweet chestnut, Virginia creeper, marjoram, ling heather and ivy.

A book which I have found useful is *The Beekeeper's Garden* by Ted Hooper and Mike Taylor. Here you will get information on siting hives in the garden as well as a useful list of plants. My own hives are in the orchard of a friend less than a kilometre from my garden. My own garden is too small to fit a hive. That said, I know a number of larger suburban gardeners who have hives. However, the range of a bee is about a 5 km radius from a hive, so many gardens nearby, including mine, will benefit from the pollination services the bees provide.

OTHER JOBS FOR THE WEEK THAT IS IN IT:
🌿 Take further cuttings of herbs such as rosemary, sage and

thyme, taking semi-ripe softwood as stem cuttings. Stick each in a pot of good soil or potting compost. Water and keep moist in a sunny spot or in the greenhouse or polytunnel. When you see new growth you know the cutting has taken and new roots are forming.

🍃 To extend the harvest into late autumn, plant lettuce, oriental salads, radish, leaf beet, spinach, beetroot, etc.

BEEKEEPING COMPLEMENTS FOOD GROWING

THE NATIVE IRISH DARK BEES WHICH I KEEP, LIVE IN A FRIEND'S ORCHARD NEARBY. I HAVE SPOTTED THEM IN MY GARDEN AS THEY FORAGE FOR NECTAR, POLLEN, PROPOLIS AND WATER. BEES FLY UP TO 3 km AND, IF REQUIRED, CAN VENTURE UP TO 8 km BEFORE RETURNING TO THE HIVES.

← ROOF WITH METAL TOP. BEES TOLERATE -35°C BUT WILL NOT SURVIVE DAMPNESS.

A 'SUPER' WHERE BEES STORE HONEY →

HIVE ENTRANCE WHICH WORKER BEES GUARD AGAINST WASPS, etc.

THE BROOD BOX WHERE THE QUEEN LAYS EGGS AND WHERE THE COLONY LIVES.

USEFUL STAND WHICH KEEPS THE HIVES OFF THE GROUND →

T.S.

The Bigger Picture:
Beekeepers gather from far and wide for the annual beekeepers' summer course

There are currently between 1,500 and 2,500 beekeepers in Ireland, and there are 46 associations affiliated with the Federation of Irish Beekeepers' Associations. Most are not commercial beekeepers but enjoy learning and practising the ancient craft of keeping a few hives

My garden in its early days. Using measuring tape, posts and string tied between them, I marked out the garden design and laid out the paths.

Laying the bricks to form an edging to the herb and fruit beds and the pond.

(BELOW)
Presenting a cabbage cutting from my garden to then President of Ireland Mary McAleese and Senator Martin McAleese during Bloom 2011 in the Phoenix Park, Dublin.
Photograph courtesy of Steve Humphreys and the *Irish Independent*.

Frosty morning: a blue tit forages on the apple tree against the 'Dig for Victory' poster on the garden shed.

Digging out a batch of almost mature compost. The uncomposted sticks, if small, are mixed in with the new batch of raw compost. The larger sticks are removed to dry for use as tinder in the wood stove.

Discussing varieties of tomato seed to grow at home with award-winning *Irish Times* journalist Miriam Lord.
Photograph: Ciarán Finn

Discussing GM-free food policies with US campaigner Erin Brockovich in University College Dublin during National Organic Week 2008.
Photograph: Ciarán Finn

A cross-party meeting in 2010 at Dáil Éireann to promote the merits of a GM-free clean, green food island policy, with the support of Columban missionary Fr Seán McDonagh, chef Darina Allen and John Brennan of the Leitrim Farmers' Co-op. TDs present are Jimmy Deenihan (FG), Éamon Scanlon (FF), Michéal Kitt (FF), Michael Mulcahy (FF), Michael D. Higgins (Labour) and Trevor Sargent (Green).

Visiting Iain Tolhurst, founder of the Organic Growers Alliance (UK), who supplies 400 families in Oxford and Reading with weekly vegetable box deliveries from his 18-acre stock-free organic farm. Photograph: Ciarán Finn

Selling organic produce from my kitchen garden and from the walled garden at Sonairte at Balbriggan Fish and Farmers' Market.
Photograph courtesy of Brenda Fitzsimons and the *Irish Times*.

An overview of my back garden
in winter, showing radishes
growing in window boxes on top
of the brick composter.
Photograph: Ciarán Finn

With chef Richard Corrigan,
who called to my garden with the
RTÉ 'Corrigan's City Farm' crew
to discuss kitchen gardening and
to take away some organic
produce for his restaurant.
Photograph: Ciarán Finn

on their own land or in another suitable location. Orchard owners and farmers are often glad to have somebody mind hives on their land as the pollination services provided by the additional bees lead to greater crop production.

There is much to learn for anybody who, like myself, is new to the craft. During the spring and summer months you will need to visit the hives at least once a week to inspect that all is well in the hives and to see if you still have a queen bee. At the height of the season, the queen lays about 1,500 eggs a day at 30-second intervals. If the queen is not laying eggs, then the colony will try to replace her by hatching out a new queen, which is real miracle of nature to me. You should prevent the colony from swarming as this significantly reduces the number of bees left in the hive. Learning the lessons about swarming is best done in the company of an experienced beekeeper. I am lucky to have the advice of Milo Doyle and John Holland who help me understand what my bees are doing and how I can help them overcome problems, for example, what to do if the queen is not laying eggs.

Luckily for me and many novice beekeepers, the Federation organises a summer course at Gormanstown College in Co. Meath, up the road from where I live, during the fourth week in July. For over fifty years this event has hosted expert speakers from Ireland and other countries such as the UK and the USA. You can study for apiculture (beekeeping) qualifications and sit exams during the summer course. Many go to just attend the lectures on various aspects of beekeeping, such as how to effectively inspect a hive, rear a queen, extract honey, make equipment and so on. There are generally a number of beekeeping providers in attendance, who sell equipment, books and magazines. The informal aspect of Gormanstown is important too. Chatting with other beekeepers can be invaluable in helping you decide what you need to do to help your own bees. Understandably, the numbers attending the Gormanstown Summer Course are growing year by year. For more information, see www.irishbeekeeping.ie.

Thoughts from other kitchen gardeners

JASON HORNER

A professional organic market gardener, Jason is also a founder member of Organic Growers of Ireland (OGI), which works to develop the organic horticulture sector. Jason's sells his produce from his farm in Rathclooney, Cruskeen, Co. Clare at a number of local markets as well as supplying food to his family. With no degree course in organic horticulture available yet in Ireland, Jason went to Aberdeen to earn a degree in modern organic farming.

Describe the location in which you grow your own food:

On the side of a drumlin in Co. Clare where we are surrounded by trees. The soil ranges from clay to bog. There is lots of wildlife and biodiversity; it's a shame about the weather.

Which food do you look forward to harvesting most and why?

Cherry tomatoes for their taste and colour. Also, they are popular on the market stall.

Which garden tool do you value most and why?

My planting trowel is like part of my right arm. I would be totally lost without it.

What motivates you to undertake the work involved in growing food?

I have been doing it for so long I have forgotten what motivates me. Originally, it was the taste. Now it's what I do, who I am.

What advice would you give to a person considering growing their own food?

Start small. Pay attention to detail. Keep good notes. Don't worry if it doesn't work – there is always next year.

Have you an aspiration for the future in relation to food?

I would like to see Ireland being self-sufficient in all foods and seeds, and free from genetically modified organisms, with food markets in all centres of population.

NICKY KYLE

From a Welsh farming background and now growing organically in Ireland for over three dozen years, Nicky started up the first commercial organic vegetable 'box scheme' in the Dublin area. A leading light in the Irish Organic Farmers and Growers Association and the Organic Trust through the years, Nicky grows, gives courses and maintains a well-respected organic growing tutorial website (www.nickykylegardening.com), as well as being a portrait sculptor.

Describe the location in which you grow your own food:

My kitchen garden lies at the heart of 5 acres, which thirty years ago I specifically designed to encompass a broad range of habitats for encouraging biodiversity, thereby attracting a rich variety of wildlife. This helps the whole garden ecology to work in a balanced and natural way, which supports organic food growing and ensures that I have no pest problems. There are roughly 4 acres of meadow and woodland, with two large wildlife ponds, a natural stream, an orchard with many old varieties of apple, plum and pear trees – some rare – a fun 'jungle garden' and a bee and butterfly border. The potager/vegetable garden is designed in a cruciform shape, with three 4 ft x 28 ft raised beds in each quarter. I have three large polytunnels.

Which food do you look forward to harvesting most and why?

I look forward with equal anticipation to every fruit and vegetable in its own proper season. The tending, anticipation and harvesting of your own naturally grown produce – at its freshest and seasonal best – teaches you how to truly appreciate and savour one of life's great experiences.

What motivates you to undertake the work involved in growing food?

The garden tool I most value is my hands! As G.K. Chesterton once said: 'To learn how to value anything – imagine losing it.' Twenty-eight years ago, after an accident, I was gradually losing the use of my hands and faced possible paralysis until I had miraculous and life-changing spinal surgery. That experience taught me never to take anything for granted. In terms of an actual garden tool – my late father's spade would be the one I most value.

What motivates you to undertake the work involved in growing food?

Greed mainly – I love eating delicious food. And knowing that all my food is as fresh, pure, nutritious and environmentally friendly as it can possibly be! I have grown food organically for thirty-six years since my daughter was born with multiple allergies.

What advice would you give to a person considering growing their own food?

I would advise that growing your own food is one of the most basically satisfying, empowering and rewarding things you can do. But don't take on too much. Start in a very small way and encourage Nature to help you – she will, trust me! Don't be tempted to start by killing everything off with weed killers first. Weed killers destroy all the micro-life in your soil which can take years to recover. Heavy mulches and timely cultivations are far better.

Have you an aspiration for the future in relation to food?

First, I would like to see a reduction in the obscene amount of food that is wasted globally – 30–50 per cent of all food produced annually. This would then nullify the argument many use that GM technology is needed to feed a growing world population. Second would be to stop the massive environmental degradation and destruction of precious habitats worldwide by chemical and carbon intensive industrial farming – purely in order to feed our greed and waste. Third would be a fairer distribution of that food. I could go on...

Lúnasa ❧ August

Month of Lugh, the Celtic God of Harvest

A T LAST, Lúnasa, the first month of the harvest. In the Celtic calendar, autumn has arrived. The god Lugh is held in some affection for a number of reasons. First, he is believed to have organised the first Lá Lúnasa, on 1 August, to be a harvest celebration before the hard work got underway. He declared the festival to be in honour of his foster mother Tailtiú, who was exhausted, having singlehandedly cleared the farmland of forestry so people could grow crops. Second, Lugh was known as being *lámh fhada* (long armed) and so he was a great help in the cornfield or on the battlefield. Third, he was a god of light and genius, and had power over thunder and storms. Indeed, if a soft rain fell on Lá Lúnasa, people thought that Lugh was blessing the proceedings, as he was well capable of much worse.

However, our ancestors believed that Lugh, associated with the purifying qualities of water, murdered his grandfather Balor (of Bealtaine fame), who was linked to the hotter sunshine of summer. This usurping of Balor was how the waning of the sun during harvest was explained. Lugh was forgiven for this dreadful crime as the sun could not be allowed to continue shining with such strength for fear of drought!

The man commemorated by the word August had some blood on his hands also. Augustus Caesar was a grandnephew of Julius, which seemingly gave him a bit of an inferiority complex. To make his mark, so to speak, he set about overthrowing the ruler of Egypt, Queen Cleopatra and her lover, the Roman General Marc Antony, to bring Egypt under Roman rule in the month of Sextillus, as it was known then. The Roman Senate agreed to rename the month

Augustus in his honour. Not happy with that, Augustus insisted that his month should have thirty-one days, just like his uncle's month. The Senate reluctantly agreed, but no further requests by emperors Claudius or Nero to have their own month were entertained.

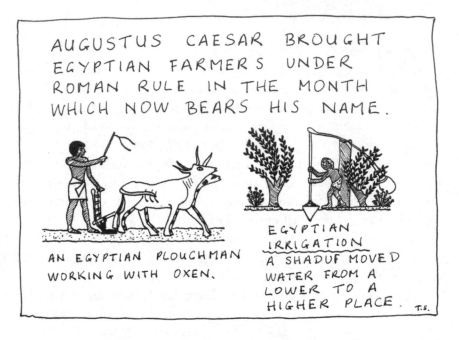

AUGUSTUS CAESAR BROUGHT EGYPTIAN FARMERS UNDER ROMAN RULE IN THE MONTH WHICH NOW BEARS HIS NAME.

AN EGYPTIAN PLOUGHMAN WORKING WITH OXEN.

EGYPTIAN IRRIGATION
A SHADUF MOVED WATER FROM A LOWER TO A HIGHER PLACE.

T.S.

An overview of the work ahead in the garden this month:
Sow out: winter radishes, winter lettuce, spring cabbage; successional sowings – turnips, endive, onions and corn salad.
Harvest: as in July, plus runner beans, sweetcorn, tomatoes, cucumber and garlic.

FIRST WEEK IN AUGUST

Creating new herb plants for free is very satisfying

'Cuireann tú an féar ag fás don bhólacht,
agus luibheanna ar mhaithe leis an duine, chun go mbaine sé
arán as an talamh.'

Salm 104:14

GIVEN the antiquity of the story of herbs, the Biblical quote above is appropriate and reads in English: 'He causeth the grass to grow for the cattle, and herb for the service of man, that he may bring bread out of the earth' (Psalm 104:14). The story of the interaction between herbs (*luibheanna* in Irish), and humans is probably as old as stories go. The cave paintings of Lascaux in France depict herbs and have been carbon dated back to between 25,000 and 13,000 BC. During Biblical times, in the fifth century BC, Hippocrates, the Greek physician, listed about 400 herbs which were in common use back then. The uses of herbs were, and are, very varied. The Ancient Greeks and Romans crowned their leaders with dill and laurel leaves. The use of herbs in medicine was a key priority in Ireland when the Dublin Society, later to become the Royal Dublin Society, established the National Botanic Gardens in Glasnevin, Dublin in 1790. However, propagating herbs mainly for culinary use is the focus of this week in my garden.

AUGUST

GROWING HERBS FROM CUTTINGS

My first lesson in propagating plants from cuttings was given to me by a parent of a pupil in the Model School, Dunmanway, Co. Cork, where I was teaching in the early 1980s. This man, a seller of plants, had an entrepreneurial spirit, but I can understand why he was a little coy about his methodology. I used to spot him playing tennis in the early morning as I, on my Honda 125cc, passed the public park and tennis courts on the way to work.

I asked him one day why he played tennis so early in the morning. He told me his main purpose was to take cuttings from any landscaping shrubbery in the park, before the park ranger came on duty. While taking clandestine cuttings in a public park is not on, there is nothing wrong with the idea of taking cuttings from many of your own plants or from those of others, if you have permission, of course!

How herb cuttings root

Herbs and other shrubs can be propagated from healthy sprigs, either cut, carefully pulled or snapped off a leafy stem of the plant. The sprig will want to heal that wound and make new roots. The job of the gardener is to provide a suitable environment – water, light, air, sufficient warmth and good soil – to keep the green leafy stem alive during this healing process.

If the stem wound is in firm contact with moist soil, roots should form in a couple of weeks. You should then notice some new leaf growth. This is a good sign that the sprig has taken and roots are beginning to form. At this point, it can help the new plant if lower leaves and any flower buds are removed. Make sure to leave some top leaves. In this way the plant can use all available energy to grow new roots and a strong stem.

When to take stem cuttings

Generally cuttings are taken during the growing season from spring to autumn. Early August is my chosen time because:

1. Chosen plants are growing strongly at this time.
2. The vigorous growth means I need to chop back certain plants like sage or rosemary anyway.
3. The fairly warm weather gives new cuttings a good chance to become established plants before growth slows down as winter approaches.

Preparation and taking cuttings:

🌿 Water the chosen plant or plants at least twelve hours before you take any cuttings.

🌿 Fill the required number of plant pots, 8–12 cm (3–5 inches) in diameter, with good soil.

🌿 Otherwise, use a larger pot filled with potting compost or soil, and stick the cuttings around the edge of the pot at 5 cm (2 inch) intervals.

🌿 Choose 12–15 cm (5–6 inch) healthy growing tips or side branches of a similar length to become the new cuttings.

🌿 Each chosen growing tip is cut with a clean sharp knife at a diagonal angle.

🌿 Each healthy side shoot can either be cut, or else gently pulled off, creating a heel from which the cutting will hopefully root.

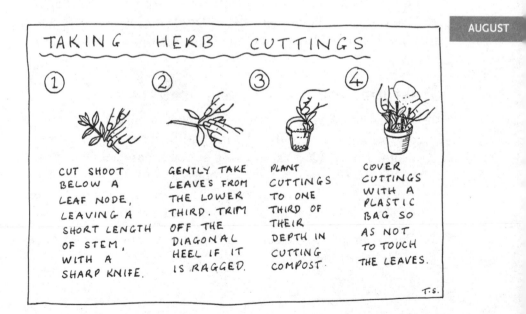

TAKING HERB CUTTINGS

① CUT SHOOT BELOW A LEAF NODE, LEAVING A SHORT LENGTH OF STEM, WITH A SHARP KNIFE.

② GENTLY TAKE LEAVES FROM THE LOWER THIRD. TRIM OFF THE DIAGONAL HEEL IF IT IS RAGGED.

③ PLANT CUTTINGS TO ONE THIRD OF THEIR DEPTH IN CUTTING COMPOST.

④ COVER CUTTINGS WITH A PLASTIC BAG SO AS NOT TO TOUCH THE LEAVES.

T·S·

Aftercare for newly planted cuttings:

🍃 Keep pots in moist and warm conditions but out of direct sunlight.

🍃 Some people create more humid conditions by putting a clear plastic freezer bag over the pot (kept clear of the cutting by a framework of twig supports). This can look like a chef's hat. Seal the plastic around the rim of the pot with an elastic band.

🍃 When cuttings start to grow vertically (as rosemary does), snip the tip of the leading stem to create a bushier looking plant if you wish.

Some herbs worth propagating from cuttings

Taking cuttings is sometimes experimental. As the parent plant is intended to continue growing, there is no big loss if a cutting does not work out. Nonetheless, practice improves the success rate.

The herbs which I have propagated from cuttings include rosemary, sage, lavender, bay, thyme, mint and lemon verbena. I am planning to try taking a cutting from a geranium, when I get a plant.

OTHER JOBS FOR THE WEEK THAT IS IN IT:

🍃 Time is nearly up for sowing if you want a harvest this autumn and next spring. Spring cabbage and Swiss chard can be sown around now. Late varieties of spinach can be sown if the weather is not too dry. Spinach tends to go to seed quickly if the weather is too hot and dry. Also, it is your last chance to sow Oriental leaves, lettuce and rocket outdoors this year.

🍃 Pinch out the tops of climbing beans to encourage new growth lower down the plant.

Those of us who have been bitten by the gardening bug know instinctively that growing plants, especially food plants, gives us a particular level of satisfaction and fulfilment. We would probably venture to say that gardening is good for us overall – if we overlook the perennial battle with slugs for a moment.

However, the academic, medical and psychiatric professionals have cottoned on to that elusive smile which gardeners can sometimes wear. The health benefits are now being quantified and analysed. The National Health Service (NHS) in Southampton, England, now prescribes 'horticulture therapy' as a treatment for low-level depression. I am amazed at the various ways in which tending a kitchen garden in particular is now credited with a multitude of health benefits. Here are a few examples of how gardening can contribute to good health:

AUGUST

- **As a treatment for depression:** 'Gardening on Prescription' is an eight-week course funded by the Southampton NHS in England to help treat people with low-level depression. The course has succeeded in curing people to the point where they can go back to paid employment. The NHS sees the course as very cost effective, given that the incidence of depression in the general population and the costs of medication are all on the rise.

- **Increases 'zest for life':** in the USA, a University of Texas study showed that gardeners have significantly higher levels of optimism and fortitude than non-gardeners.

- **Creates healthy bones:** a University of Arkansas study of 3,310 mature women, again in the USA, found that the gardeners amongst them had lower rates of osteoporosis than the joggers, swimmers and those who did aerobics. The study deduced that this was due to the weeding, digging and general weight-bearing activities involved in gardening.

🍃 **Lowers diabetes risk:** a Kansas State University study showed that American gardeners tend to get the required 150 minutes per week of exercise. This combination of exercise, as well as a healthy diet of fresh home-grown fruit and vegetables, helps to keep diabetes at bay.

🍃 **Ensures a good night's sleep:** the International Society of Horticultural Sciences found in research that people with anxiety, dementia or other serious illnesses like cancer, who used gardening as a coping strategy, had less stressful lives and better sleep patterns than equivalent non-gardeners.

As a former teacher, I relate also to the benefits of gardening in childhood development and in a fully rounded education. This realisation was a key part of the initiative to introduce 'Meet the Spuds' and the 'Incredible Edibles' food-growing programmes into every primary school and many secondary schools in the Republic, as well as the teacher training colleges in Ireland, north and south.

However, when talking to fellow organic grower and political colleague, former Senator Mark Dearey, he spoke about himself and his three-year-old daughter Stella gardening together. The quality of the interaction between father and daughter as they weeded a row of young carrots brought home to me some more tangible benefits for family life which gardening can bestow. Whatever about all these tangible, not so tangible and even anecdotal benefits, the essential draw for me, which keeps me coming back to the kitchen garden again and again, is very simple – enjoyment!

Using some crops to fertilise the soil

'...nature is never spent;
There lives the dearest freshness deep down things...'
(From 'God's Grandeur', Gerard Manley Hopkins, 1844–1889)

ONE key requirement of organic horticulture is that the soil is nurtured and fed. If the soil is healthy, then it follows that the plants growing in it will be healthy too. To keep the soil alive and healthy, it is good for it to be covered either by a crop or a mulch like cardboard and grass clippings after a food crop has been cleared.

Once a crop of potatoes, for example, has been lifted, the bare earth should be covered to keep life in the soil, for instance earthworms, in good dark living conditions. Apart from preferring to be in the dark, useful microbes in the soil also prefer a root system as part of the soil cover.

AUGUST

GREEN MANURE CROPS

You can find packets of seeds called 'green manures' in garden centres. These are generally plants which are not for human consumption, like red clover or phacelia. Instead, they are sown with a view to digging them into the soil when they flower, but *before* they seed, in a similar way that farmyard manure might be dug into the soil to prepare the ground in advance of sowing potatoes.

Now is a good time to rake over and weed a patch where a crop has finished growing. My garlic harvest has left a space which I can now sow with red clover. If this is sown after the end of August, it may be too late to get a good start. This is what I found when I sowed it in September a few years ago.

Benefits of using green manure crops:

- Increases the organic matter, earthworm activity and beneficial microorganisms in the soil.
- Increases soil available nitrogen and helps moisture retention.
- Stabilises soil to prevent erosion and leaching of soil nutrients.
- Brings deep minerals to the surface and breaks up any deep hardpan.
- Provides habitat, nectar and pollen for insect allies who in turn prey on pests.
- Improves water, root and air penetration in the soil.
- Smothers weeds.
- Gives the gardener a rest from tending a patch temporarily!

Sowing and digging in green manure crops

I know some kitchen gardeners who broadcast the seed all over the vacant patch of soil. If your soil is relatively weed free, this can work. In my case, I prefer to sow the green manure in parallel rows so the weeds emerging from the bare earth will be identifiable and can be hoed or weeded so the green manure gets the space to germinate and develop.

Remember to cut down and dig in the crop as soon as it flowers. Do not wait for seeds to form as the crop may well become a weed in years to come if the seeds fall and lie dormant in the soil for the next and subsequent years. I cut the crop down with a hedge clipper on my small patch. I leave the mown crop to lie like a mulch in situ for about a month before removing the stalks to the compost heap. I then dig in the stubble and roots, turning the soil so the surface is easy to prepare as a seedbed for the next edible crop.

Ranges of green manure crops

The first range of green manure crops is good at fixing nitrogen in the soil because each is a legume similar to garden peas.

🌿 **Alfalfa/Lucerne (*Medigo sativa*):** a deep-rooted, tall perennial, alfalfa is extremely useful in the garden as long as you have enough space to let it occupy land for a whole season. If you have, it provides plenty of green matter, is very deep rooting indeed and, being a legume, adds nitrogen. Sow at 15 g per square metre in spring, then dig it in in the autumn. If you want to sow now, that is fine too. Alfalfa can also be sown in late summer and dug in in the spring.

🌿 **Broad, fava or field bean (*Vicia faba*):** this is an excellent green manure crop in every way. It will stand the winter almost everywhere. It produces plenty of organic matter and is a nitrogen fixer. The beans can be harvested and eaten. Sow in the autumn or early summer. Space out the seeds by 10 cm (4 inches) in rows 30 cm (12 inches) apart, if you wish to harvest the beans as well. In any case, it is as well to allow a row or two to produce beans because they can be used for seed for later crops of green manure.

🌿 **Red clover (*Trifolium pratense*):** a low-growing nitrogen fixer with an extensive root system that will supply plenty of organic matter, red clover is best sown in spring or late summer, but always before the end of August. Scatter the seeds in rows 15 cm (6 inches) apart and dig in when the land is needed.

🌿 **Lupin (*Lupinus Angustifolius*):** deep-rooting tall legume that will add nitrogen and large amounts of phosphates to the soil. Sow in spring in rows about 15 cm (6 inches) apart, with about 7 cm (3 inches) between each seed. Cut down and dig in in summer. A second crop could even be sown and dug in eight weeks later.

🌿 **Winter tare (*Vicia villosa*):** another tall plant, this is one of the most useful crops because it grows during winter when land is vacant. Sow in rows, as for lupins, during late summer, and dig them in in early Spring. It can also be sown during spring and summer if land is vacant; 80 g will sow 100 m of row. Winter tare produces a large amount of green matter, has an extensive root system and fixes nitrogen.

The second range has many benefits as a green manure crop, but these plants do not fix nitrogen.

🌿 **Buckwheat (*Fagopyrum esculentum*):** useful only where space is available for the whole summer. Sow when the weather is warm, in spring or summer, and dig in during the autumn; sow in rows about 15 cm (6 inches) apart. Buckwheat is tall and has a very extensive root system. It makes copious organic matter. Although it does not fix nitrogen, it does attract hoverflies, which eat greenfly by the thousands.

🌿 **Rye (*Secale cereale*):** a non-legume which has an extensive root system and produces a useful amount of green material to dig in. Sow the perennial variety in late summer and dig in during spring. Sow in rows 2 cm (1 inch) apart. Rather than cutting the whole crop, leave a few plants to mature in the summer and save the seed for sowing the next crop.

🌿 **Phacelia (*Phacelia tanacetifolia*):** one of the best of all green manure crops in spite of the fact that it does not fix nitrogen and has roots of only medium vigour. It is fast growing and, if dug in when still soft, will not rob the soil of nitrogen. (More woody material requires nitrogen to break down, thus robbing the surrounding soil, unless it is first broken down in the compost heap before being dug into the soil.) It does not withstand cold, so sow it after the threat of frost has passed and dig it in after about eight weeks. About 30 g of seed will cover an area of 4 sq. m.

🌿 **Mustard (*Sinapis alba*):** a quick-growing, short and shallow rooting crop that will make plenty of organic matter for digging in and is a good weed suppressor. Used widely in gardens where land cannot be spared for long. Sow in spring and summer and dig in before flowering. It has a big disadvantage in that it is a member of the cabbage family, so it could harbour clubroot. It must only be sown if it complies with the rotation plan wherever cabbage family crops are being sown. Sow in rows 15 cm (6 inches) apart.

🍃 **Italian ryegrass** *(Lolium multiflorum)*: fast growing and bulky, this is a good crop for sowing early in the spring. It will germinate quickly, even in cold soils, and it can be dug in before the ground has warmed up sufficiently to plant out tender vegetables. It is essential to ensure that you use the annual strain, for example, westerwolds, rather than the perennial or biennial ryegrass, which will cause endless problems by re-growing. Be sure also to dig it in before it produces seed. About 30 g of seed will cover 4 sq. m.

OTHER JOBS FOR THE WEEK THAT IS IN IT:

🍃 Plant new strawberry plants as soon as possible, in soil where strawberries have not grown for at least three years.

🍃 Continue to pinch out tomato side shoots which appear in the 'V' between leaf stems and the main stems. When watering, mix in some liquid comfrey feed in the watering can, especially for tomatoes.

The Bigger Picture:
Grow food for a peaceful future

Even though Ireland exports considerable quantities of meat and dairy produce – and mushrooms – the Central Statistics Office calculates that approximately two thirds of all food eaten in Ireland is imported. Each year we import approximately 250,000 tonnes of vegetables, 10,000 tonnes of fruit and 1 million tonnes of grain. (See www.cso.ie.)

In effect, we are also importing the energy and fresh water taken to grow, harvest, process, pack and transport all this food. This energy imported is very conservatively estimated to be 1.5 million tonnes of oil equivalent (TOE) per annum, which would be the equivalent of the energy used to heat about half of all the housing stock in Ireland.

Can this reliance on food importation continue indefinitely? The same question was asked about the property bubble. Will we be blind-sided by a sudden change in the global food market, just as we were by the collapse of the property bubble?

Local food economies are essential for other food-exporting countries also. When I was in Ethiopia with Irish Aid and the World Food Programme, I passed many industrial flower-growing export enterprises. The employment they created was welcomed in the short term, but the water they consumed was water that was not available to grow food locally for the communities living there.

FOUR REASONS WHY GROWING FOOD LOCALLY WILL HELP ENSURE THE FUTURE IS MORE PEACEFUL

1. Food scarcity and the consequent higher food prices are pushing poorer countries into economic and social chaos.

2. These suffering societies generate large numbers of refugees and are prone to outbreaks of civil war, terrorism, illicit drug trading, wildlife and human trafficking, and a proliferation of military hardware.

3. Water shortages, soil losses and rising temperatures, which cause droughts from global warming, are placing severe limits on food production.

4. Without massive and rapid intervention to address these

environmental factors, the ripple effect from these chaotic, suffering and volatile countries will overwhelm their governments and threaten the current world order.

Meanwhile, to avoid greater chaos in the future, the grossly unequal world food order has to be transformed to sustain more locally resilient food economies. Globalisation has to make way for localisation. Everyone can help by sowing the seeds of this survival strategy. As my favourite T-shirt says, 'Give peas a chance!'

🍂 THIRD WEEK IN AUGUST 🍂

Time for light pruning of plums and raspberries

'Do not be afraid to go out on a limb…
That is where the fruit is.'

(Anonymous)

INEVITABLY, with good growth rates in the garden, I find myself dodging wayward raspberry canes or overgrown apple boughs reaching across paths. Particularly in a small garden, there is a need to lightly prune over-zealous apple, pear, plum and cherry trees, if you have them.

PRUNING: TRAINING THE PLUM TREE AS A FAN AGAINST THE WALL

Members of the cherry family (essentially fruit with a stone in it), like plum or cherry trees, are not keen on being pruned. Any wounds can get infected, especially in winter. The safest time to prune them is around now when they are growing well and any pruning cuts can heal before the colder weather sets in. If new shoots appear, cut them out with a sharp secateurs.

If your plum tree, for instance, is growing against a wall, as mine is, then keep in mind the desired shape of the tree while pruning. Plums fruit on young wood growing out from the stem. Therefore, the best shape for a plum tree against a wall is a fan shape. Imagine the trunk of the tree is a roundabout and the branches are roads radiating 180 degrees in all directions. When older wood stops fruiting, remove it and train a new branch nearby in its place. Tie in the radiating branches so they are well spaced for optimum fruiting.

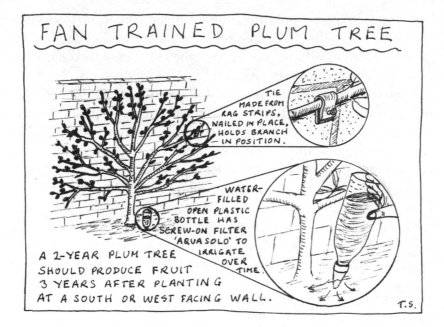

FAN TRAINED PLUM TREE

TIE MADE FROM RAG STRIPS, NAILED IN PLACE, HOLDS BRANCH IN POSITION.

WATER-FILLED OPEN PLASTIC BOTTLE HAS SCREW-ON FILTER 'AQUA SOLO' TO IRRIGATE OVER TIME.

A 2-YEAR PLUM TREE SHOULD PRODUCE FRUIT 3 YEARS AFTER PLANTING AT A SOUTH OR WEST FACING WALL.

T.S.

Wall-trained trees need watering as the wall both soaks away moisture and also shelters plants from rainfall, depending on wind direction. Keep trees watered with a diluted comfrey liquid feed over the summer. My trees get an occasional basin of dishwater thrown around their roots at this time also – and they appreciate it.

PRUNING SUMMER-FRUITING RASPBERRY CANES AND DECLUTTERING THE RASPBERRY PATCH

Raspberries are bred to be summer fruiting or autumn fruiting. I love them so much I could not wait for autumn so I planted the summer-fruiting Glen Moy variety. I pick a dry day to prune my Glen Moy raspberries because I like to lie at the base of the canes to see what I need to do.

The older brown canes which fruited over the early summer are now finished and need to be cut out at the base to make room for the new green canes, upon which fruit will hopefully grow next year. Looking from a standing position, I can see lots of leaves but the canes are hidden. Looking up from below, while lying on the ground, I can clearly see the green canes to keep and the brown canes which need to be cut out.

Once the brown canes are gone, I tidy up the green canes. Some new growth is wayward and any stray green canes should be cut out too. As raspberry roots spread, I also prune out the wayward shoots which pop up outside the confines of the raspberry patch, known as 'suckers'. Too many of these stray suckers dilute the plant's energy and would reduce the potential for fruit growth the following year. My aim is to have about eight canes at each plant location and, using string wound around the canes, to create what looks a little like a boxing ring. This keeps the canes tidy and prevents them from blocking the narrow pathway.

OTHER PRUNING CAN WAIT FOR WINTER

Blackcurrant bushes, apple trees and pear trees may be lightly pruned now to prevent paths being overgrown, but the time to prune these plants is in winter. For a start, winter pruning with no leaves about makes life easier as I can see clearly what has to be done.

OTHER JOBS FOR THE WEEK THAT IS IN IT:

- Water regularly to prevent plants from going to seed.
- Keep picking any vegetables, especially beans, peas, courgettes, spinach, chard and other cut-and-come-again vegetables. Regular picking encourages the plant to continue growing. The plant is trying to reproduce and harvesting means that the plant tries again and produces more harvest as a result.

The Bigger Picture:
Preparing a garden for a summer break

Being keen to take a holiday with a chance of fine dry weather, I have found that this time of year is good for taking a week away from the garden.

PREPARING THE GARDEN TO BE LEFT WITHOUT A GARDENER FOR A WEEK

The priority for a gardener-less garden in the summer is watering. Those upturned mineral bottle 'funnels' are handy at a time like this. Some years ago I bought cone-shaped porous bottle-top devices designed to release the water bottle contents into the soil over a week, or longer, depending on the model. This is a patented watering device called an Aquasolo. All I do is screw the porous cone device to the bottle, stick the cone into the soil and fill it with water. Remember not to use a water bottle which is sealed; air must be able to get into the bottle if you want the water to be released over the holiday time.

Other priorities include:

🌿 Cut the grass. Grass can grow so fast at this time of year that I fear a homecoming where a machete may be needed to restore my garden to a manageable state.

🌿 It is good to leave the ground weeded and mulched with the grass clippings, for example. This cuts down on water evaporation from the vegetable patches. It also avoids weeds going to seed.

🌿 If you are lucky, like me, to have friendly neighbours, then a happy arrangement can be discussed. For example, your neighbour gets any ripe tomatoes in return for topping up the slow release watering bottles.

HOLIDAY IDEAS – THE WORLD OF WALLED GARDENS CONTINUES TO INSPIRE

A chance a visit to somebody else's garden while on holidays is both enjoyable and educational. As mentioned in the First Week in April, the walled-garden head gardeners of old developed their craft to have year-round supplies of the freshest food available. I tend to search these gardens out, regardless of their state of repair. The ghosts of gardeners past can evoke knowledge of thinking and techniques which may seem out-of-date now. However, present-day food security issues mean that all manner of food-growing skills must be considered to meet our future needs. Here are just some of the gardens I have visited in recent times and which continue to inspire me:

Kylemore Abbey, Connemara, Co. Gaillimhe:
www.kylemoreabbeytourism.ie

Strokestown House, Co. Roscommon:
www.strokestownpark.ie/gardens

Lissadell House, Co. Sligo: www.lissadellhouse.com

The Botanic Gardens, Glasnevin, Dublin: www.botanicgardens.ie

Ardgillan Castle, Co. Dublin: www.ardgillancastle.ie

Airfield House, Dundrum, Dublin: www.airfield.ie

The Organic Centre, Co. Leitrim: www.theorganiccentre.ie

Sonairte Ecology Centre, Co. Meath: www.sonairte.ie

Wexford Organic Centre, Cushinstown, Foulksmills, Co. Wexford: www.wexfordorganiccenter.com

Irish Seed Savers Association, Co. Clare: www.irishseedsavers.ie

The Nano Nagle Centre, Co. Cork: www.nanonaglebirthplace.ie

An Gairdín, Portumna, Co. Galway: www.angairdin.ie

Kinvara Sustainable Living, Knockakillen, Doorus, Kinvara, Co. Galway: www.kinvarasustainableliving.com

Kerry Earth Education Project (KEEP), Gortbrack Organic Farm, Ballyseedy, Tralee, Co. Kerry: www.gortbrackorganicfarm.com

🍂 FOURTH WEEK IN AUGUST 🍂

Apple harvesting, storage and juicing

'What wond'rous life is this I lead!
Ripe apples drop about my head.'

(Andrew Marvell, MP, 'The Garden',1681)

EVEN with just one apple tree in the garden, I have more than enough apples to eat, bake and cook with, as well as juice to drink. I freeze the surplus juice. By thawing the frozen juice one container at a time, the flavour of the garden fruit is available throughout the year. Nowadays, even a balcony garden can grow a few apples, with the modern upright miniature varieties of tree I see at the garden centres.

The tree variety in my garden – James Grieve – is well regarded in orchards as it is a reliable pollinator of the more commercial varieties like the Bramley, an old cooker variety going back to 1813. The value of this cooker in Ireland reached sales of €5.2 million recently, a year-on-year increase of 9 per cent.

Most apples sold in Ireland are dessert apples, for example, Royal Gala, Golden Delicious and even Granny Smith. These apples are generally imported at the cost of about €57 million per annum. But the Irish climate is perfect for apple growing.

I am convinced, also, that eating older varieties of apples has nutritional benefits. In his book *In Defence of Food*, Michael Pollan quotes research saying that apple varieties in the 1940s had three times the iron content of modern varieties. Adrian Myers, in *Organic Futures – the Case for Organic Farming*, quotes research which found that, in 1916, the average person needed to eat two apples to meet their daily iron requirement, whereas today that person would need to eat twenty-three apples to benefit from the same amount of iron.

IF YOU HAVE ONLY SPACE FOR ONE APPLE TREE, CHECK YOU LIKE THE VARIETY YOU CHOOSE

I am lucky in that I planted a variety of apple tree which I subsequently discovered that I liked, when it had grown and produced fruit. It would have made sense for me to visit the Irish Seed Savers Association in Scariff, Co. Clare (www.irishseed savers.ie), or Sonairte, the ecology centre at Laytown, Co. Meath (www.sonairte.ie), or the Organic Centre, Rossinver, Co. Leitrim (www.theorganiccentre.ie), all of which have 'apple days' – when one can sample the flavours of the varieties in their respective orchards. My solitary apple tree is now well established and thankfully healthy and productive. Luckily, the pollinating insects exchange pollen from my trees with other apple trees in other gardens around the town. As mentioned, my tree is of the James Grieve variety.

WHO WAS JAMES GRIEVE AND HOW DID HE GET AN APPLE NAMED AFTER HIM?

James Grieve was a Victorian nurseryman, a grower of horti-cultural stock, in Scotland. He succeeded in crossing two apple varieties, Pott's Seedling and Cox's Orange Pippin, to create a new second-early variety, which ripens before the main crop apples in the autumn. Each apple grew to a large size and became sweeter as it ripened. It could therefore be used as a cooker early and as a dessert apple when fully ripe. It also turned out to be a good pollinator.

AUGUST

Grieve was less effusive about the short keeping life of his new apple. Nonetheless, he had a winner on his hands, and, like a new father, he proudly announced in Edinburgh in 1893 that his new creation was to be called 'James Grieve'. He received the Award of Merit from the Royal Horticultural Society in 1897. James Grieve (the apple, that is!) went on to father many other good varieties like Katy or Katya (crossed with Worcester Pearmain) and Greensleeves (crossed with Golden Delicious).

STEWED APPLE WITH YOGHURT, SULTANAS & NUTS

500g 'BRAMLEY', OR APPLES WHICH WILL
   NOT KEEP, LIKE 'JAMES GRIEVE'.
100ml WATER
25g SUGAR (NO SUGAR IF APPLE IS SWEET)
50g TOASTED HAZELNUTS AND ALMONDS
50g DRIED FRUIT eg. SULTANAS.
2 OR 3 tbsp HONEY.
   METHOD
PEEL, CORE AND SLICE THE APPLES.
PLACE IN A SAUCEPAN, ADD 100ml WATER.
COVER WITH A LID. COOK OVER A
LOW HEAT UNTIL SOFT. ADD SUGAR
IF YOU WISH. COOL THE APPLE.
   WHEN READY, FOLD IN YOGHURT.
PUT IN SERVING DISH (ES). SPRINKLE
WITH THE FRUIT, NUTS AND HONEY.

P.S. STEW APPLE IN BULK AS IT
FREEZES WELL FOR FUTURE USE. T.S.

NAUL & DISTRICT GARDENING CLUB
NAME: TREVOR SARGENT
ADDRESS: BALBRIGGAN
SECOND PRIZE
CLASS NO: 97

AUTUMN HORTICULTURAL
SHOWS ARE GREAT
MEETING PLACES FOR
GROWERS AND BAKERS.

WHAT CHOICE HAVE I GOT WHEN CHOOSING TO PLANT AN APPLE TREE?

The pioneering work of breeders like James Grieve has left us with a massive range of apple varieties, about 3,000 in all. Some of these were completely naturally bred, such as the Golden Delicious variety, which was initially a chance seedling found in West Virginia, USA, in 1899. The famous Bramley cooker began as a seedling, grown from a pip by a young girl, Mary Ann Brailsford, in her garden in Southwell, England in 1809. So the choice is yours. Planting a pip means you will be waiting a while for it to grow and fruit, but you may end up with a lucrative new variety which can be named after you. On the other hand, you may be impatient, as I was, and you can buy a young tree in a pot to plant, either to be trained against a wall or to grow in the open garden as mine does.

WHEN SHOULD I PICK THE APPLES?

To avoid bruising the apples when they fall on the ground, give the ripe apple a gentle lift and twist while on the tree. If the apple comes away, you know it is ripe and almost ready to fall. Otherwise, you can leave it a while or pull it off if you do not mind the possibility of an unripe sour taste. As I have a bed of black peppermint, raspberries and a lawn under my apple tree, the apples are cushioned and hardly bruise if they drop naturally. The apples fall over a period from the middle of August to the end of September. This suits me well. Every couple of days, I collect up the fallen apples, wash them and juice them. Some juice is bottled and chilled for drinking, or poured into containers and frozen to be stored in the freezer until needed.

STORING YOUR OWN APPLES

You may have an apple variety or varieties which store better than James Grieve. As a rule, early-maturing apples and pears do not store well, so eat them, use them, sell them or give them away as soon as you can. Later varieties can be stored if picked gently and laid carefully in a basket. Spread them out gently in an airy place to dry overnight. Then wrap each fruit in paper to isolate any mould or bacteria. Remove any fruit with a blemish, cut, bruise or missing stalk as you wrap. Then store the fruit in a dark well-ventilated place at a temperature of 2–4°C (35–40°F). By the way, pears like it very slightly warmer. Well-stored apples can keep until springtime, but only if the store is checked each week to remove any apples which are becoming overripe.

JUICING YOUR OWN APPLES

The clear apple juice which is sold commercially has to be treated to extend its shelf life. Before packaging, it is generally treated with vitamin C (ascorbic acid) as an antioxidant and is heat sterilized to destroy natural oxidising enzymes, as well as spoilage organisms.

Naturally, there is some loss of nutrient value and taste with this treatment.

The freshly juiced apples pack a punch in the taste department. I never fail to be amazed at the astounded look on people's faces when they taste actual freshly squeezed apple juice for the first time. They say things like, 'It is really *apple-y*!'

Now for the bad news. A good juice extractor can cost a few hundred euro. I had a cheaper electric centrifugal juicer which flung the fruit at the fast-moving sieve-like bowl as it spun. It gave me very little juice and lots of pulp. The better option by far is the masticating juicer, which slowly pushes the pulp through a metal gauze, forcing out the juice and automatically expelling the pulp separately.

Bottled in clean screw-top bottles, this juice keeps for three or four days in a fridge. Most of my juice, however, goes into the freezer labelled with the date. Once it is thawed and decanted into a jug, I keep it in the fridge and drink it over a day or two. It is almost as good as the freshly squeezed juice but looks a little darker due to oxidation.

OTHER JOBS FOR THE WEEK THAT IS IN IT:

After rainfall and/or a good watering, lay down a mulch of grass clippings on top of cardboard or paper. Rotted-down compost is also good if you have it. This helps to keep moisture in the soil.

The Cabbage White butterfly may be less frequent now but the Cabbage Root Fly may still be a threat. Make up some 12 cm (4.7 inch) square mats from carpet, felt or card. Cut a slit from the side to the centre, and then slot them around the stem of each brassica plant at ground level like a collar. This is a good defence against the Cabbage Root Fly which likes to burrow down and eat the roots of the cabbage if there is no obstacle.

The Bigger Picture:
Making a living from horticulture

With the lack of paid employment in many communities, it is understandable that many people are looking at ways of turning a hobby into a career. Making a living from large-scale horticulture is harder than ever, even for the highly trained mechanised farmer with a tradition of farming in his family going back generations. However, I have seen opportunities for hard-working people who can correctly judge the emerging trends in horticulture and who have an efficient yet flexible business model.

The globalised food trade has effectively put farmers from Ireland, Scotland, Spain, Kenya, Mexico, China, etc. in direct competition with each other. Mexican scallions, Chinese garlic, Kenyan beans, Spanish tomatoes and Scottish carrots all arrive into Ireland to compete with Irish produce. Often imported produce comes from countries where production costs are lower than in Ireland.

Opportunities or gaps in the market for a grower to make a living:

Growing organically for import substitution: over 90 per cent of the organic fruit and vegetables consumed in Ireland has to be imported as there is simply not enough Irish-grown organic horticulture to satisfy demand. The Irish organic market has been growing year on year at 11 per cent and stands at around €120 million in value, compared to €66 million in 2006 and €38 million in 2003. Bord Bia commissioned a survey of how modern Irish consumers view organic food in 2008. When customers were asked in what food categories they purchased organic produce, 91 per cent prioritised organic vegetables. Next most popular were fruit and dairy produce, at 70 per cent each. Then came meat at 66 per cent, cereals and baked goods at 30 per cent, drinks at 18 per cent, confectionery at 10 per cent and other organic products (honey, jam, soup, etc.) at 35 per cent.

213

This survey suggests that a great proportion of that €120 million is being spent on imported organic vegetables as well as other organic imports. Irish organic growers are needed to satisfy a clear demand for organic vegetables.

🍃 **Growing for farmers' markets:** on a related point, I have some experience of establishing farmers' markets. It is generally straightforward enough to interest bakers, jam makers and people selling refreshments, but getting a grower, organic or not, is very difficult. Horticulture has become large scale and specialised. This is first and foremost to satisfy the central distribution needs of supermarkets. As a result, a farmer growing a diversity of vegetables and fruit to grace a stall at a market is a rare person indeed. Yet, with about 130 farmers' markets established in Ireland and more at planning stage, the potential exists for growers to tailor their production to suit the seasonal and diverse requirements of running an attractive stall at a number of markets.

🍃 **Growing for restaurants:** the idea of growing to order has been taken to a new level of sophistication by Gold River Farm just south of Aughrim, Co. Wicklow. Here, the farm canvasses the needs of restaurants and other markets as to their customers' requirements for particular lines of organic herbs, baby carrots, salad leaves and even organic pork. The orders are agreed and the farm produces to order. This is a dynamic form of agriculture which engages with the market and, indeed, with the individual buyer. It is a market in which there is little competition, so far.

🍃 **Growing for the community directly:** farmers who are not shy have found a new lease of life by meeting non-farming families in their community and agreeing to an arrangement to grow for thirty or forty families. In return, these families pay at the start of the farm year for seed and other requirements, including the wages of the farmer and his or her family. There is reassurance on both sides of the deal. The families get a regular and diverse pre-paid supply of fresh produce in season. The farmer gets the peace of mind of a wage which is not dependent on the vagaries of the global market. This phenomenon has become known as Community Supported Agriculture (CSA). My neighbouring community in Skerries, Co. Dublin has set up a very good CSA through their Community Harvest Group. See more at www.sustainable skerries.wordpress.com. John Peterson from Illinois, USA is another amazing farmer who has embraced biodynamic farming and is a very innovative CSA farmer, in spite of his conventional farming background. His CSA website is www.angelicorganics.com.

🌿 **Joining up kitchen gardens to produce enough to sell:** another gap in the local food market has been identified by kitchen gardeners in Saskatoon, Canada, and in Philadelphia, USA. Enthusiastic growers have hit on the potential of growing vegetables in a number of gardens and selling the produce locally. This new business model is being called SPIN Horticulture, which stands for Small Plot InteNsive. For example, a half acre of combined garden makes $26,100 for an enterprising grower as a wage for the year. Naturally, the grocery bill for the grower is low as he does not need to buy fruit and vegetables, which is an added bonus. So far there are about 200 SPIN farmers in the USA and Canada and the idea is taking hold in South Africa, Australia and the UK now as well.

WHERE CAN I GO TO GET A QUALIFICATION IN HORTICULTURE?

Courses in horticulture are available at:

🌿 The Institute of Technology, Blanchardstown, Co. Dublin runs a Bachelor of Science in Horticulture course (see www.itb.ie).

🌿 Teagasc run FETAC Level 5 and 6 Certificate in Horticulture courses at Kildalton College, Piltown, Co. Kilkenny and at the Botanic Gardens, Glasnevin, Dublin 9 (see www.teagasc.ie).

🌿 Dublin City University runs a Bachelor of Science degree in Horticulture also (see www.dcu.ie).

🌿 An tIonad Glas, The Organic College, Drumcollogher, Co. Limerick runs a FETAC Level 5 Certificate in Organic Growing and Sustainable Living Skills
(see www.organiccollege.com).

Less time-consuming courses are run over a weekend or on a part-time basis at other centres. These can help to extend your skill base and can also lead to employment in due course. Such courses are available at various centres, including:

🌿 The Organic Centre, Rossinver, Co Leitrim
(see www.theorganiccentre.ie)

🌿 Sonairte, the National Ecology Centre, Laytown, Co. Meath
(see www.sonairte.ie)

🌿 Irish Seed Savers, Capparoe, Scariff, Co. Clare
(see www.seedsavers.org)

🌿 Kerry Earth Education Project, Gortbrack Organic Farm, Ballyseedy, Tralee, Co. Kerry
(see www.gortbrackorganicfarm.com)

🌿 The County Wexford Organic Centre, Cushinstown, Foulksmills, New Ross, Co. Wexford (email: rmee@eircom.net).

🌿 Nano Nagle Centre, Ballygriffin, Mallow, Co. Cork
(see www.nanonaglebirthplace.ie)

🌿 Airfield House, Dundrum, Co. Dublin (see www.airfield.ie)

🌿 Carraig Dúlra Organic Education Centre, Gleanealy, Co. Wicklow (see www.dulra.org)

If you need to take some time and ponder your options as well as gain relevant farming experience, then there is always a 'WWOOF-ing' experience to consider. WWOOF stands for World Wide Opportunities on Organic Farms and gives volunteers a chance to see if they like the reality of farming organically. WWOOF-ers are also helping a farmer in a very tangible way in return for free board and lodgings. A WWOOF experience also provides informal opportunities to discuss courses in and experiences of farming, and perhaps to get a good reference for your CV with a view to future employment. It is worth noting that the current EU Agriculture Commissioner Dacian Ciolos spent over thirteen months volunteering on organic farms in Brittany in northern France. He went on to become the Romanian Minister for Agriculture in 2007 before his promotion to the European Commission. Details are available at www.wwoof.ie or www.wwoof.org.

Thoughts from other kitchen gardeners

DERMOT CAREY

Renowned as a professional cultivator of old walled kitchen gardens, Dermot trained as both a grower and a mechanic. Now based mainly in Connaught and Ulster, Dermot is in demand to tend kitchen gardens and give courses in organic growing in the Organic Centre, Co. Leitrim, and elsewhere. As head gardener, he transformed the organic walled garden at Lissadell House, Co. Sligo, which hopefully will be open to the public again some day. Dermot can be contacted at +353 87 228 6145.

Describe the location in which you grow your own food:

I currently have a couple of gardens on the go. One is 'Harry's Walled Garden' at Burt House, the famous restaurant on the Inishowen Peninsula in Co. Donegal. I spend on average two days a week there, depending on the weather. I also tend a private garden in Lower Rosses, Co. Sligo, which feeds four families.

Which food do you look forward to harvesting most and why?

I always look forward to harvesting potatoes as they come with an element of surprise. One is never quite sure what lies in wait beneath the soil. In a way, it is like opening a gift at Christmas.

Which garden tool do you value most and why?

As a mechanic and a grower, I get great use from a two-wheeled tractor, which I walk behind. This machine can quite quickly turn pasture into seed drills. It can take attachments such as a rotavator, plough, potato lifter and drill plough. Once an area over a quarter of an acre is being cultivated, some form of tractor takes over from the spade as the preferred tool of cultivation.

What motivates you to undertake the work involved in growing food?

Food growing is a legacy of my upbringing, as my father and mother farmed 100 acres as market gardeners near Clondalkin, Co. Dublin, which is now all covered in housing. I trained as a mechanic and this now stands to me in working with machinery. All my life, my real passion has been to grow the best food possible.

What advice would you give to a person considering growing their own food?

I would advise serving your time as an apprentice to the best grower or gardener you can find. To make a living from growing on a small acreage (2–5 acres), you need to have ways of adding value to your produce, such as making preserves or drinks, running a restaurant, or some other innovative business idea.

Have you an aspiration for the future in relation to food?

My aspiration is that organic and good quality food in general will be available to everybody at affordable prices. The more householders and food and hospitality businesses grow their own food – and the more shops network with local farmers – the more affordable good food will be. More direct selling by producers will also ensure a fair price is received by the farmer.

SÍLE NIC CHONAONAIGH

Síle Nic Chonaonaigh – láithreoir *Garraí Glas*, clár déanta ag Abú Media do TG4. Tá Síle tar éis spreagadh mór a thabhairt do phobal na hÉireann glasraí agus torthaí a chur ag fás go horgánach, lena cláracha seachtainiúla. Is léir, agus í ag bualadh isteach ar gharraíodóirí eile, go raibh Síle ag foghlaim faoi phlandaithe le linn na sraithe, mar a bhí mise agus tusa, is dócha. Anois, tá Síle ag baint triall as na cleasanna talmhaíochta sin, ina garraí féin.

Déan cur síos ar an láthair ina mbíonn tú ag saothrú do chuid bia féin:

Tá mo gharraí suite ar bharr chnoic i gCois Fharraige. Tá radharc álainn agam amach at an Atlantach go hÁrainn, ach faraor ciallaíonn sé sin go bhfuil an suíomh uafásach gaofar, rud nach dtaithníonn le garraíodóirí riamh.

Cad é an sort bia is fearr leat a bhaint agus cén fáth?

Píseanna agus fataí. Tá draíocht faoi leith ag baint le fataí a bhaint. Ní churann tú sa talamh ach ceann amháin agus fáigheann tú suas le deich gcinn ar ais! Níor chur mé fataí riamh go dtí anuraidh agus ní raibh mé ag súil leis an mblas aoibheann a thagann ó do chuid féin. Píseanna mar go bhfuil siad chomh milis go n-itheann tú ansin sa ngarrai iad – luach do shaothair.

Cad é an uirlis gharraíodóireachta is tábhachtaí duit agus cén fáth?

An ghrafóg, nó an *oscillating hoe*. Tá sé iontach. Ciallaíonn sé go bhfuil sé i bhfad níos éasca salachar a bhaint. Ní gá duit a bheith ag cromadh síos an t-am ar fad, rud atá tábhachtach má tá spás mór le glanadh agat.

Cad é an spreagadh a bhíonn agat chun tabhairt faoi shaothrú bia?

Níor thosaigh mé ag garraíodóireacht go dtí go raibh mé ag obair ar an gclár *Garraí Glas*. I ndáiríre níor thuig mé cé chomh mór is atá an 'duais' ag deireadh an lae, nuair is féidir siúl amach sa ngarraí agus do bheile a phiocadh. Fiú i lár an gheimhridh tá mé ag ithe glasraí geimhridh ar nós biatas bán, cabáiste agus sailéid geimhridh ar lá Nollag fiú.

Cén chomhairle a thabharfá do dhuine a bheadh ag smaoineamh ar a gcuid bia a shaothrú?

Tosaigh le ceithre no cúig rud. Ní obair mhór é glasraí a chur a fhás – níl i gceist ach deich nóiméad sa lá do gharraí beag.

Cur síolta orgánacha. I mo thuairmse beidh an glasra níos folláine.

Cur glasraí a thaithníonn leat – ní fiú a bheith fágtha le glasra bith nach bhfuil suim agatsa ithe.

Tabhair aire don ithir agus tabharfaidh na glasraí aire dóibh féin – simplí ach réasunta fíor. Má bhíonn an ithir leasaithe beidh an garraí go maith.

Iarr comhairle ar do chuid comharsan. Má tá garraí acu beidh siad sásta cabhú leat.

Cad é an cuspóir mór atá agat don todhchaí maidir le bia?

Ba bhreá liom níos mó daoine a fheiceáil ag fás a gcuid bia féin. Chomh maith le sin sílim go mba cheart go mbeadh garraíodóireacht á mhúineadh i ngach scoil sa tír. Is scil den scoth é a bheith in ann bia a fhas duit féin agus do chlann. Ba chóir go mbeadh chuile theaghlach ar domhan in ann agus i dteideal a gcuid bia féin a fhás, ach ár ndóigh tá fadhbanna ollmhóra ar nós athrú aeráide ag cur isteach go mór ar chúrsaí talmhaíochta.

Meán Fómhair ❧ *September*

The Month of Mid-Harvest

*L*á *Lúnasa* (1 August) is also called *an chéad lá d'fhómhar* (the first day of harvest). The English translation of 'Meán Fómhair' is 'middle of harvest', a further reminder of the central importance, in times past, of gathering the ripe crops for storage, processing and preservation, to carry the community through the hungry winter, spring and early summer periods to come. Strength was not everything when it came to harvest work, as this saying reminds us: 'Ní hiad na fir mhóra a bhaineann an fómhar go huile' (It is not big men only who gather the harvest). Not every farmer or kitchen gardener can be, or needs to be, a Lugh lámh fhada look-alike!

'Blackberry day' falls on 12 September, and *ag piocadh sméara dubha* (picking blackberries) is still a family harvest activity, where children pick the lower berries on the hedge while adults reach for the higher fruit. Typically, hungry children would eat as many berries (*sméara*) as they put in the bucket, with the result that, in Irish, one word for a dirty-faced person is *sméarachán*.

Traditionally, by Michaelmas (29 September), no more *sméara dubha* are picked for fear of the Devil's spit! This belief refers to the story of St Michael the Archangel, which the feast day of Michaelmas remembers. St Michael, we are told, expelled the Devil out of Heaven on this day. The Devil ended his fall from grace by landing on a blackberry bramble. None too happy, he cursed and spat on all the blackberries, making them inedible.

Other crops remain to be gathered in, however. A great help in extending the bright hours for harvesting is the harvest moon. This is the nearest full moon to the autumn equinox, 21–22 September,

BLACKBERRY JAM (WITH APPLE JUICE)

2 kg BLACKBERRIES : JUICE OF 1 LEMON
2 kg SUGAR : 500g APPLES TO MAKE JUICE
METHOD
PREPARE THE APPLE JUICE BY BOILING
TO A PULP THE APPLES IN ½ litre OF WATER.
   ADD 150 ml WATER AND LEMON
JUICE TO THE BLACKBERRIES. SIMMER
UNTIL TENDER. (BARELY RIPE BLACK-
BERRIES WORK BEST AS THEY HAVE
GOOD PECTIN LEVELS.) ADD SUGAR AND
JUICE FROM STRAINING THE APPLES.
   BOIL, STIRRING CONSTANTLY,
UNTIL IT SETS WHEN TESTED.
SKIM AND FILL CLEAN STERILISED
HOT JARS. SEAL AND LABEL JARS.

THIS RECIPE IS FROM 'WILD AND FREE-
COOKING FROM NATURE', BY KIT AND
CYRIL Ó CEIRÍN, THE O'BRIEN PRESS, 1978.

"Is cuimhne liom
laethanta m'óige,
ag baint sméara
dubha san Fhómhar"
YOUTHFUL MEMORIES
PICKING BLACKBERRIES.

and has romantic associations as well. 'Ag déanamh fómhair' literally means 'making the harvest', but for those in the know it also means 'courting'.

An overview of the work ahead in the garden this month:
Sow out: successional sowings – spinach, winter radish and lettuce.
Harvest: onions, tomatoes, marrows, potatoes, carrots, celeriac, spinach, runner beans and French beans.

Bottling beetroot and other storage methods

'It may sound grandiose, but in many ways the history of civilisation is the story of our progressive mastery of food preservation.'

(Nick Sandler and Johnny Acton, from *Preserved*, 2004)

GROWING food is only half the battle when it comes to food security or, on a personal level, self-sufficiency. It is all very well visiting the kitchen garden in August or September and witnessing a landscape of bountiful crops. Happy days! A visit to the same garden in January or March paints a less rosy picture of meagre rations, unless the summer surplus has been bottled, dried, frozen, or turned into juice or something stronger.

The Grow It Yourself (GIY) organisation (www.giyireland.com) has become a phenomenal nationwide movement and it is great to see it promote food preservation techniques as well as food growing. There is a need for more of us to rediscover the forgotten skills of food preservation. Meanwhile, we keep our fingers crossed that the freezer containing all those valuable summer fruit and vegetables does not break down. Apart from being a way to store food, food preservation adds new flavours to meals in any season. Chutneys, jams, sauerkraut, cider, dried herbs, cassis, etc. are all flavoursome dishes and drinks in their own right, as well as being ways to keep food from going off. Continental countries with seriously frozen winters tend to practise their food preservation traditions out of necessity as their soil becomes as hard as ice for months on end and digging outdoors is not possible. There are no guarantees that, in winter, Ireland will indefinitely have access to imported food from tropical countries or that freezers will have the capacity and uninterrupted electricity supplies to keeps our winter stocks of food

SEPTEMBER

on ice. As important as the GIY movement is, I see a growing need to help more of us to 'Store It Yourself' (SIY), or even Preserve It Yourself (PIY). Is there an opening for a 'PIY Ireland' movement, I ask myself!

START WITH A TRADITIONAL RECIPE FOR BOTTLING BEETROOT

Having been used to fairly bland pickled beetroot bought in shops during my childhood, I was a little underwhelmed by the prospect of pickling my own home-grown beetroot, until a great cook, Mrs Butterly in Rush, Co. Dublin, gave me the recipe some years ago – and when I tried it out, my eyes were opened. I've included the recipe in the Fourth Week in May. Try it yourself and let us know what you think! Leave a comment on www.trevorskitchengarden.ie.

These jars of beetroot are a great addition to many meals, not just salads. Preserved beetroot in a salad sandwich is a personal favourite of mine. These jars of beetroot also make a handy gift. I brought a couple of full jars along to a function in the Brooklodge Hotel and Spa, in Aughrim, Co. Wicklow. I gave them to the renowned organic grower and chef Evan Doyle in the depths of an icy winter, when driving, not to mention gardening, was treacherous. As such, Mrs Butterly's beetroot bottling recipe was on the menu at a Slow Food banquet in the Strawberry Tree, Ireland's only officially organic restaurant, at the famous Brooklodge Hotel and Spa.

OTHER ADVICE AVAILABLE ON PRESERVING HOME-GROWN PRODUCE

A casual search on the internet under the search terms 'preserving fruit and vegetables' revealed no less than eight-one pages of website links. Most of the websites are American, with talk of 'home canning' aplenty. This topic is big elsewhere, going by the number of Australian and British websites also. Some of the more

PRESERVING FRUIT WITHOUT A FREEZER

MAKE A BLACKCURRANT LIQUOR CALLED 'CRÈME DE CASSIS'.

THIS IS LIKE 'RIBENA' FOR GROWN-UPS! IT IS POPULAR MIXED WITH WHITE WINE.

THE REMAINING BLACKCURRANTS CAN BE USED AS AN INGREDIENT IN (ALCOHOLIC) DESSERTS!

LEAVE AT LEAST 4-5 MONTHS BEFORE BOTTLING

T.S.

① FILL ½ A Le Parfait PRESERVING JAR WITH WASHED BLACKCURRANTS.
② FILL NEXT ¼ WITH SUGAR.
③ TOP UP WITH GIN OR VODKA.
④ AGITATE EVERY FEW DAYS.

useful sites I hit on were www.pickyourown.org, www.hobby farm.com, www.growveg.com and www.makeitandmendit.com. A good start for food preservation information in Ireland would be www.theorganiccentre.ie.

OTHER JOBS FOR THE WEEK THAT IS IN IT:

🍃 Watch out for the second brood of Cabbage White butterfly. Rub off any eggs laid on the underside of brassica leaves or remove the caterpillars if you are too late. Vigilance now will help plants to survive the lower light and temperature drop in the coming months.

🍃 Sow spring cabbage plants in ground which has been cleared after the end of the broad bean harvest.

🍃 Around this time of year is your last chance to sow rocket, radish and other winter salads to ensure fresh salads as late as possible before the winter frosts, or longer if you can grow under glass or in a polytunnel.

The start of the academic year brings to mind food literacy as well as academic literacy. Of concern to many parents is what to put in the lunch box as well as how to pay for the school books, transportation, uniforms, etc. Knowing many teachers in Ireland, England and a few in France, I realise that the absence of school canteens in many Irish schools is an oversight in our education system. Those schools lucky enough to have a school canteen have the potential to instil in students, not just a taste for healthy freshly cooked meals, but also the experience of sitting down with peers at a table to partake in meals, which is a healthier habit than 'grazing' or snacking. How we eat is important, as is what we eat, for long-term health.

ARE SCHOOL MEALS POSSIBLE WHERE SCHOOLS HAVE NO CANTEEN?

Other countries have managed to provide school meals without a school canteen and a pilot scheme could test the feasibility of such a plan in Ireland. Fresh ingredients can be prepared in one dedicated location for a cluster of schools using a sous vide (under vacuum) cooking method. This French technique has been adopted by a Co. Waterford food company called Dunhill Cuisine (www.dunhillcuisine.com), which has the facility now to provide 100,000 school meals per week. The company says that this method of cooking maintains the integrity of the ingredients. Each school would essentially need a sufficiently large fridge and a bain-marie stainless steel hot food serving trolley, as well as the associated delph, cutlery, dining and wash-up facilities. In Rome, for example, 150,000 school meals are served each day. The average cost per meal is €5.28. The criteria for ingredients are that they are locally grown and, where available, organic. The switch to organic ingredients made the average meal cost 16c more than the non-organic alternative. There are many other examples from which to learn: in the UK – the London Borough of Camden, Shropshire Council's school meals service and Jamie Oliver's school dinner campaign; in the USA – Alice Waters' school lunch initiative; in Italy – the school meals services in Udine.

MAKING PROGRESS

The nutritional advice is to eat a minimum of five portions of fruit and vegetables a day for children and adults alike. The Food Dudes Programme is a Bord Bia programme to provide fresh fruit and vegetables to children in a few hundred schools. In 2006 the Food Dudes Programme won a Counteracting Obesity Award from the World Health Organisation. The Agri Aware Incredible Edibles Programme, with the help of private sponsorship, complements the Bord Bia initiative by showing primary school students how to grow at least five types of fruit and vegetables, in containers initially. Many schools have gone on to develop school kitchen gardens from these initiatives.

THE BEST SCHOOLS HAVE A HEALTHY EATING POLICY WHICH ENJOYS THE SUPPORT OF PARENTS

School healthy eating policies are not just about banning junk foods – usually sweets, bars and canned minerals. At lunch break in the most health conscious schools, both teachers and pupils often eat their lunch in the school room before going out to the school yard. Any food not eaten is returned to the lunch box and brought home. In this way, parents can know what is eaten and how to plan future school lunches. Variety can be the key to an enjoyable school lunch. As with the growing of a wide variety of food in the kitchen garden, it is important to ask children about the foods they like and involve them in making the school lunch.

> **Tip for sandwich making:** keep bread for sandwiches pre-sliced in the freezer. This means each slice is frozen solid when being buttered. In this way the bread will not tear, even when you spread hard butter from the fridge. Once the sandwich is made and cut with a bread knife, it thaws slowly in the lunch box. The cool bread helps to keep the salad leaves and other sandwich contents fresh.

🍂 SECOND WEEK IN SEPTEMBER 🍂

Selecting seeds for autumn sowing

'Where are the songs of Spring? Ay, where are they?
Think not of them, thou hast thy music too.'
(John Keats, 1795–1821, *from* 'To Autumn')

GARDEN centres tend to strongly promote spring as the time to sow most seeds. Autumn sowing tends to be overlooked as a result. However, autumn sowing makes much more sense for a school garden as the horticultural year then ties in with the academic year. Also, predation by slugs and snails is generally less of a problem with autumn-sown plants, I find.

A harvest before the end of the school year (in summer) is a key requirement for school gardeners and indeed for many third level institute kitchen gardens. I recall visiting the community garden run by students and staff at the National University of Ireland (NUI) in Galway City. In England, the University of Essex has turned an ex-tennis court into an allotment; Bath University students are growing vegetables in a number of under-used gardens attached to student accommodation premises; and Plymouth University students are working with other schools in their area to grow food.

Autumn sowing makes sense for a more even availability of crops all year round.

EXAMPLES OF AUTUMN SOWING:

🌿 Grow kohlrabi in a pot: this is like a small cabbage with a swollen turnip-like base. You eat its swollen root at golf-ball size and peeled, grated raw or in cooked dishes. Sow in early September as it needs heat to get going. You need a peat-free soil and compost mix; a container at least 20 cm (8 inches)

229

deep; a mineral bottle type of cloche (a bell-shaped cover to protect young plants); slug defences; a watering can; and labels. Sow the seeds 2 cm (1 inch) deep. When seeds germinate, thin the plants out to allow about 20 cm (8 inches) between them. Protect them from the cold at night with cloche or horticultural fleece. Varieties of kohlrabi to try include Azure Star or Blusta.

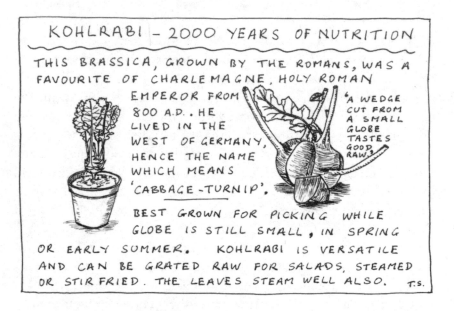

KOHLRABI – 2000 YEARS OF NUTRITION

THIS BRASSICA, GROWN BY THE ROMANS, WAS A FAVOURITE OF CHARLEMAGNE, HOLY ROMAN EMPEROR FROM 800 A.D.. HE LIVED IN THE WEST OF GERMANY, HENCE THE NAME WHICH MEANS 'CABBAGE-TURNIP'.

'A WEDGE CUT FROM A SMALL GLOBE TASTES GOOD RAW.'

BEST GROWN FOR PICKING WHILE GLOBE IS STILL SMALL, IN SPRING OR EARLY SUMMER. KOHLRABI IS VERSATILE AND CAN BE GRATED RAW FOR SALADS, STEAMED OR STIR FRIED. THE LEAVES STEAM WELL ALSO. T.S.

Grow coriander in a bright porch or an unheated greenhouse: this is a versatile culinary herb which makes a carrot soup very special and enhances many other dishes. Sow in a similar way to the kohlrabi above but keep the plants moist with a little more protection. Coriander grows slowly so is not likely to go to seed. A variety to try is Calypso, for its long period of growing.

A final sowing of radish and winter lettuce will add crunch to your salads as the days get shorter. There is a wide range of salad leaf crops which can be sown around now. Check the back of the seed packets for the optimum time to sow.

🍂 Sow annual flower seeds now, and again next spring, to compare the success of each. Cornflowers, nasturtiums, calendula and other hardy annual flower seeds can be sown directly into a prepared seedbed or in pots at this time with a view to them flowering next spring or in early summer. Keep some seed back, and reseal and store the packet so more can be sown under glass in early spring.

🍂 Other autumn-sown vegetables include carrots – Autumn King; spinach – Crocodile; spring onion – White Lisbon (Winter Hardy); cabbage – Frostie and Spring Hero; and lettuce – Winter Gem.

BUY ONION SETS, GARLIC, BROAD BEANS AND PEAS, INCLUDING SWEET PEA, TO SOW LATER

There is just enough time to order by post the late autumn-sown seeds, if they are not available at a garden centre or shop. Garlic is planted at the end of September or in early October, likewise onion sets such as the varieties Radar or Electric. To sow onions from seed, I would wait until next January and sow them under glass, if possible. Some beans (e.g. Super Aquadulce) and peas (e.g. Excellenz) are hardy enough to start in September or October. They stop growing during the coldest weeks and then start again when the warmth returns in the early spring.

OTHER JOBS FOR THE WEEK THAT IS IN IT:

🍂 Harvest onions: some growers bend over the stem on each mature onion gently a week or so before harvesting, in the hope that this will further swell the bulb. Others, like me, have yet to notice this making any difference, and simply wait for a fine day to lift their mature onions. Let the lifted onions dry for a couple of hours on a concrete path. Then you can gently rub off the dry soil and place the onions on a griddle on a shelf in the greenhouse until the stalk leaves shrivel. Then plait five or six at a time so each string of onions can hang in the cool, dark, dry shed without any bulb touching the ground or anything else.

- 🍂 Lift and store carrots: my garden quantity of carrots can normally be stored in dry sand in a cool dry shed (or a garage if you have one).

- 🍂 Gather fallen leaves: these will become useful leaf mould in a year or two if collected after rain and packed into old black plastic bags (see the Fourth Week in June).

- 🍂 Harvest apples and pears: enjoy the harvest in desserts, salads, sauces, chutneys and juices. I have yet to embark on cider making, but I look forward to having a go!

The Bigger Picture:
Abandoning my garden for GIY Ireland

No greater love has a kitchen gardener than to abandon his or her garden for a whole weekend and travel to Waterford, or wherever, and join in the workshops, lectures and general camaraderie of the annual GIY gathering. The fact of the matter is, this is a weekend I look forward to for months in advance.

The annual GIY gathering is generally a mid-September affair and the first one in 2009 was in Waterford (the GIY movement has its origins in Waterford). Since then, the range of activities has become (and I do not use this word lightly) awesome. The full gambit of sessions, events and workshops range from 'Cook it Yourself' to 'Pop-up Allotments'.

Making the weekend enjoyable is clearly a key objective of the organisers, hence events like 'Picnic in the Park' and the 'GIY

Street Feast'. The overall objectives of GIY Ireland are nothing if not ambitious. How else does one explain sessions entitled 'Can GIY Save the World?' Irish and international gardeners, food writers and broadcasters are well represented. I have been delighted to meet organic broadcasting gurus like Bob Flowerdew, who gives me food for thought every time I hear him answer questions on *Gardeners' Question Time*, BBC Radio 4, on a Sunday at 2.00 p.m.

Ultimately, the best way to appreciate the full extent of a GIY gathering is to be there. Check out the website for plans, reports and inspiration (www.giyireland.com).

THIRD WEEK IN SEPTEMBER

Enjoy taking part in a local horticultural show

'Entries are to be staged between 8.00 p.m. and 10.00 p.m.
on Friday night and between 9.00 a.m. and 11.30 a.m. on the
day of the show, Saturday.'
(Rule 1 in the Naul and District Horticultural Show programme)

JULY, August and September in North County Dublin (Fingal) are when most of the horticultural shows near me take place. Contact the Royal Horticultural Society of Ireland (details below) for information about horticultural shows in other places. If I am not otherwise busy, there is nothing I enjoy more than selecting a few pea and bean pods, courgettes or a few sprigs of parsley – whatever is in best condition at that time – and entering whichever nearby horticultural show happens to be on.

In one year or another I have had the chance to enter almost every show in Fingal. The various local horticultural associations stagger their shows at different weekends, so you tend to see some of the same faces turning up in each place.

- Dublin 5, Rush and District, and Malahide generally exhibit in July.

- Fingal (Swords), Cameron and St Brigid's (Finglas) generally exhibit in August.

- Balbriggan, Lusk, Clontarf and Naul generally exhibit in September.

I am particularly fascinated by the Naul and District Horticultural Show in late September. Here one hears accents from all parts of Ireland, north as well as south of the border. The competition can be quite (but quietly!) intense between growers of flowers as well as fruit and vegetable growers – not to mention knitters, jam, bread, cake and biscuit makers, and flower arrangers.

Recently, I was chuffed to come away with a little prize for parsley grown in Trevor's Kitchen Garden! It is a boost to your self-confidence as an amateur grower if you get a prize for your courgettes, for instance, or your lovingly grown Rondo peas.

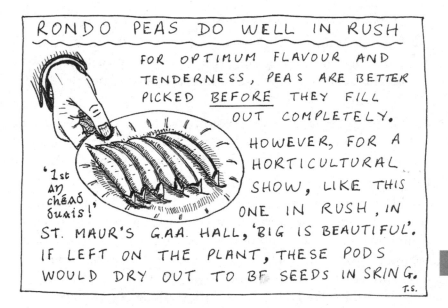

RONDO PEAS DO WELL IN RUSH

FOR OPTIMUM FLAVOUR AND TENDERNESS, PEAS ARE BETTER PICKED BEFORE THEY FILL OUT COMPLETELY.

HOWEVER, FOR A HORTICULTURAL SHOW, LIKE THIS ONE IN RUSH, IN ST. MAUR'S G.A.A. HALL, 'BIG IS BEAUTIFUL'. IF LEFT ON THE PLANT, THESE PODS WOULD DRY OUT TO BE SEEDS IN SRING.

'1st An chéad Duais!'

T.S.

However, the real enjoyment of the horticultural shows lies in meeting other exhibitors and gleaning some tricks of the trade. Here are some of the 'secrets' of exhibiting I picked up over the years:

- Quality, cleanliness and uniformity are important for any exhibit.
- Apples should never be polished, but vegetable roots should be carefully washed.
- Currants and grapes should be shown in bunches, as grown.

235

- All fruit, except peaches and nectarines, must have stalks attached; likewise for tomatoes.
- Flowers are best cut the evening before the show, then stored in a cool place in deep water overnight.
- Naming an exhibit enhances its show value and counts if the competition is close. If the variety is not known, state 'variety unknown'.
- Jam jars and lids must not have any trade names showing.
- Lift onions approximately one week before the show, trim off roots and remove split skins. Wash, dry and sprinkle them with unscented talcum powder. To stage, remove all powder and tie tops tightly with raffia.
- On the other hand, I was recommended not to trim leek roots, but to wash them thoroughly – and to water them well a few hours *before* uprooting them with a garden fork.

I would love to see the day when every town and village in Ireland would have a local annual horticultural show. Thankfully, many already do. The Lusk Horticultural Society, for example, is a sub-committee of Lusk Community Council Ltd. Perhaps other community councils could develop a local horticultural society. For more information, contact the Royal Horticultural Society of Ireland, Cabinteely House, The Park, Cabinteely, Dublin 18; tel: +353 1 2353912; email: info@rhsi.ie.

OTHER JOBS FOR THE WEEK THAT IS IN IT:

- Save seed, starting with peas: mature pea and bean pods being grown for seed can be pulled up while leaving their roots in the ground, as the soil can use the nitrogen the root nodules have fixed from the air. The haulms (as bean and pea stalks are called) are tied in bunches and hung up in the shed. When the pods turn brown and the leaves wither, remove the dry seeds and store them in a paper bag placed in a sealed and labelled glass jar and put this in the fridge. These are your (cost-free) seeds to be sown next spring. The resulting pea plants are more likely to suit the climate and conditions of the garden better than those grown from bought seed.

🍃 Plant winter onion sets such Radar or the red-skinned Electric.

🍃 This is a good time to set about making or buying a compost bin, where you can put all those stalks and left-over growth from the harvesting of crops.

The Bigger Picture:
Remember Johnny Appleseed's birthday

One of my historic heroes was a man who spent his whole adult life planting apple seeds wherever he went, not for money, not for glory, but to leave the world in a better state than when he came into it. Johnny Appleseed, whose real name was John Chapman, was born on 26 September 1774 in Massachusetts, USA. He died aged seventy. Throughout his adult life he planted orchards, some of which still survive, in Indiana, Pennsylvania, Ohio and Kentucky.

His reputation for planting seeds, not just in spring or in autumn, but all the time, earned him the name Johnny Appleseed. He is said to have slept outdoors and his favourite reading material was the Bible. His exploits are remembered as legendary and some say he planted orchards in far away California as well. He walked everywhere barefoot and dressed in clothes made from sacking, or so I am told.

As an organic apple grower, I relate to Johnny Appleseed, whose legacy was born long before chemicals or even genetic modification became factors in world agriculture. Johnny Appleseed's legacy still lives on today in many ways, not least in that his birthday is remembered in the USA as 'Johnny Appleseed Day'. As we sow seeds this September, let us sow an extra one in honour of Johnny Appleseed.

Sorting out the garden shed and the bird table

'During the day he stayed in his garden shed, writing…'
(Sophie Dahl speaking about her late grandfather
and giant of children's literature Roald Dahl)

I CAN relate to Roald Dahl to the extent that I studied for my Leaving Certificate in a garden shed, built by my handyman dad and lit after sunset by a Tilley lamp.

'With all the garden sheds that are on the market today, you have an excellent chance of finding what you are looking for in both price and size,' says one website which wants to sell pre-built sheds. Unfortunately, I could not find that elusive product to suit my narrow elongated space in my kitchen garden. Apart from the narrowness of the space, I also wanted the shed to be a lean-to structure and to have a grass roof.

HOARDING CAN BE HEAVEN...

IF YOU CAN FIND ANYTHING QUICKLY!

SCREW-TOP JARS MAKE GOOD HOMES FOR DRILL BITS, SCREWS, NAILS, etc, ONCE THE LIDS ARE SCREWED TO THE UNDER-SIDE OF A BEAM IN THE GARDEN SHED.

T.S.

To tell the truth, I would have been surprised if I found what I was seeking in any shop. So, as I mentioned in the Fourth Week in July, I had a bash at building my own homemade garden shed, again with vital help from my dad.

When the shed was built back in 1998, I designed it to have a space allotted to every garden tool. There was ample shelving to keep items, packets and whatnot off the ground. Jars of assorted screws and nails were easily seen and accessed as their lids were screwed to the wooden shed roof beam.

By this stage in the gardening year, I have been in and out of that shed a lot, hastily retrieving and depositing all manner of seed trays, plant pots, buckets and tools. As a result, the place is now a bit of a dumping ground, I'm afraid. So a tidy-up is needed and now is a good time, while the days are still warm enough and the light is good.

SEVEN STEPS TO A TIDY GARDEN SHED:

1. Set aside a day for a serious tidy of the shed and to preserve garden furniture and fences.
2. Empty the shed, sweep the floor and check for rot or any other damage, such as leaks. Check for signs of rodent damage. If evidence is found, alert your cat or set a trap yourself.
3. Reuse or recycle unwanted items (especially items not used in the last two years!). Pass on any unwanted plant pots to a school garden, a garden centre, a neighbour or an organic centre.
4. Repair any leaks; fix and oil wobbly hinges; and paint or preserve any woodwork if necessary.
5. Now is the time to put up extra shelving, or put a bracket here or a nail there to hold any newly acquired tools or equipment. Consider having a seat in the shed to sit on in case of a rain shower when you are gardening.

6. Before putting all your bits and pieces back in the shed, use a security marker kit to label mowers and tools with your name and address. This will help identify them in case of theft.
7. Finally, decide if you need a strong rust-proof lock on the shed to prevent, or at least minimise, break-ins.

A newly painted shed shows up the weathered bird table and the benches, so when I set aside time to tidy and preserve the exterior wood of the garden shed, I take the chance to also fix up the bird table. The birds will not miss it at this time of the year with the hedgerows fruiting so generously. While the paint brush is out, I apply a new coat of non-toxic, water-based wood preservative to the bird table, as well as to the wooden benches and fences in the garden.

OTHER JOBS FOR THE WEEK THAT IS IN IT:

Lift potatoes, especially if leaves show any sign of blight. Cut off leaves and stems and compost this greenery. I checked this with a Teagasc advisor and was told that, because the blight fungus is airborne, it will not affect the compost adversely. However, soil-borne diseases, like clubroot, should not be introduced to compost bins. Once the potatoes are dug on a dry day, I normally leave them for a couple of hours in the open air to dry off before storing them in a paper bag or in a cardboard box in the fridge, if I have space. The ideal, for the best flavour, would be to cook and eat them immediately, of course.

Around now, I take the final cut of comfrey before winter. These leaves are stuffed into the comfrey barrel and topped up with water. This concoction will be ready for the start of the growing season next spring, so I can mix it in with the water in the watering cans, especially if the weather is dry.

Do not be tempted to prune plums or cherry trees when you see them shedding leaves. I did this before and inadvertently killed a lovely Victoria plum tree which caught silver leaf as a result. If you must prune back any untidy plum or cherry branches, wait until next summer when the tree is strong and in full leaf.

I remember when I was teaching how much I appreciated the help given by parents and others, whether it was helping with computer lessons, dance lessons or refereeing a football match. Teaching has changed since my time during the 1980s and 1990s. One of those changes is that almost all of the schools I have visited now have school gardens. Even schools with no grass or soil are planting up containers to ensure growing and nurturing plants is a part of every child's education.

Another change since the 1980s is the growing epidemic of obesity and type 2 diabetes now affecting more and more children. No one measure will fix this problem but there are worthwhile efforts being made locally and internationally. Oregon State University in the USA has developed a curriculum and lesson plans under the heading Garden Enhanced Nutrition Education. Another set of lesson plans for school garden-based education can be found at www.grannysgardenschool.com. America's famous Cornell University in New York State even has a distance learning course called Teaching and Learning in the School Garden.

In a way, Johnny Applewood (see Third Week in September) was an eighteenth-century pioneer of distance learning through his example. Perhaps we need a few more modern-day 'Johnny Appleseeds', be they parents, amateur gardeners, farmers or local authorities, who can offer plants, tools or any form of help to the principal of the local school. There is every likelihood that that school is developing, or would like to develop, a garden and would like to undertake garden-based education.

To quote the website of one very impressive school, Knockanean National School near Ennis, Co. Clare: 'At this busy time of year in the garden, and to help our children get the most out of this brilliant facility at the school, we need a few more volunteers to help out' (see www.knockaneannationalschool.com).

Thoughts from other kitchen gardeners

EAMON RYAN

Better known as a former Minister for Communications, Energy and Natural Resources, and leader of the Green Party (An Comhaontas Glas), Eamon also cultivates an allotment. Growing food nearer to the house would be easier, but since he has four young sons, the garden is required for play at present. However, an allotment has other compensating advantages.

Describe the location in which you grow your own food:

I have the great good luck of having an allotment which is all my own space and a great escape from my office and my home. The land is not the best after the topsoil was scraped off a few years before the council took it over. Five years on, with the occasional lump of seaweed and manure thrown on top, it is coming back to life a little. The site is in Goatstown with views looking over Dublin City. There are some 100 other plots on the site so there is a lot of chat and swapping of seeds and produce.

Which food do you look forward to harvesting most and why?

I love picking potatoes, especially when the dreaded blight or slugs haven't got to them. It is one of the activities that my young boys volunteer for, without us having to have a major row. I have also been lucky in the last two years with sweet corn and I tend to cluck around for the last few weeks as I try and guess whether they are ripe enough.

Which garden tool do you value most and why?

A great friend who has one of the best organic gardens in the country gave me a present of a hoe with a flexible head which can take out weeds like nothing else. Other than that, the only thing I use is a simple spade, but I have been through a good few of those. They never seem to last the full weight of my big boot and the gluey soil I am trying to turn over.

What motivates you to undertake the work involved in growing food?

I have always loved the miracle of seeing a seed germinate and, a few weeks later, a green shoot coming out of the ground. I like the exercise in digging and the way it allows my mind to chew over whatever is the concern of the day. I have a romantic notion of myself and my children working away together as a happy co-operative. I love walking back to my house with a big clump of something under my arm, letting my wife know that she has a real hunter–gatherer on her hands.

What advice would you give to a person considering growing their own food?

Start small and work your way up from there. Plant things that you like eating yourself. Buy a really strong spade.

Have you an aspiration for the future in relation to food?

I need to eat less but hope that by growing more I will get enough exercise to tip my health balance in the right direction. I would like to be able to grow grapes. I love seeing those big polytunnels all around the country and would love to see our local markets going from strength to strength.

MICHAEL CONNOLLY

Michael is a family man living in Co. Monaghan. Acutely aware of the way in which finite fossil fuels, more than human labour, give humanity the present levels of food production, Michael logically advocates food growing for everyone.

Describe the location in which you grow your own food:

I live in a converted church on a one-acre site which I share with some dead people and some thirty or so large mature trees. I have the use of about one-eighth of an acre, which is south facing, on which I have two polytunnels, a chicken enclosure and some raised beds. In addition, every nook and cranny in the acre has either a nut tree, fruit tree or fruit bush. The earth is what Kavanagh called 'stony grey soil of Monaghan' and yields only reluctantly to the sweat of your brow.

Which food do you look forward to harvesting most and why?

Potatoes – they are fantastic, cheap, easy, tasty and, in terms of EROEI (energy return on energy invested), are beaten only by cobnuts.

Which garden tool do you value most and why?

I have a scythe which was my father's and grandfather's and which brings tears to my eyes on the rare opportunities I get to use it.

What motivates you to undertake the work involved in growing food?

I do many things, but have only one real job, which is to raise my three children to maturity and teach them the skills they will need to feed themselves.

What advice would you give to a person considering growing their own food?

Get started. You have a lot to learn and you will need these skills in the coming years. It can be immensely satisfying to grow your own food and, as someone once said, 'Civilization is only three meals deep.' It would be wise to have a fallback position in the event of food shortages. Ask the former members of the USSR or the people of North Korea today.

Have you an aspiration for the future in relation to food?

The brutal facts are that our species has exceeded the capacity of this planet to support us in our numbers and our consumptive habits. It is my earnest hope that there will be enough of humanity left at the end of this century, and that we will have retained enough knowledge and be intelligent enough to bring our food production systems into balance with nature. In so doing, we could live up to the name the Swedish scientist Linnaeus gave us – *Homo sapiens* ('Man the wise').

Deireadh Fómhair ✿ October

The Month of Harvest Thanksgiving

OCTOBER, OR DEIREADH FÓMHAIR (meaning 'end of harvest'), is the month when the Christian calendar overlaps with pagan traditions, in terms of appreciation of the natural world, and where and how food is provided. Churches are decorated with fruit, vegetables, jars of jam, bunches of flowers, sheaves of wheat and whatever else is produced locally, to provide a context for the services of Harvest Thanksgiving. These celebratory events are often tied in with the feast day of St Francis of Assisi, who understood human interdependence with the rest of creation more than other Christian leaders of his time or since. In 1225 AD, the year before he died, aged around forty-five, he wrote his celebrated 'Canticle of the Sun', which includes the lines:

> Be praised, My Lord, through our sister Mother Earth,
> who feeds us and rules us, and produces various fruits with
> coloured flowers and herbs.
> Praise and bless my Lord, and give thanks,
> and serve him with great humility.

Most people relate to St Francis as the Italian saint who loved birds, wolves and other animals. In the light of the modern environmental challenges we face, Pope John Paul II declared St Francis of Assisi the patron saint of ecology on 29 November 1979. This was a good start in mobilising Christian communities to live in a way which respects the natural limits of a finite planet. Some churches have gone on to make the connection between living ecologically, social justice, fostering a good community spirit and growing food organically, by having an allotment in the grounds of their parish church.

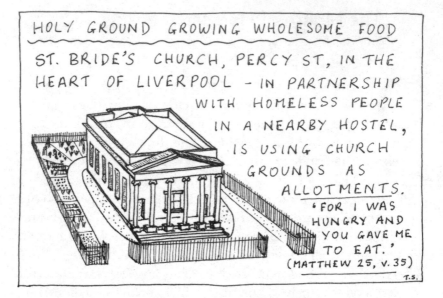

HOLY GROUND GROWING WHOLESOME FOOD

ST. BRIDE'S CHURCH, PERCY ST, IN THE HEART OF LIVERPOOL - IN PARTNERSHIP WITH HOMELESS PEOPLE IN A NEARBY HOSTEL, IS USING CHURCH GROUNDS AS ALLOTMENTS.

'FOR I WAS HUNGRY AND YOU GAVE ME TO EAT.' (MATTHEW 25, v. 35)

T.S.

An overview of the work ahead in the garden this month:
Plant: garlic cloves and autumn onion sets, e.g. Radar
Sow out: successional sowings – spinach, winter radish and lettuce
Harvest: onions, tomatoes, marrows, potatoes, carrots, celeriac, spinach, runner beans and French beans

🍁 FIRST WEEK IN OCTOBER 🍁

Coping with powdery mildew on my apple tree

'I said to Heart, "How goes it?" Heart replied:
"Right as a Ribston Pippin…."'
(Hilaire Belloc, Anglo-French writer and parliamentarian, 1870–1953)

THERE is an implication from Belloc (above) that there is never a problem with the Ribston Pippin apple tree and that it is always in perfect health. All I know about the Ribston Pippin is that it was raised from a pip brought from Rouen in France and planted at Ribston Hall, at Knaresborough in Yorkshire, England. It first produced a worthwhile late harvest of yellow (streaked with red), sweet and aromatic fruit in 1709. However, it is not just humans who feed on apple trees. Pigs, health conscious bugs and fungus get sustenance from apple trees too. From time to time, apple trees, like any of us, require some first aid.

KEEP A REGULAR EYE ON THE LEAVES AND BARK TO ENSURE EARLY DETECTION

Powdery mildew on an apple tree is easy to notice. It is a fungus disease and looks like talcum powder spinkled on the bark of affected branches and on leaves. I have noticed it on my tree at this time of year, but it can also overwinter in the tree and appear first thing when the tree comes into leaf in the spring. The affected leaves fall off and the tree is unable to store up the sun's energy, so it cannot, therefore, produce fruit.

OCTOBER

FIRST AID FOR AN APPLE TREE SHOWING SIGNS OF MILDEW

Affected buds and boughs should be cut away altogether. Take care not to disturb the powdery mildew and so contaminate unaffected parts of the tree. All affected parts should be destroyed by burning.

Having a wood-burning stove comes in handy as a way to burn diseased wood.

HOW TO PREVENT MILDEW OCCURRING OR RECURRING

Mildew is a sign that a tree is stressed. It can be due to a hot, dry growing season. This is not the case with my tree, as I give it a regular drink of dish water from the kitchen. Mildew can also be due to the soil being too light. I doubt that this is the problem with my tree, with the amount of compost I dig in at planting time and the annual mulch I put around the tree each autumn. Another cause of mildew can be that the tree is too close to other plants and the air flow is restricted. Now, that is a possible cause of the mildew problem on my apple tree. I have raspberry canes on one side of the tree and mint growing around the base. The mildew acts like a warning to cut back the nearby vegetation and allow air to circulate. De-cluttering is part and parcel of managing a small garden – especially when mildew is giving me that message loud and clear!

WHY NOT JUST GET A CHEMICAL TREATMENT FOR MILDEW?

Most wildlife and life in the soil is beneficial to producing healthy crops. An agri-chemical company advertiser might attempt to persuade me to purchase a poison to 'zap' a pest. However, it is likely, as in any war, that 'friendly fire' will kill the beneficial wildlife as well as the villain. Once the food chain becomes poisoned, the consequences are not always predictable. I am reminded of the seminal publication *Silent Spring* by Rachel Carson (see the Fourth Week in May).

> 'Humankind has not woven the web of life.
> We are but one thread within it.
> Whatever we do to the web, we do to ourselves.
> All things are bound together,
> All things connect.'
>
> (Chief Seattle (known to his tribe as Si'ahl), 1854)

CREATURES IN 'THE WEB OF LIFE' THAT BENEFIT KITCHEN GARDENERS

🍃 **Bees:** their pollinating skills are irreplaceable, even if we had the time to physically transfer pollen from one flower to another by hand. There are 101 or 102 species of bee in Ireland. Twenty are bumble bees and eighty or so are solitary bees. Only one species, the native honey bee, lives in a hive of 60,000 or so bees. However, the honey bee colonies only now survive thanks to beekeepers' disease control management of their man-made hives. Half the bumble bee species are in decline and 45 per cent of solitary bees are declining also. The clear priority is to encourage all bees (see the Third Week in July).

🍃 **Birds:** feeding birds, especially in winter, combined with non-use of poisons, encourage smaller birds like tits, sparrows, blackbirds, robins, thrushes and starlings, which feed on a variety of insects, caterpillars, slugs and snails.

🍃 **Centipedes:** feed on insects, mites and slugs.

🍃 **Frogs and toads:** voracious eaters of slugs.

🍃 **Ground beetles:** devour many soil insects, including the cabbage root fly grub.

🍃 **Hedgehogs:** famous for reducing slug populations.

🍃 **Hover flies:** looks like a wasp but is smaller and hovers over plants. Their larvae are voracious eaters of aphids, eating several hundred each before pupation. They are attracted to yellow flowers.

OCTOBER

🍃 **Lacewings:** these are beautiful insects with delicate wings, large eyes and a metallic sheen. Their larvae consume large quantities of aphids, mites and other soft-bodied insects.

🍃 **Ladybirds:** both adults and larvae feed on aphids, scale insects and mites.

🍃 **Worms:** Charles Darwin appreciated the importance of the earthworm and their intelligent behaviour, which improves soil fertility. The arrival of the New Zealand flatworm, in the soil of imported pot plants, to parts of Ireland and Britain needs vigilance as these carnivorous worms consume our native earthworms.

🍃 **Wasps:** wasps eat various insect pests in the garden. They do not spread disease. If their nest is not in the way, I would leave well enough alone. Wasps do not return to old empty nests but build new ones. The hornet is less common than the wasp and can be identified as it is a larger insect.

HEDGEHOGS NEED HABITATS

THESE SLUG, SNAIL, CATERPILLAR AND INSECT EATING MAMMALS (Erinaceus europaeus) ARE BECOMING SCARCE. HELP THEM BY REMOVING LITTER (THEIR HEADS GET STUCK IN PAPER CUPS AND TINS). ALSO, PROVIDE PILES OF LEAVES WHERE THEY CAN HIBERNATE FROM OCTOBER TO MARCH.

T.S.

OTHER JOBS FOR THE WEEK THAT IS IN IT:

🍃 Sweet pea can be sown now in pots for flowering next year. Germinate under a cloche or in the greenhouse.

🍃 Likewise, sow lettuce for winter use, either under a cloche or in the greenhouse.

🍃 Complete planting of spring-flowering bulbs.

The Bigger Picture:
World Vegetarian Day, 1 October

It is difficult to estimate with accuracy the number of vegetarians in the world. Estimations that place the world's vegetarian population at 50 per cent have been published. Most of these people do not eat meat for economic reasons, others for religious reasons, while others would have secular reasons such as taste, health, environmental considerations, and so on.

The *American Journal of Clinical Nutrition* reckons that two billion people worldwide live primarily on meat-based diets, while four billion live primarily on plant-based diets. Even so, the UN Food and Agricultural Organisation (FAO) confronts us all with a very uncomfortable finding: that livestock production is responsible for more climate change gases than all the motor vehicles in the world, as well as being a major cause of land and water degradation. Climate change is now reducing the world's agricultural output when we need more, not less, food.

Between 1950 and 1994, global meat production increased fourfold, rising faster than the human population, and that trend looks like continuing. Given that far fewer people can be fed on a meat-based diet than a vegetarian-based diet, based on the amount of agricultural land available to humanity, this trend towards more meat production is alarming.

OCTOBER

WHERE IS THE WATER FOR ALL THIS MEAT PRODUCTION GOING TO COME FROM?

At present, about one billion people are short of fresh water, which contributes to many avoidable diseases and deaths. By 2025 AD, according to the UN Environmental Programme, more than 2.8 billion people in 48 countries will face water stress or scarcity conditions. This water crisis is made worse by a growth in meat production.

Dr David Archer, Professor of Geophysical Sciences at the University of Chicago, USA, compares the amount of fresh water used to produce 1 pound of various foods (see below):

Lettuce	23 gallons
Wheat	25 gallons
Apples	49 gallons
Chicken	815 gallons
Pork	1,630 gallons
Beef	5,214 gallons

Dr Archer also found that meat diets are wasteful in terms of energy requirements also. Even in terms of calories, 90 per cent of the energy in the grain fed to livestock is lost to the human consumer. Thankfully, in Ireland, our long grass-growing season makes Irish meat less grain dependent, but there is still a reliance on imported animal feed to satisfy the twelve-month demand for meat. Less hardy breeds of animals are used, which require overwintering in sheds and consequently eat costly grain-based feed.

EATING LESS MEAT AND MORE LOCAL VEGETABLES IS A HUMANE RESPONSE TO WORLD HUNGER

Each year within the EU, about 300 million cattle, sheep and pigs, and about 4 billion chickens are slaughtered, and still the EU imports meat from elsewhere. Compassion for animals is one obvious reason why many people choose a fruit- and vegetable-based diet. Dr Rajendra Pachauri, the chief of the UN International Panel on Climate Change (IPCC), advocates a meatless diet in the interests of dealing with climate change and being better for human health. Dr Pachauri also advises us to adopt a diet of food associated with much lower levels of greenhouse gas emissions and urges governments to put a price on the carbon footprint of each food produced. Such a move could make local horticulture, arable farming and kitchen gardening even more cost effective, as vegetable growing generally consumes less water and energy than other more processed food production.

Ex-Beatle Sir Paul McCartney can certainly afford as much beef steaks as he fancies, but he has other reasons to advocate a meatless diet: 'If anyone wants to save the planet, all they have to do is stop eating meat. It's staggering when you think about it. Vegetarianism takes care of so many things in one shot: ecology, famine, cruelty' (interview in the *Animal Times*, 2001).

I occasionally eat meat, but I enjoy vegetarian cooking most days. Mahatma Gandhi summed up the case best with his mantra: 'Live simply so others can simply live.'

OCTOBER

🍁 SECOND WEEK IN OCTOBER 🍁

Foraging in the garden for a lunch no money could buy

'The real power in the future will not be nuclear power, or even energy, but will belong to whoever possesses the sources of food.'

(Ismail Sabri Abdullah, Egyptian Minister of State, 1980)

SEVERAL decades spent at the political coalface have got me into the habit of making a packed lunch before leaving the house in the morning. Experience soon taught me that mornings became afternoons which became evenings very quickly, with back-to-back meetings and other parliamentary obligations. Often there was no time to visit a canteen for lunch.

Apart from the advantage of having some lunch to hand regardless of where I might be on a given day, the ingredients for some great sandwiches and salads were there to be gathered in my kitchen garden at almost any time of the year.

The garden in October is beginning to slow down noticeably for the winter. However, this is the time when foraging is generally in the news. Before going very far to forage, it is worth seeing what lies outside the back door – herbs, salads, and even some edible flowers and so-called weeds can make a mundane sandwich taste a bit wild and mysterious.

WHAT MIGHT BE ON THE LUNCH OR SANDWICH MENU FOR A KITCHEN GARDEN FORAGER?

October–November

🍁 A few stray cherry tomatoes sliced in a sandwich

254

🌿 Chopped fennel leaves give an exotic aniseed flavour.

🌿 Rosemary sprig thinly chopped and spread with the butter gives an instant herb-flavoured sandwich.

🌿 Blackberry in an apple crumble or jam makes a wonderful autumn treat.

🌿 Home-grown apples chopped and put in a lunch box; they bruise easily if left whole in a briefcase.

December–January

🌿 This is a lean time in the garden so take out the stored produce, like sliced beetroot, from the jar.

🌿 Being evergreen herbs, rosemary and sage are available throughout the winter.

🌿 Sprouted beans grown indoors provide good crunchy fresh food (see the First Week in December).

February–March

🌿 Lamb's lettuce is not crunchy and is a little bland, but fresh greens now are rare and welcome.

🌿 Dandelion leaves are not bitter as they are still young; these are good in sandwiches.

🌿 Bottled beetroot is always a good staple for salads or sandwiches.

April–May

🌿 Radishes sown in March are almost ready to harvest, bringing a peppery crunch to lunch.

🌿 Larger lettuce is now ready, and cut-and-come-again leaves can replace lamb's lettuce.

🌿 Nasturtium leaves growing semi-wild are peppery in a salad or sandwich.

June–July

- Lettuce leaves, radishes and an increasing diversity of young edible plants

- Chives, fennel, parsley, basil and a growing range of herbs

- Tomatoes and peppers if the greenhouse has been well planted in early spring

- Edible flowers like borage, nasturtium, calendula and even organic rose petals

- Strawberries, raspberries, blackcurrants, plums – this is the season of desserts in lunch boxes.

August–September

- Plenty of tomatoes and basil – delicious. I have never been bored by these two yet!

- Nasturtium leaves, like a sandwich damp-proof membrane, prevent bread becoming soggy when using sliced tomatoes, etc.

- Slices of courgette give an interesting crunch to a sandwich.

- A full range of herbs and vegetables make lunch possibilities almost endless.

- There is no shortage of apples for juicing, stewing or cutting into wedges – always a handy snack.

OTHER JOBS FOR THE WEEK THAT IS IN IT:

- Thin out pond plants and remove debris from the bottom of the pond. Then spread a net over the pond, if it is small enough, to collect any falling leaves. Rotting leaves, especially in a small pond, are a problem for fish.

- To have fresh herbs throughout the winter, lift and pot plants of parsley, mint, chives and lemon balm, and bring them into the greenhouse. Any excess pots of herbs make good gifts.

🍃 Close up the greenhouse or tunnel completely in cold or stormy weather, but be sure to open it up again in any sunny weather. Do not water much at all.

The Bigger Picture:
Foraging for wild food

I love blackberries, so this is a magical time of year for me. Although the blackberry is sometimes grown as a specially cultivated thornless garden plant, I enjoy the traditional activity which reminds me of childhood – picking blackberries.

A reminder of early adulthood is the picking of elderberries, which went to make elderberry wine. This looks like a regular red wine, but tastes much stronger! My preference would be for elderflower wine as it is more refreshing, but that means foraging in May.

FORAGING FOR FUNGI – LEARNING TO IDENTIFY A FEW SAFE MUSHROOM SPECIES

There are several thousand mushroom species in Ireland, of which many are inedible and a very small number are deadly poisonous. Four are fatal to humans – so be warned! Another like the Shaggy Ink Cap can affect a person if alcohol was consumed in the previous couple of days. However, there are many mushrooms which are not just safe to eat, but unique and delicious, compared to any other shop-bought or home-grown vegetable or fruit.

Where to start

Become an expert in just two or three species, or even just one species for a start. Learn to identify beyond any doubt, for example:

🍃 The Hedgehog mushroom

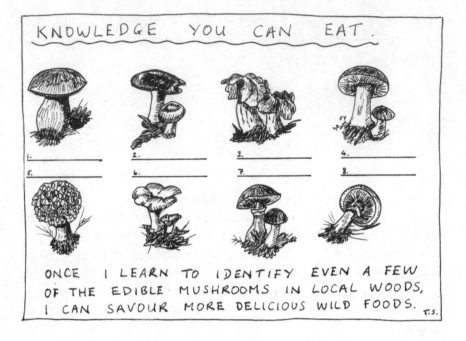

ONCE I LEARN TO IDENTIFY EVEN A FEW
OF THE EDIBLE MUSHROOMS IN LOCAL WOODS,
I CAN SAVOUR MORE DELICIOUS WILD FOODS. T.S.

🍂 The Winter Chanterelle

🍂 The Girolle

You will need a sharp knife, a small brush, an identification manual, a pen, paper and a collection basket.

Choose a dry day to commence foraging. Record the time and other observations on the day; these details are useful to read back over next year. Just pick healthy intact mushrooms and pick the full stem as well. Clean off the mushrooms in the forest. Transport them carefully in an airy basket, packed so as to avoid damage from rolling around.

Preparation of the wild harvest of mushrooms

🍂 As an absolute precaution, keep one specimen aside with an emergency medical number!

- Clean the mushrooms with a knife and brush – do not wash them if possible as mushrooms absorb water.

- Do not eat them raw.

- Slice them and put them in a pot with a lid; gently cook them in their own juices for ten minutes.

- Now they are ready for further cooking, for example, frying in a bit of butter and salt.

LEARNING MORE ABOUT FORAGING IN IRELAND

In many continental countries, it seems that most families go foraging. There is a growing interest in foraging in Ireland, however. Courses can now be found at the Organic Centre in Leitrim and in other similar centres elsewhere. Roger and Olivia Goodwillie at Lavistown House, Lavistown, Co. Kilkenny have been running such courses for over thirty years now and have a good website (www.lavistownhouse.ie).

OCTOBER

THIRD WEEK IN OCTOBER

Sowing autumn garlic and onion sets

'Where would we be without onions?
How many recipes begin with "take an onion"?'
(Greg Wallace, *The Greengrocer's Cookbook*)

THE onion (*Allium cepa*) is a member of the lily family. Thought to have been first cultivated in central Asia, it was brought to Europe by traders in ancient times. The onion was part of the staple diet of the Greek and Roman civilisations, the latter possibly giving it the name 'unio', meaning 'only', for its singularity.

Garlic (*Allium sativum*) is thought to have been indigenous to the southwest of Siberia, from where it was brought to southern Europe, where it has become naturalised. History records that, during the building of the great pyramids in Egypt, garlic, along with onion and radish, was given to the slaves to increase their stamina and protect them from disease. The name garlic is of Anglo-Saxon origin, being derived from *gar* (a spear) and *lac* (a plant), in reference to the shape of its leaves.

WHERE TO GET GARLIC FOR SOWING

Resist the temptation to plant garlic cloves from garlic sold for eating. No kitchen gardener wants white rot infecting their alliums, hence the need to select your garlic for planting carefully. Not only would such a disease cost this year's crop of onions and garlic, but white rot remains in the soil and will infect any subsequent allium crops for ten to twenty years. There is no easy cure for white rot, so prevention is important. That means a strict adherence to rotation. Always be sure to plant certified disease-free alliums, but never in the same plot more often than once every four years. Greengrocer garlic may well give a crop if sown, but it may not have been screened for white-rot risk, unlike the horticultural garlic sold in the garden centre.

Most garden centres at this time stock horticultural garlic bulbs. I sometimes go online to www.fruithillfarm.com and order garlic bulbs and onion sets from mail order supplier Manfred Wandel in West Cork. Otherwise, email sales@fruithillfarm.com or phone +353 27 50710.

HOW MUCH TO SOW

Garlic is normally sown by breaking up a bulb gently so that the cloves are separated and intact. With about ten cloves to a bulb, I need only two bulbs to grow enough garlic to give me one bulb a week from August to March. After that, I find my stored garlic starts to sprout.

SOWING GARLIC – WHERE AND HOW?

Garlic needs a frosty spell to trigger full growth in the spring, so planting now is better than waiting until spring. I reserve a space (1 m x 2 m) for autumn-sown garlic. I try to leave about 20 cm (8 inches) between each clove. With a trowel, I make a narrow hole to sit the clove in so that the tip is about 2 cm (1 inch) below the surface. Light but well-composted soil is best. Garlic likes to grow in full sun, but try growing it in the best location you have. Whatever your harvest, the chances are it will be the only Irish-grown garlic you will be able to get. Garlic was grown commercially in Co. Wexford, and hopefully will be again in the future.

CARE AND HARVESTING

Unlike wide-leaved plants, garlic has spear-like leaves which do not exclude daylight from the soil, so hoe between the garlic plants to keep your plot weed free. Water the plants if the soil is dry. When the leaves go brown next June or July, the crop is ready to harvest. With a garden fork, lift the garlic bulbs. Allow them to dry on a concrete path, or spaced out on a garden riddle raised off the ground to help air to circulate around the garlic. Nowadays, I put the riddle containing the new garlic bulbs on a shelf in the greenhouse.

STORAGE OF GARLIC

Low temperatures and dry conditions are optimum for garlic storage. Leaving the leaves attached also prolongs storage. This is why at this stage I plait the garlic using the dry leaves, which look like raffia. Hang the string or plaits of garlic in a cool, dry dark place like the garden shed.

DIVIDING CERTIFIED GARLIC BULBS INTO CLOVES TO GROW A YEAR'S SUPPLY OF GARLIC.

SOWING OF ONION SETS

The sowing and growing of onions sets are very similar to the sowing and growing of garlic. Some years, I grow onions beside the garlic patch; other years, I leave the existing leaf beet to feed me over the winter, and plant leeks there instead next spring. I have a plan to grow onions from seeds some January in a heated propagator in the greenhouse, but have not got around to it yet. Meanwhile, I buy onion sets by mail order or, more often, from a garden centre.

BUYING AND GROWING ONION SETS

Choose small healthy onion sets; larger ones tend to bolt. Sow them using a similar method to that described for the garlic above. The difference is to have the tip of the onion set showing above the soil. Some people find that birds pick out a set or two from the ground, but this has not happened to me. Netting might be needed if your onion sets are prone to disturbance. Another small difference with the onions is that their root system is shallow, so they should sit higher in the soil. When weeding, be careful with the hoe or, better still, weed by hand.

OTHER JOBS FOR THE WEEK THAT IS IN IT:

🌿 Cut and clear pea and bean haulms (tops/stems). With the pea and bean harvest now over, the haulms will be added to the next batch of greenery for compost making. The roots of these legumes are traditionally left in the ground. The next crop in the rotation, the brassicas, may benefit from the extra dose of nitrogen which will be in this soil, fixed from the atmosphere by the roots of the bean and pea plants. This clearance also means putting away as neatly as possible the canes and string which supported these tall climbers. It is worth taking a bit of time to clean off excess soil from canes, etc. Next spring will be busy enough, and ready-to-go supports for young legume plants will be appreciated.

🌿 Divide clumps of chives which have become too big for their position. The benefit is a free extra clump of chives for another part of the garden or as a gift for a chive-less friend. With the soil hopefully soft and damp, a garden fork can easily lift the chives. Gently, using two hands, tease apart the clump to become two clumps. Plant one clump back in the original spot and plant the other elsewhere, or pot it up using good garden soil. Water both new plants so they grow a little before the winter dormant period.

The Bigger Picture:
Giving thanks for a good harvest

For as long as humans have settled in any one place long enough to cultivate the soil, communities have had thanksgiving ceremonies to celebrate that the barns are full once again for the lean winter months ahead, until extensive cultivation is possible again the following spring.

The Ancient Romans paid tribute after the harvest to Ceres, the goddess of cereals, at the festival of Cerelia. The Greeks likewise paid tribute to their goddess of the soil, Demeter. In China, a three-day festival of thanksgiving called Chung Ch'ui has a long tradition, while in Ancient Egypt, a statue of Min, the god of vegetation, was erected in the harvested fields in thanksgiving.

A similar tradition is recorded in Christianity as early as the third century AD. Erntedankfest (harvest festival of thanks) occurred whenever the autumn harvest was gathered. Over the centuries, the festival became more associated with carousing and the excessive consumption of alcohol.

In Victorian Britain, a dim view was taken of this wild behaviour around harvest time. Reverend Robert Hawker in Cornwall came up with the idea of a specific service of Harvest Thanksgiving for his local Church in Morwenstow to involve his congregation in the festival. He invited kitchen gardeners, farmers, bakers and flower arrangers to decorate the church in advance of the service. The tradition spread throughout Britain and Ireland and much of the English-speaking world.

'All Things Bright and Beautiful', a favourite hymn sung at harvest thanksgiving services, was composed by Dublin-born woman Cecil Frances Alexander (1818–1895), née Humpreys, who married the Bishop of Derry William Alexander. He later became the Church of Ireland Primate of All Ireland. Being married to such a prolific hymn writer did no harm whatsoever to the future Archbishop's career path. I would be curious to know if the Alexanders had a well-tended kitchen garden to inspire their preparations for the annual harvest thanksgiving.

Sowing broad beans
– a favourite autumn activity

'Ancient broad-beanlike seeds 8,500 years old have been
found in the Middle East, and the seeds probably reached
northern Europe in the hand luggage of a Roman centurion.'
(Bill Laws, from *Spade, Skirret and Parsnip: The Curious History of Vegetables*)

MANY vegetable seeds are as small as a pinhead and care is
needed to ensure one seed, and not three or four, is sown in
any one place. With the broad bean, there is no such problem. The
seed is about the size of a Euro coin, but the return from your
investment is probably going to be healthier when sowing a broad
bean seed.

The value of a broad bean in the Middle Ages is clearly reflected
in the legal statutes of the time. The crime of stealing beans from
open fields carried the death penalty. Mind you, the black fly
aphids, which sometimes attack the growing tips of my bean plants,
know a bit about the death penalty, as I knock them to the ground
with jets of soapy water, where birds and beetles finish them off.

PLANNING A PLACE TO SOW THE BROAD BEANS

I need just one square metre in which to sow my new crop of broad
beans. Having cleared away the legume remnants which were
harvested in the last few months, it is time to eye up the next plot
(from where the last season's garlic crop was taken out) to be the
new legume patch from now until next October.

I am in the habit of digging in compost before planting garlic and onions. This residue of compost is enough to keep the new broad bean seeds happy. Like all legumes, they create some of their own fertility by fixing airborne nitrogen into the soil. All I need to do, therefore, is to fork over the former garlic bed, breaking up any lumps of soil, and rake it to create a good level tilth in which to sow the seeds. Broad bean seeds can be sown any time in November also.

SOWING THE BROAD BEAN SEEDS

My one square metre patch will accommodate sixteen broad bean seeds, which means leaving at least 15 cm (6 inches) between the plants. So four rows of four seeds is my sowing plan. These seeds can be soaked in water overnight to trigger a quicker germination, but this is not essential. With a trowel, sow each seed 5 cm deep and press the soil down by hand afterwards. Water the patch well to settle the soil and soak the bean seeds. I expect the seedlings to be above ground before the colder weather of December and January. The broad bean seedling will go dormant in winter but survives -8°C temperatures.

SUPPORTING THE YOUNG BROAD BEAN PLANTS WHEN THEY START TO GROW

The upright growing habit of the broad bean plant can survive unsupported in a calm environment. However, a sudden gust or a hailstone blizzard is enough to blow it over. Like boxers in the ring, broad bean plants appreciate containment, although they have no tendrils like peas to hang from and climb skyward.

I find that the best way to give the plants support is to drive about eight canes around the bean patch. Wind string around these supports to create what looks a little like a boxing ring. By criss-crossing string across the bean patch to form a lattice network, the bean plants have free movement to grow, but they are supported in a strong wind.

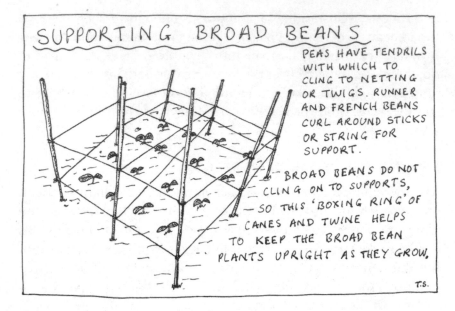

SUPPORTING BROAD BEANS

PEAS HAVE TENDRILS WITH WHICH TO CLING TO NETTING OR TWIGS. RUNNER AND FRENCH BEANS CURL AROUND STICKS OR STRING FOR SUPPORT.

BROAD BEANS DO NOT CLING ON TO SUPPORTS, SO THIS 'BOXING RING' OF CANES AND TWINE HELPS TO KEEP THE BROAD BEAN PLANTS UPRIGHT AS THEY GROW.

T.S.

CARING FOR THE GROWING BROAD BEAN PLANTS

The broad bean plant is quite hardy, but I notice that in warm weather the growing tips can be attacked by the black fly, also called the black bean aphid. If the plants have grown fully and are in flower, I nip out the growing tips, as the aphid goes for this new soft growth. If the plant still has growing to do, then I bring out my hand-held pump action mist sprayer.

One setting on the mist sprayer creates a jet of water. I add some crushed garlic and a drop of washing-up liquid to the sprayer and blast the blackflies off the plant growing tips, holding the tips steady with one hand. Once knocked to the ground, the hapless black flies become dinner for garden predators like ladybirds, dunnocks or various species of beetles.

HARVESTING THE BROAD BEANS

By next May or June, the beans should be ready to harvest. Pick them before they get too old. They taste better when young and can become tough if left too long. The consolation is that healthy beans left too long can be dried later and used as seed for next year. This is a tradition which goes back to Stone Age times.

OTHER JOBS FOR THE WEEK THAT IS IN IT:

🍃 Take final cuttings of bay and lavender, and other such woody herbs and shrubs. Plant the cuttings in pots filled with a mixture of horticultural sand and soil. Put them in the greenhouse, if you have one, under a cloche or on a windowsill to root and grow on as new plants. Next spring, these rooted cuttings can be transferred to their own pots to be given away as presents, or they can be planted up in a vacant part of the herb patch.

🍃 Complete the planting of strawberry runners with a view to them fruiting next year.

🍃 Lift the beetroot crop to use or store in moist sand in a dry frost-free place like the garden shed.

The Bigger Picture:
Avoiding food waste and saving money

A 'Stop Food Waste' survey was carried out by the Environmental Protection Agency (EPA) in November 2010 and had a total of 1,100 respondents. The results showed that 30 per cent of all food bought is thrown away, costing up to €1,000 per household per annum. The advice is to shop with a list of grocery requirements and not to shop if you are hungry.

However, it is probably no harm to be a little bit hungry in the kitchen garden. Eating food fresh from the garden is not wasteful at all. In the case of beans or peas, regular picking encourages the plants to produce more. Once carrots, potatoes or leeks are eaten,

OCTOBER

269

the leftover greenery forms important ingredients in the compost later on. However, what does cause wastage in a garden is when too much food is ready to harvest at the one time. It is better to stagger sowing and planting times to alleviate this problem next year. However, this need not be a problem and need not be wasteful.

AVOIDING WASTE IN THE KITCHEN GARDEN

The likes of parsnips or leeks are never wasted as they can stay in the ground over winter, until they are needed. In a small garden, however, leaving crops in the soil after they mature is a bit of a luxury, as space is at a premium.

On the other hand, carrots and beetroot can bolt if left in the ground too long and they can turn 'woody' as well. Making soup or meals for the freezer is an option, as are pickling, drying, juicing and other preservation techniques.

Cool storage for the winter

To put vegetables into cool storage, first acquire a non-plastic clean container, like a metal dustbin, and a supply of clean, pure coir fibre compost (extracted from the husks of coconuts), which is available from garden centres. Avoid storing damaged vegetables as these may rot and spread the rot to the good vegetables. Clean the harvested vegetables with a dry brush and place them in layers between the coir fibre. Top up the container with the coir fibre and fit the lid. Store it in a dry cool shed. Some claim this storage actually improves the taste of carrots and potatoes, but avoiding waste is the main satisfaction for me.

Freezing leafy herbs

Drying herbs by hanging up herb bunches is a well-established practice. It does alter the flavours, however. In the case of parsley, coriander, dill or fennel, those trays used to make drink cubes in the freezer can be useful for preserving something of the fresh flavours over winter. Some herbs stuffed in each cube space, which is then filled with water and frozen, keeps the colour and flavour of the herb better than drying, in my opinion. I choose not to wash these garden-cut herbs, also to keep more flavour.

Courgette chutney or 'glutney' – The answer to a glut of courgettes

INGREDIENTS:
Thumb-sized piece of ginger
12 garlic cloves
12 black peppercorns
1 tsp coriander seeds
A few blades of mace
1 kg courgettes cut into 1 cm cubes
1 kg red or green tomatoes, scalded, skinned and roughly chopped
1 kg cooking or eating apples, peeled and diced
500 g onions peeled and diced
500 g sultanas or raisins
500 g light brown sugar
750 ml cider vinegar, made up to 1 litre with water
1–3 tsp dried chilli flakes
1 tsp salt

METHOD:
Make a spice bag from muslin or cotton and place in it the ginger, garlic cloves, peppercorns, coriander and mace.

Put the vegetables and fruit in a large saucepan with the sugar, vinegar, water, chilli flakes and salt. Place the spice bag in the centre of the mix.

Heat the mixture gently, stirring to dissolve the sugar. Simmer for 2–3 hours uncovered, stirring occasionally to avoid burning the pot. When the chutney is thick and reduced enough to show the pot base when parted by a wooden spoon, it is ready.

Pot up the chutney while still warm (not boiling) in sterilised glass jars. Seal with plastic coated screw-top lids. Do not allow the vinegar to interact with metal lids, as metal can taint the chutney flavour. Leave the chutney to mature for at least two weeks – ideally, two months – before serving.

Thoughts from other kitchen gardeners

ART O'HARE

Originally from Co. Down, school teachers Art and his wife Pauline, and their family, have a great appreciation of education and sport, as well as the historic heritage of Balbriggan, Co. Dublin. This all led to their purchase and careful restoration of an historic eighteenth century townhouse. The south-east facing large garden has been put to good use, as Art explains.

Describe the location in which you grow your own food:

We are lucky enough to have an old walled garden in Balbriggan about 300 m from the sea. This means that we rarely have frost and can grow early crops of most vegetables. The downside is that, since we are right on the east coast, the east wind, when it comes, can do considerable damage in a very short time. The main part of the garden contains vegetables, but we have also planted pear and apple trees as well as raspberries.

Which food do you look forward to harvesting most and why?

Potatoes! This is for two reasons: when I gather the potatoes I feel that I have made my provision for the winter and so the growing season has been successful; and, second, because it is a great thrill to see eight or ten nice potatoes emerge from where one was planted.

Which garden tool do you value most and why?

It is a tie between a long handled spade and a similarly handled fork. I suppose this is because I am still a 'digger' rather than a 'no-tiller', so a lot of satisfaction comes from seeing a freshly dug and forked-over piece of ground, ready for planting with the new crop. The long handles make digging and tilling much easier than the standard pattern short 'T' handles generally found on these tools.

What motivates you to undertake the work involved in growing food?

For me, it isn't work; it is a pleasure – the pleasure of newly tilled earth, the pleasure of planting out seedlings, of sowing seed and seeing it germinate, the pleasure (sometimes) of outwitting pests and diseases, and finally the pleasure of gathering in my own produce.

What advice would you give to a person considering growing their own food?

Go right ahead and try it. It should be well worth it from several points of view – exercise, fresh air and fresh food. Start with a smallish area, and grow simple and dependable crops to begin with: potatoes, peas, beans and perhaps onions. Buy a few good quality tools and keep good records of what worked and what didn't, for guidance in future years.

Have you an aspiration for the future in relation to food?

I would like to produce enough fruit and vegetables to feed our family for six months of the year but, so far, this only works for potatoes and onions. I suspect that this will need more careful planning and better storage methods than I have at the moment.

MICHAEL KELLY

An author and feature writer for the *Irish Times,* Michael is known to many as the founder of Grow It Yourself Ireland (GIY Ireland). His vision and dedication to the common good have won him awards as a social entrepreneur. Meanwhile, he organises his time to make sure he can grow food for his family in Co. Waterford. His humorous take on growing food in his books *Trading Places: From Rat Race to Hen Run* and *Tales from Home Farm* makes for good reading. He blogs at www.michaelkelly.ie.

Describe the location in which you grow your own food:

We grow our own food in our back garden. Our house is on a site of about three quarters of an acre. The vegetable patch is fenced off in a corner of the back garden. It's about 10 m x 20 m. We also keep hens, chickens, turkeys and occasionally a few pigs, so the garden is a busy spot.

Which food do you look forward to harvesting most and why?

I love cropping potatoes – rummaging in the soil feels like Christmas morning to me. You just never know what you are going to get. I also love harvesting sweet corn – it's one of those vegetables that has to be eaten immaculately fresh, otherwise it doesn't taste as sweet. And I do also adore my first crops of tomatoes and peas. God, I love it all really.

Which garden tool do you value most and why?

A hoe – the single biggest and most valuable lesson I ever got as a GIYer was a demonstration of how to hoe properly from Jim Cronin over in Clare. Get yourself a sharp Dutch hoe and, once a week, run it over your entire vegetable patch. You simply run the hoe lightly back and forward slightly under the surface of the soil, standing upright (easy on the back). You hoe before weeds get a chance to become weeds – it makes keeping the vegetable patch weed free a lot easier.

What motivates you to undertake the work involved in growing food?

Initially it was because I didn't see any sense in the way our food chain was set up. It seemed so bizarre to be importing food from all over the world that grows perfectly well here in Ireland. I hate things that don't make sense and I am a stubborn git, so I decided to grow it myself. These days, I don't really see it as work – I enjoy the process itself. I could sow seeds quite happily all day long, and it wouldn't really matter to me whether they became plants or not.

What advice would you give to a person considering growing their own food?

Just get started. It's as simple as that. Don't be daunted or worried about potential failures. Stick a seed in the ground and see what happens. The very worst that can happen is that it won't grow, and that's pretty unlikely.

Have you an aspiration for the future in relation to food?

That home-grown food would become the norm.

Samhain ❧ November

The Month of the Celtic New Year

HALLOWEEN (Oíche Shamhna – 31 October) still reminds us of the priorities which our Celtic ancestors attached to the month of November. Samhain was regarded as the first month of winter. Living close to the elements without modern comforts, it was likely many people would not survive a harsh winter. As a life insurance policy, it made sense to be kind to the spirit world, just in case you might die and end up there yourself before long.

The slaughter of some livestock at Samhain served two purposes. First, it reduced the herd size and saved on fodder during the winter, as well as sustaining the post-harvest celebrations. Second, it became a sacrifice to give thanks for the harvest and placate the forces of nature going into winter.

The bonfire was central to cooking the meat, providing warmth and light, as well as being a sacred ritual. We are talking about a time when a fire was kept lit in the hearth for cooking all year round. Before Oíche Shamhna, the day of All-Hallows' Eve, or Halloween, the fire was quenched and the hearth cleared out. The following morning, to start the 'Celtic New Year' (Lá Samhna – 1 November) at home, embers were taken from the ashes of the bonfire and a new fire was re-kindled in the hearth. The ultimate sacred bonfire, from which you were lucky to get embers, was the fire at Tara, the seat of the High King. St Patrick recognised the prestige associated with High King Laoghaire's fire, when he audaciously lit his Christian paschal flame within sight of Tara.

The bonfire was also a chance to clear out the house of broken furniture or unwanted clutter. However, reducing old clutter was

NOVEMBER

not about the modern malaise of buying new clutter, it was to make room to accommodate the shepherds and herders, now returning to the bosom of their families for the winter.

The table was set for the whole re-united family, and also for a guest from the spirit world. A 'dumb supper' or 'feast with the dead' was served and windows and doors were left unlocked to welcome a passing spirit. Whether the passing spirit said 'trick or treat' when he or she called is not recorded! One thing we can assume is that the food on the table for the living and the dead was home-grown and home-cooked.

THE SAMHAIN TRADITION OF SCARING AWAY MALEVOLENT SPIRITS CONTINUES TODAY WITH THE DISPLAY OF A FACE ON A HOLLOW PUMPKIN.

T.S.

An overview of the work ahead in the garden this month:
Plant: garlic cloves
Sow out: broad beans
Harvest: spinach, endive, winter cabbage, cauliflowers, Brussels sprouts, celery, leeks, parsnips, Jerusalem artichokes and pumpkins

🍁 FIRST WEEK IN NOVEMBER 🍁

Treat yourself to an organic garden visit and learn more

'You ask me where I get my ideas. That I cannot tell you with certainty. They come unsummoned. Directly, indirectly – I could seize them with my hands – out in the open air, in the woods, while walking in the silence of the night…'

(Ludwig van Beethoven, 1770–1827)

As the gardening year slows down and October or Deireadh Fómhair ('end of harvest') is over, you might find yourself with time to look at other gardens, even bigger gardens. See how they grow; see what they grow. Techniques and ideas used by other gardeners may be learned from discussing experiences. Visiting gardens can be a unique learning opportunity that cannot be equalled by even the best gardening books.

IF YOU HAVE THE TIME, SPEND A FEW DAYS ON AN ORGANIC FARM

Around Ireland, a number of organic farmers and growers encourage guests to visit, stay for a few days or longer, and work on the farm in return for accommodation and a learning experience of growing on a larger scale than in most kitchen gardens. Such volunteers are known as 'WWOOF-ers' (World Wide Opportunities on Organic Farms). WWOOF Ireland co-ordinates the host farms and those wishing to volunteer in Ireland. Contact WWOOF Ireland at www.wwoofireland.ie or by post at WWOOF Ireland, Coomhola, Bantry, Co. Cork. The telephone number is +353 27 51254 (Tueday–Thursday, 9.30 a.m.–1.00 p.m.).

NOVEMBER

JOIN UP WITH YOUR LOCAL GIY GROUP AND TAG ALONG ON GARDEN VISITS

I have greatly enjoyed the visits organised by my local GIY group in Balbriggan – from the walled kitchen garden at Ardgillan Castle to large rural gardens and smaller suburban gardens like my own. The exchange of views can be very educational. The similar climate and soil of nearby gardens makes the visiting experience even more relevant. Information about all the GIY groups around the country can be found at www.giyireland.com.

LEARN ABOUT GROWING ORGANICALLY BY VISITING YOUR NEAREST ORGANIC CENTRE

We are fortunate in Ireland that there are a number of visitor centres around the country which provide demonstrations and train growers of all ages, including primary and secondary students, about growing food organically. These centres are generally run by dedicated volunteers who welcome enquiries (and help), provide a range of courses related to food and gardening, and cater for visitors.

The following are a few organic centres worth checking out:

- The Organic Centre: set in the heart of the north-west on a 7.7-hectare site with an organic garden, orchard and woodland, café, bookshop, seed catalogue and numerous useful courses (including FETAC Level 5), the Organic Centre is a great resource and major tourist attraction in the area. Details: Rossinver, Co. Leitrim; tel: +353 71 9854338; email: info@theorganiccentre.ie; www.theorganiccentre.ie

- Sonairte, the National Ecology Centre, is on a 4-hectare site near Laytown, Co. Meath. It includes a fabulous 250-year-old south-facing organic orchard and walled garden on the banks of the River Nanny. Many kitchen gardeners drop by to the garden, café or bookshop, or to stroll along the river bank woodland trail. Courses are available, too, and are well worth attending. Details: The Ninch, Laytown, Co. Meath; tel: +353 41 9827572; email: info@sonairte.ie; www.sonairte.ie

🍂 The Irish Seed Savers Association is on an 8-hectare site near Scarriff, Co. Clare, and was set up in 1981 to conserve and promote the many fruit and vegetable varieties which were near to extinction. The calendar of events and courses suits the nearby gardener well and are also, in my experience, very sociable. Details: Capparoe, Scariff, Co. Clare; tel: +353 61 921 856/866; email: info@irishseedsavers.ie; www.irishseedsavers.ie

🍂 Kerry Earth Education Project is based at Gortbrack Organic Farm near Tralee, Co. Kerry. It hosts farm visits and demonstrates a range of habitats and food production techniques. The main activities include helping schools nationwide to grow organic school gardens. To this end, with Bord Bia, it produced a DVD, which was sent to every school in Ireland, on setting up an organic school garden. Details: Gortbrack Organic Farm, Ballyseedy, Tralee, Co. Kerry; tel: +353 66 7137042 or 087 9246968; email: gortbrackorg@gmail.com; www.gortbrackorganicfarm.com

🍂 The County Wexford Organic Centre is on a 16-acre site near New Ross, Co. Wexford. It is run by former organic inspector and soil scientist Richard Mee, and grows food for a number of farmers' market stalls nearby. It also provides courses in small- and large-scale growing and sustainability generally. I have visited it a few times and the attractive wooden hall and shop are well used by visitors of all ages. Details: Cushinstown, Foulksmills, New Ross, Co. Wexford; tel: +353 51 428375; email: rmee@eircom.net; www.wexfordorganiccenter.com

NOVEMBER

🍂 The Nano Nagle Centre is between Mallow and Fermoy, Co. Cork. It is located on an organic mixed farm with livestock, fruit and vegetables. It also runs a wide range of courses about food growing and sustainability in general. Kitty Scully, who I know

SOME PLACES TO GO TO SEE FOOD GROW

1. THE ORGANIC CENTRE
19 ACRES OF GARDENS
www.theorganiccentre.ie

2. SONAIRTE ECOLOGY CENTRE
ORGANIC WALLED GARDEN
www.sonairte.ie

3. CARRAIG DÚLRA FARM
GLENEALY, CO. WICKLOW
www.dulra.org

4. WEXFORD ORGANIC CENTRE
NEAR NEW ROSS
www.wexfordorganiccenter.com

5. NANO NAGLE CENTRE
32 ACRES NEAR MALLOW
www.nanonagle
birthplace.ie

6. KERRY EARTH EDUCATION
PROJECT, BALLYSEEDY, TRALEE
www.gortbrackorganicfarm.com

7. AN t-IONAD GLAS
DROMCOLLOGHER, CO. LIMERICK
www.organiccollege.com

8. IRISH SEED SAVERS
SCARRIFF, CO. CLARE
www.irishseedsavers.ie

9. TRY WORKING ON AN
ORGANIC FARM.
www.wwoof.ie

10. JOIN A G.I.Y. GROUP TO
VISIT LOCAL GARDENS
www.giyireland.com

11. O.P.W. VICTORIAN
WALLED KITCHEN GARDEN
www.phoenixpark.ie

12. WALLED KITCHEN GARDEN
GLASNEVIN, DUBLIN 9.
www.botanicgardens.ie

13. COASTAL WALLED GARDEN
BALBRIGGAN-SKERRIES RD.
www.ardgillancastle.ie

14. AN GAIRDÍN, ORGANIC
ECOLOGY CENTRE, PORTUMNA
www.angairdin.com

T.S.

from visiting the centre, now co-hosts the RTÉ TV programme *How to Create a Garden*. Details: Mallow, Co. Cork; tel: +353 22 26411; email: enquiries@nanonaglebirthplace.ie; www.nanonaglebirthplace.ie

❧ Carraig Dúlra Organic Growing and Permaculture Farm, Glenealy, Co. Wicklow. Suzie and Mike Cahn encourage people to visit their farm, which is no ordinary organic farm (if there is such a thing). The farm is located on the slopes of Carraig Mountain near beautiful Glenealy on the road to Moneytown. They have also established an OOOOBY store (see the Third Week in July). Details: Glenealy, Co. Wicklow; tel: +353 404 69570; email: info@dulra.org; www.dulra.org

❧ An tIonad Glas, The Organic College, is situated in Drumcollogher, Co. Limerick. It runs courses on growing food and developing students' skills with a view to becoming professional growers. The courses run from October to September, and are supported by Co. Limerick VEC. Founder Jim McNamara is often seen on the TG4 series *Garraí Glas*, sharing his enthusiasm and expertise with Síle Nic Chonaonaigh and all of us watching at home. Details: Drumcollogher, Co. Limerick; tel: +353 63 83604; email: oifig@organiccollege.com; www.organiccollege.com

OTHER JOBS FOR THE WEEK THAT IS IN IT:

🌿 Cover outdoor growing parsley with a cloche to prolong availability of fresh parsley in winter. If the parsley is in a pot, then move it into the greenhouse or a bright porch.

🌿 Prepare any sites for hedge planting. I am planting box hedging in the front garden to frame the rowan trees and the rhubarb bed. The box will also complement the hornbeam hedge already growing at the front boundary of the garden.

The Bigger Picture:
Consider an Italian view of food

Food and talk of food occupies conversations in Italy in a similar way that GAA and the weather keeps conversation lively in most of Ireland. I was fortunate as Minister for Food and Horticulture to be able to represent Ireland with Bord Bia in Italy, given the importance of Italian restaurants and shops to Irish food exports. In Italy, however, the local people rarely talk of Italian food as a generic brand. Their loyalty to regional dishes takes precedence over national dishes and levels of food production.

In a restaurant in Turin, the capital of the Piedmont region, the favourite dessert is *panna cotta*, a regional speciality of sweetened cream served in gelatin. In eastern Liguria, a request for soup of the day will probably evoke claims of excellence for the regional *mesciua* made from chickpeas, beans and wheat grains. In Puglia, in the south, *purè di fave*, a broad bean purée, is a famous regional dish, while in Sicilia *panelle*, a chickpea fritter, is a popular street vendor food.

It is noticeable that the local food dishes are a result of generations of tradition and celebration of local ingredients in culinary evolution. There are also local fruit and vegetable varieties, such as the cherries of Modena in the north, which are the nearest thing to the proverbial Garden of Eden for any lover of cherries.

The Italian reaction to the homogenisation of food inspired by McDonald's was to counteract a 'fast food culture' with a 'slow food culture'. The founder of the Slow Food Movement is Carlo Petrini, a chef and (as he might say) an eco-gastronomist. He advocates that food education should begin with the 'pleasure principle' and says agriculture and nutritional culture are part of our identity. He describes genetic modification of food as the highest expression of unsustainable farming, based on monoculture and in conflict with biodiversity.

The objectives of the Slow Food Movement are to promote:

1. Taste
2. Clean and sustainable food production
3. Fairness for all involved

Carlo Petrini believes, not in producers and consumers, but that we are all 'co-producers'. A little like the GAA, the Slow Food Movement has spread to other countries. The world could do with more of the awareness which the Slow Food Movement brings to the production and enjoyment of many diverse drinks and dishes. I would describe Carlo Petrini as a kind of Italian Micháel Ó Muircheartaigh in terms of the reverence in which he is held throughout his country.

❧ SECOND WEEK IN NOVEMBER ❧

Propagating heritage cabbage cuttings and saving seeds

'Good hudwifes in sommer will save their own seedes,
Against the next yeere, as occasion needs.
One seede for another, to make an exchange,
With fellow lie neighbourhood seemeth not strange.'

(Thomas Tusser, farmer, 1573)

WHEN you begin to examine the diversity of crop varieties, you see that certain types suit large field-scale production, such as commercial Brussels sprouts, which all come good at the same time to suit the logistics of mechanical harvesting. Other crops like purple sprouting broccoli generate better value in a small garden as they produce florets little and often, ensuring a continuity of supply for daily hand harvesting.

Kitchen gardeners traditionally favour perennial fruit trees and bushes, as well as crops which are easily propagated from one year to the next or from which, when a crop goes to seed, some of that seed can be saved, stored and sown in the next growing season.

As I have mentioned in passing before, one variety of perennial cabbage which I have propagated is nigh impossible to buy at a garden centre or even online. It is a cut-and-come-again cabbage which grows like a bush. It is very sweet tasting – I know of children who think they hate all cabbage, but they eat and enjoy the sweet flavour of this heritage variety. Slips or cuttings of this cabbage have been passed along my mother's side of the family from John Flower in the nineteenth century, a great grand uncle who farmed at Colehill in Co. Longford, near Mullingar. John passed it on to his children, one of whom, Annie, passed it on to my mother's parents. In turn, my parents passed it on to me. Over three centuries, this

NOVEMBER

cabbage has been grown organically and has fed us through two world wars and all the other trials of life.

WHERE CAN ONE GET THIS VENERABLE PERENNIAL CABBAGE?

I am aware that Irish Seed Savers in Scariff, Co. Clare have this cabbage growing but their stocks are limited. Signing up for a course there may well be your best chance to take a cutting home (see www.irishseedsavers.ie). From time to time, I have a large bush of cabbage from which I take cuttings. I give these away at the Bord Bia Bloom Festival, for example. I presented one such cutting to then President of Ireland Mary McAleese in 2011, when she was visiting the GIY stand at Bloom. Mary and Martin McAleese have become renowned organic kitchen gardeners in their own right at this stage. Let me know if you wish to grow this perennial cabbage and I will send you a cutting when I have some to spare (see www.trevorskitchengarden.ie).

PLANTING A CUTTING TAKEN FROM THE PERENNIAL CABBAGE BUSH

Cuttings can be taken easily from the cabbage bush, once it has been growing through a year. It roots quite easily once the parent plant is growing well. At this time in November the peas and beans have been cleared from their patch where they grew throughout last summer. This is the patch I now lightly fork over and rake to start off the new brassica patch. Three cuttings from the parent cabbage bush is usually enough to grow new cabbage bushes which fill half of the brassica patch. The other half of the patch will be planted with purple sprouting broccoli next spring.

To make a cutting, I pull a healthy side shoot downwards towards the roots. It easily tears away from the parent plant. Ideally, the cutting will have leaves, a stem and a 'heel' with a long wound where the cutting was attached to the parent plant. If I just remove the older outer leaves to leave just four of the newest leaves, this cutting can be planted as is. The leaf removal is to ensure the cutting is under less pressure and can retain moisture, which evaporates from the leaf surface. If the cutting is larger than 15–20 cm (6–8 inches), then I get out a sharp kitchen knife to shorten it.

A sharp knife is useful for cutting a long diagonal slice from below the point where a leaf could grow down as far as possible towards the bottom of the cutting. This exposes as much fresh plant tissue as possible. This 'heel', as it is called, will hopefully become the root of the new plant. With a trowel, make an 8–10 cm (3–4 inch) thin hole in the soil and stand the cutting in the hole. Press in the soil around it to steady the cutting. Water it and leave it to take root.

After a few days, the leaves on the cutting may droop, but in a couple of weeks new leaves should start to appear. This indicates the cutting has rooted and the plant should grow from then on, especially when the days get a bit warmer in the spring.

If everlasting cabbage cuttings were taken last February and grown on in pots, they too can be planted in the new brassica patch now (see the Third Week in February). This perennial plant is very tolerant of being propagated at various times of the year, once the soil is not too wet or cold.

OTHER JOBS FOR THE WEEK THAT IS IN IT:

- Clear weeds from around apple and other fruit trees, and mulch with compost or leaf mould.

- Send for seed catalogues or check seed supplier websites to see what varieties might be worth ordering for spring planting.

NOVEMBER

The Bigger Picture:
Saving seed saves money and makes sense

As with the perennial cabbage above, there is no other way to preserve a non-commercially available variety other than by propagating the plant, saving seed from a parent plant or getting a present from somebody else who saves seed. Under EU rules, seed for sale has to be registered. Registration costs money. If that seed is not commercially in demand, the seed is unlikely to be registered. These threatened unregistered seed varieties need you and me, as well as organisations like Irish Seed Savers, to keep our diverse fruit and vegetable heritage alive.

Kitchen gardeners of yore knew all about saving seed. Those were the days long before garden centres, mail order companies and GIY meetings, when spare seeds were often swapped. Harvesting was not the end of the process for a medieval gardener; they then turned their attention to removing seeds from selected pods or fruits, and drying and storing them for sowing next year.

In the past, gardeners were also like talent scouts. If a plant showed unusually good characteristics, its seed could be the start of a new variety. The names of these new varieties were often called after the gardener or the gardener's employer or place of work. Mind you, I am curious to know how a French bean variety came to be called 'The Lazy Housewife'!

SAVING SEED: MAKING A START

Peas and beans are good plants from which to save seed in the beginning. Because they are largely self-pollinated, they are most likely to yield seeds which will be like the parent plant. Other self-pollinating vegetables include chicory, endive, lettuce and tomatoes.

Once pods of peas appear, tie a piece of string around the healthiest looking pods you wish to retain for seed, while you eat the rest. Before uprooting the plant after the harvest is finished, cut off the branch to which the seed pods are attached. Hang them in a dry dark shed in a loosely tied brown bag. In a week or two, check to see if all is well and dry. Separate out the seeds when dry and store them in a labelled paper envelope in a lunch box and in a cool place. I make space to store seeds in the fridge. Sow next year following the same instructions as those for the shop-bought seeds of a similar variety.

WHAT ABOUT WIND-POLLINATED OR INSECT-POLLINATED FRUIT AND VEGETABLE SEEDS?

The beet family and spinach reproduce by wind pollination, while the cabbage and onion families need insects like bees to pollinate them. As a result, there is an unpredictability to the offspring of these plants. In a way, this makes the seed saving involved with beets and brassicas more interesting. However, with my small garden, I will leave that experimentation to friends with spacious farms or big gardens. When you see the size of an enormous cabbage plant going to seed, you will see what I mean.

CAN SEED BE SAVED FROM AN F1 HYBRID VARIETY OF BRUSSELS SPROUT, FOR EXAMPLE?

The answer is yes, but the offspring could be very different from the parent. The F1 refers to the fact that it is a first generation cross. First crosses give predictably vigorous uniform plants with the best qualities of both parents. So saving seed will result in a variation of the traits of the parent plant. In other words, the process is a bit of a lottery. However, this is an aspect of what plant breeders do for a living, so sometimes the result is worth the effort.

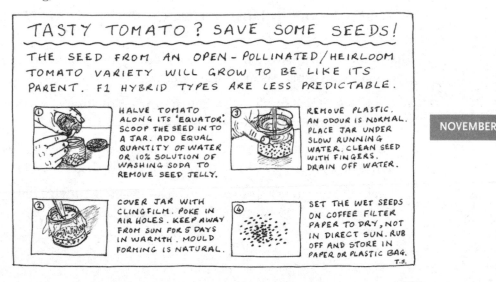

TASTY TOMATO? SAVE SOME SEEDS!

THE SEED FROM AN OPEN-POLLINATED/HEIRLOOM TOMATO VARIETY WILL GROW TO BE LIKE ITS PARENT. F1 HYBRID TYPES ARE LESS PREDICTABLE.

① HALVE TOMATO ALONG ITS 'EQUATOR'. SCOOP THE SEED INTO A JAR. ADD EQUAL QUANTITY OF WATER OR 10% SOLUTION OF WASHING SODA TO REMOVE SEED JELLY.

③ REMOVE PLASTIC. AN ODOUR IS NORMAL. PLACE JAR UNDER SLOW RUNNING WATER. CLEAN SEED WITH FINGERS. DRAIN OFF WATER.

② COVER JAR WITH CLINGFILM. POKE IN AIR HOLES. KEEP AWAY FROM SUN FOR 5 DAYS IN WARMTH. MOULD FORMING IS NATURAL.

④ SET THE WET SEEDS ON COFFEE FILTER PAPER TO DRY, NOT IN DIRECT SUN. RUB OFF AND STORE IN PAPER OR PLASTIC BAG.
T.S.

❧ THIRD WEEK IN NOVEMBER ❧

Choosing an apple tree to suit soil, climate and your own needs

'Even if I knew that tomorrow the world would go to pieces, I would still plant my apple tree.'

(Dr Martin Luther, German monk and theologian, 1483–1546)

WHEN planning my kitchen garden, I reckoned there was just enough space for one apple tree. I kept my fingers crossed that, living in a housing estate, there would be a couple of other apple trees growing nearby which flower at the same time for cross-pollination to take place. My neighbour had an apple tree but it had to make way for a building extension. Nonetheless, my solitary James Grieve apple tree has fruited beyond my wildest expectations. Local bees must know of other apple trees for cross-pollination to continue when my apple tree is in flower.

FACTORS TO BEAR IN MIND WHEN GROWING AN APPLE TREE:

- Choose a variety which has been successful in a similar soil, climate and aspect as in your garden.

- If another local apple grower is happy cultivating the same variety, chances of success are good.

- Ensure a good flow of air around the tree; mildew fungus likes damp and muggy conditions (see the First Week in October).

- Water the tree in dry spells to stop blossoms prematurely falling. Watering also helps to swell the ripening apples.

BEFORE CHOOSING A VARIETY, CONSIDER THE SIZE OF THE TREE

The cultivation of apple trees over thousands of years has become quite sophisticated. Breeding has resulted in over 3,000 varieties. Apart from the multiplicity of apple varieties, a branch of science (so to speak) has been developed where high-performing roots, like those of the native crab apple, have been grafted onto separate cultivated stems. This is a bit like a saloon family car being given a sports car engine, but the result is a diversity of dwarf trees, columnar trees, cordon trees, miniature container trees, vigorous rootstock trees, and so on.

Left to its own devices, my James Grieve tree, which has a very vigorous rootstock, would by now (almost twenty years on) have taken over the garden. To check the growth, the tree is pruned each winter so branches do not poke anybody's eye out and so that the height is kept at around 3 m. This is as far as I can reach by standing on the step ladder to pick the highest apples. See below for more about pruning.

A FEW VARIETIES I WOULD PLANT IF I HAD MORE SPACE:

Katya: this variety is Swedish but is known as Katy in the English speaking world. It is a daughter, one could say, of the James Grieve and Worcester Pearmain varieties. It has a refreshing flavour and texture, is medium sized, red and ripens well, even in a poor summer. The harvest is from late August to mid-September. The fruit keeps well on the tree over 2–3 weeks. Some people like to store the fruit in a fridge as the flavour is even more refreshing when the apple is cooled. It is mainly a dessert variety, but is also good stewed or used in baking.

Elstar: this is maybe not the easiest apple to grow, but the flavour is beautiful. It was developed in the Netherlands. Con Traas, at the Apple Farm, Cahir, Co. Tipperary, sells it at a few farmers' markets I have frequented. It is so crunchy and sweet; I was surprised it was Irish grown. I am told it also stores well, being a late cropper.

🍃 **Worcester Pearmain:** this parent of Katya is grown as one of many varieties in the Sonairte orchard. It sells well at Balbriggan Fish and Farmers' Market and at the Dublin Food Co-op. It has a slight strawberry flavour, and this flavour improves the longer it is left on the tree. Bred back in 1870, it is an early season variety and is most prolific around mid-September.

🍃 **Lady Sudely:** another favourite variety grown in the heritage orchard at Sonairte. In the Balbriggan Fish and Farmers' Market, customers tell me that this is how they remember apples tasting years ago. Again, it is an early apple so it will not store for more than a couple of weeks.

🍃 **Cox's Orange Pippin:** a sweet apple with a great history. Richard Cox, a retired horticulturalist and brewer, bred it first at Colnbrook, Slough, England in 1825. It has since become a parent to many other varieties which retain the Cox name in their titles. It does not do so well in the north of the country, I am told.

Other sweet dessert varieties I would like to try growing are: Mrs Perry and Honeyball (both available from Irish Seed Savers in Co. Clare), as well as Fiesta, Fortune, Jupiter and Red Devil. I'd be curious about Beauty of Bath, Jonogold, Crispin, Chivers Regal, Egremont Russet and Kidd's Orange Red. So many dessert varieties of apple, so few in the shops!

If I had space for separate varieties of cooking apples, I might plant Bramley's Seedling, Grenadier or Rev. W. Wilks. However, in a small garden, some of the varieties above perform well as dual-use or even triple-use apples; in other words, they can be used for cooking, making cider and juice, or as dessert apples.

WHY ARE THESE HERITAGE VARIETIES ABOVE NOT SOLD IN SUPERMARKETS?

People at Balbriggan Fish and Farmers' Market ask me why they can no longer get Beauty of Bath in the shops as an early apple variety. Apples from the southern hemisphere like Royal Gala and Pink Lady have found favour with supermarkets, which appreciate apples with a long shelf life. Customers have, as a result, got used to apples with a denser flesh, since hotter climates tend to grow these varieties. Irish apples contain about half the cells of those grown in hotter countries. As a result, the locally grown early varieties in particular do not store long enough to travel to centralised warehouses and out to the shops to sit on shelves for long periods. Unless you live near to a community orchard, or an organic centre (see the First Week in November), then your best bet, if you want to have a supply of real Irish dessert apples, is to plant a tree yourself in the next few weeks.

HOW TO USE AN APPLE SURPLUS IF THE VARIETY YOU GROW DOES NOT STORE WELL

The James Grieve apples I harvest taste great but start to go off after a week. Therefore, I make a point of giving many away as presents. I sell some at my local farmers' market. The rest I juice. I have discovered that the apples stew beautifully with a few raisins and a sprinkle of ground cinnamon; there is no need to add sugar. This makes a lovely dessert with a topping of vanilla ice cream or custard. I am now stewing in bulk and freezing multiple desserts for a taste of autumn later in the year and next spring. Chopped and bagged apple pieces can be frozen and are handy when thawed for apple-tart baking. Finally, many chutney recipes require apple as an ingredient (see the Fourth Week in October).

PRUNING AN APPLE TREE

Pruning a tree is not like a haircut. The objective is to keep the tree open as well as in balance so it does not look lopsided. If the tree is looking fine and branches are in nobody's way, then there may be no need to prune this year. However, here are a few tips to consider if you do decide on a dry winter's day to go out to prune with saw, lopper and secateurs to hand:

- Stand back and look at the tree to pinpoint the branches that are touching or that are making the tree look out of balance.

- Using the saw more than the secateurs, cleanly cut a branch here or there, which allows nearby branches space to develop and 'breathe'.

- Cut branches which are in the way, for example, blocking a footpath.

- Cut branches which are growing higher than a fruit picker on the available stepladder can reach. This is important for my James Grieve tree as apples which fall bruise easily.

- At the end look through the tree and imagine throwing a hat from one side to the other through the spaces between branches. (I have seen an experienced apple tree pruner do this in reality!)

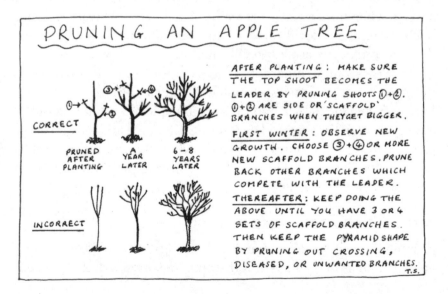

PRUNING AN APPLE TREE

CORRECT

PRUNED AFTER PLANTING / A YEAR LATER / 6 - 8 YEARS LATER

INCORRECT

AFTER PLANTING: MAKE SURE THE TOP SHOOT BECOMES THE LEADER BY PRUNING SHOOTS ①+②. ①+② ARE SIDE OR 'SCAFFOLD' BRANCHES WHEN THEY GET BIGGER.

FIRST WINTER: OBSERVE NEW GROWTH. CHOOSE ③+④ OR MORE NEW SCAFFOLD BRANCHES. PRUNE BACK OTHER BRANCHES WHICH COMPETE WITH THE LEADER.

THEREAFTER: KEEP DOING THE ABOVE UNTIL YOU HAVE 3 OR 4 SETS OF SCAFFOLD BRANCHES. THEN KEEP THE PYRAMID SHAPE BY PRUNING OUT CROSSING, DISEASED, OR UNWANTED BRANCHES.
T.S.

OTHER JOBS FOR THE WEEK THAT IS IN IT:

 Make a final cut of the lawn, or else prepare the ground if you are planning to sow a lawn next spring. The seedbed will probably sprout a few unwelcome weeds which can be hoed away before the grass seed is sown next year. My lawn is very small, but the cat appreciates lying on it on a sunny day!

 Prune raspberry canes. Cut out all the fruiting canes which have carried this season's crop as soon as possible. Tie new canes to the supporting framework so they do not catch in your clothes as you walk by. Remove weak and surplus canes.

The Bigger Picture:
Ode to the appetising apple from Asia

The genetics of the modern domestic apple can be traced back to the ancient apple forests in the mountains of eastern Kazakhstan and parts of adjacent countries. The predominant species found there is Malus sieversii and remnants of these forests still exist there today.

The Romans planted their apple trees wherever they conquered. Before the Normans took these Roman specimens to Ireland, the native Celts relied on the wild native crab apple for food and to make alcoholic beverages. As mentioned, there are over 3,000 distinct apple varieties, but only a couple of dozen of these form the bulk of commercial apple production worldwide.

WHAT IS STOPPING US FROM ACCESSING A MORE DIVERSE RANGE OF APPLES?

 A shortage of viable routes to the marketplace for any farmer or small-scale grower who has a few productive traditional apple trees. Solution: more farm shops and farmers' markets, and more local sourcing of fruit by shops, big and small.

🍃 Ireland has stricter brewing regulations compared to the UK, where small apple producers are allowed to make and sell up to 7,000 litres of cider without being liable for duty.

🍃 The lack of awareness and celebration of the diversity of taste and uses associated with all sorts of apple varieties. Currently apple promotion in Ireland is mainly about the Bramley, the green cooker which has gone to make many an apple tart in our houses down through the years. People will often have a definite opinion about their favourite car or TV programme, but how many could express their apple preferences beyond the Bramley? Now there is a conversation topic for when you are next chatting over a pint of cider or a glass of apple juice.

HOW SELF-SUFFICIENT IS IRELAND ON THE APPLE FRONT?

Bear in mind that the apple industry in Ireland, when you take away the small-scale gardeners like me, encompasses about forty professional growers. This translates to about 60 full-time jobs and just under 300 part-time and seasonal jobs. Production meets about 20 per cent of Irish demand. Although Ireland produces about 15,000 tonnes of apples, we export about 7,000 tonnes. We mostly produce cookers and yet the biggest demand is for dessert apples. Therefore, many of our Bramleys are sold abroad. Meanwhile, Ireland imports about 68,000 tonnes of apples annually. At this point in November, after all our apples have been gathered in, Irish retailers are importing from Belgium and the UK (Cox and Elstar), from China (Fuji), from France (Golden Delicious, Royal Gala, Granny Smith and Braeburn), from the USA (Mac Reds) and from Holland (Jonagored), although we have some home-produced Jonagored apples for sale as well.

FINDING IRISH-GROWN APPLES AMONG THE IMPORTS

The Irish dessert apple season starts at the end of August with Discovery (very juicy), and moves on to Worcester Pearmain (sweet), Katya (crunchy) and then Red Windsor, Elstar and Jonagored (all sweet and juicy). These latter two will carry through to the beginning of March. Meanwhile, Irish Bramley cookers will store for more than six months, so there is no excuse for not buying an Irish cooker. While waiting for the tree in the garden to grow, ask in the shops and markets for Irish-grown varieties you know to be in season.

❧ FOURTH WEEK IN NOVEMBER ❧

Going forth to divide and multiply a rhubarb crown

'Well Art is Art, isn't it? Still, on the other hand, water is water.
And east is east and west is west, and if you take cranberries
and stew them like applesauce they taste much more like
prunes than rhubarb does. Now you tell me what you know.'

(Groucho Marx, 1890–1977)

I'M not sure Groucho Marx had heard of a rhubarb variety called
Irish Giant which has stems that grow up to 1.5 m, and which
has stems as thick as a man's arm? Wherever this specimen grows,
it is unlikely to be found in a small kitchen garden. The rhubarb in
my front garden is not huge. Its ancestors, like all cultivated
rhubarb today, go back to ancient times in China where it was a
medicinal plant. The Venetian merchant traveller Marco Polo
(1254–1324), wrote about rhubarb in glowing terms and was, like
many others, keen to introduce it in Europe.

The name derives from a Greek description *rhabarbarum*
(roughly 'the plant from the River Volga area'). The eating of
rhubarb only became more popular when sugar became affordable.
The earliest recipe for rhubarb tart I could find was printed in 1807
by Maria Eliza Rundell. Only after that, in 1824, did south London
nurseryman Joseph Myatt develop the market for culinary rhubarb.
Myatt had a taste for rhubarb tarts, but also had a reputation for
growing and selling strawberry plants. He soon gained a reputation
for selling rhubarb crowns also, and the rest is rhubarb history.

Reasons for the growth of rhubarb's popularity in the Victorian
period:

🍂 Sugar became affordable for most people so they could sweeten
the sour rhubarb flavour.

🍂 Rhubarb ripened before other spring vegetables, making a change from winter-stored food.

🍂 Rhubarb was an impressive garden plant, with those big 'dinner plate' leaves.

🍂 Impressive growth was possible, helped by a good supply of horse manure (plentiful then).

🍂 Recipes for apple tarts and desserts were easily adapted to suit the exotic 'new' vegetable.

GROWING RHUBARB

My rhubarb grows in less-than-ideal conditions. The harvesting season for rhubarb is considered to be April to September. However, I do not harvest once June is out, as the oxalic acid levels rise, making the rhubarb more sour to taste. In any event, some Irish apples are nearly ripe by then and they require less sugar to make delicious desserts. Also, it is no harm to let the plant build up energy for the winter hibernation period and for growth again the following spring.

The ideal conditions for growing rhubarb are rich well-drained soil and in full sun. Lucky for me the rhubarb plant also tolerates shade, but this means the leaves are smaller and the yield is less per plant, too. With space precious in my garden, the three rhubarb plants I have are growing between a pair of rowan trees, and this patch is also in the shadow of the north-facing side of the house. However, the rhubarb still supplies me with many desserts every spring and early summer.

DIVIDING THE RHUBARB PLANT

Every four years or so, the rhubarb plant gets a notion that it is time to reproduce and go into retirement. It attempts to make flower heads and, if left alone, will go to seed and soon afterwards may die off. To give it a new lease of life, the crown can be divided to make the rhubarb think it is a young plant again with years of growth ahead. Every four years, therefore, take out a sharp spade, or even an axe, around this time of year. If you have the time and you have no axe, you could sharpen a spade. Dividing a rhubarb crown can also be done in January – if the ground is not frozen solid.

When the stems start to wither and get thinner and the leaves appear smaller, and once the leaves have rotted away and the plant is in its winter dormancy, it is time to prepare to divide the crown (the mass of roots which remain):

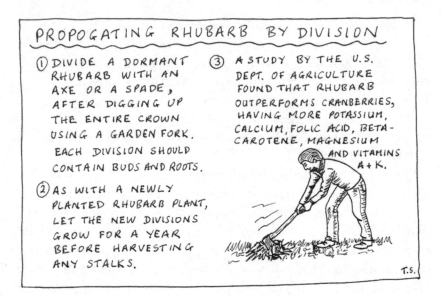

PROPOGATING RHUBARB BY DIVISION

① DIVIDE A DORMANT RHUBARB WITH AN AXE OR A SPADE, AFTER DIGGING UP THE ENTIRE CROWN USING A GARDEN FORK. EACH DIVISION SHOULD CONTAIN BUDS AND ROOTS.

② AS WITH A NEWLY PLANTED RHUBARB PLANT, LET THE NEW DIVISIONS GROW FOR A YEAR BEFORE HARVESTING ANY STALKS.

③ A STUDY BY THE U.S. DEPT. OF AGRICULTURE FOUND THAT RHUBARB OUTPERFORMS CRANBERRIES, HAVING MORE POTASSIUM, CALCIUM, FOLIC ACID, BETA-CAROTENE, MAGNESIUM AND VITAMINS A + K.

T.S.

Before dividing, prepare a hole (at least 3 ft away from any other rhubarb plant) for the spare half-crown to be planted, or, if the new spare crown is to be given to another gardener, find a pot large enough.

Dig up the existing crown. Avoid damage to the emerging buds.

- Place the crown steadily on the ground and, sharply and carefully, divide the crown in two.

- Add compost and, if drainage needs improving, add sand to the hole before replacing one half-crown in the original hole. The hole should be about 2 ft deep and 2 ft wide. The top bud should be 2 inches below the ground surface level.

- Refill the hole with fresh compost, firm it down and water it to settle the crown and soil around it.

- If planting the spare half-crown nearby to increase the size of the rhubarb bed, leave 3 ft between plants.

OTHER JOBS FOR THE WEEK THAT IS IN IT:

- Clean the glass and tidy in the greenhouse so plants can make the most of lower light levels. In this way, next spring will be less busy if the tidying is already done.

- Try out some new Christmas recipes using garden produce *before* your Christmas guests are subjected to experimental cuisine in a few weeks' time!

The Bigger Picture:
The golden age of hand tools on farms

It is hard to imagine that there are 230 types of spade. One ironworks in Co. Tyrone alone had patterns for such a range of spades, according to *A History of Irish Farming, 1750–1950* by Jonathan Bell and Mervyn Watson.

Before the Famine of the 1840s, 45 per cent of farms were between 1 and 5 acres in size. Many families cultivated and survived on an eighth of an acre. Although these farmers were very poor by today's standards in Ireland, they often had surprisingly good health. We know this from the reports of doctors who recorded the health of immigrant farmers arriving at Ellis Island in the 'New World' at that time. This reflects the all round nutritional value of the potato as a food and the value of water and some buttermilk as beverages, as this was all that most people had to live on at that time.

Hardly any of these families had a plough or a horse. A good farmer with a team of twelve men, each using a loy (a narrow traditional Irish spade), could turn one acre in one day. It was only after the Famine that, with widespread rural depopulation, larger agricultural holdings were created and ploughs became more widely used.

Records of crop yield after 1850 show yield per acre to be reduced, where ploughs replaced hand-dug tillage. A well-trained team of loy ploughmen could be more thorough per acre than one or two men with a pair of horses pulling a plough. On the other hand, the larger size of fields and holdings made dependence on the loy for ploughing too slow, as well as being very hard work.

An 1848 report of a debate at the Rotunda in Dublin highlights the popularity of the spade culture in farming at the time. The motion being debated was 'That the spade is better than the plough'. Irrespective of the debate, the demise of spade work was by that time already well underway. In 1760, there were ninety mills or ironworks making a diversity of spade designs to suit various tasks, soil types, and so on. By 1845, there were just sixty-seven such mills in operation.

So, whether we are dividing a rhubarb crown, digging out compost or making a raised bed, spare a thought for the old blacksmiths who had a working knowledge of up to 230 spade types, beyond long and short handles, and beyond whether the farmer was a 'left footer' or a 'right footer'.

Thoughts from other kitchen gardeners

GERRY DALY

The voice of Irish gardening advice, Gerry Daly's RTÉ radio and television shows were influential for many present-day gardeners. Outside of media work, Gerry has a garden design and nursery business. For over twenty years, he has written for the *Sunday Independent*, and he edits the magazine *The Irish Garden*, along with the website www.garden.ie.

Describe the location in which you grow your own food:

In the open ground of the vegetable garden.

Which food do you look forward to harvesting most and why?

Fruit is a favourite as it is varies from season to season.

Which garden tool do you value most and why?

I value the spade because it is the most important multi-purpose tool.

What motivates you to undertake the work involved in growing food?

It has been my lifetime work and career and I have a family background in growing food.

What advice would you give to a person considering growing their own food?

Don't bite off more than you can chew, in any sense!

Have you an aspiration for the future in relation to food?

I look forward to continuing to grow much of my own food as nothing beats the freshly picked sample for flavour.

NOVEMBER

DEIRDRE JUDGE

Deirdre is one of a new generation of food growers who has enthusiastically taken up the opportunities to both grow healthy food and to develop, with her husband and friends, a positive community spirit. She has an allotment under the recent allotment initiative in Skerries, Co. Dublin.

Describe the location in which you grow your own food:

I've been growing my own food since March 2011 in the Skerries allotments which are on the Golf Links Road just outside Skerries in North County Dublin. The allotments are run by Fingal Co. Council and we pay a rent of €50 per year for a 10 m x 5 m plot.

Which food do you look forward to harvesting most and why?

This is a hard question to answer as I get a thrill out of almost everything I manage to harvest! The excitement at excavating those first new potatoes, the wonderful sweetness of the first podded peas, the triumph of finally pulling some properly sized carrots (after some earlier failures), the strange thrill of unearthing something entirely new like Jerusalem artichokes (and having to learn how to cook them) – all of these and many others are things I look forward to.

Which garden tool do you value most and why?

I'm tempted to say my compost bin! It's just a simple, plastic one that we bought in a garden shop but I love it and can't imagine now how I went years without one in the garden at home. When I think of all the wonderful stuff we were throwing out and how sadly depleted the soil in the garden had become! I love the idea of putting back into the soil what I take out – this is the main way to ensure good healthy produce year after year.

What motivates you to undertake the work involved in growing food?

The desire to have good quality food on the table, freshly picked when it is at its best, and free from horrible sprays and additives continue to be my main reasons for growing my own food. Next would be the economics of it, especially in these straightened times. I have been greatly motivated and inspired by GIY Ireland and its website, GIY Skerries and its various speakers, blogs and websites such as Trevor Sargent's trevorskitchengarden.ie, and the example set by local organic growers at the Skerries and Balbriggan farmers' markets.

What advice would you give to a person considering growing their own food?

Just get out there and start somewhere, no matter how small! Get some lettuce or herb seedlings from a garden centre, plant them in a trough outside the back door or wherever you can and see them grow. Or, better still, plant some seeds, even if it's just to have a little parsley in a pot, and watch what happens. Join your local GIY group; if there isn't one, why not start one?

Have you an aspiration for the future in relation to food?

I would love to see our children being fed more healthily than most of them are at the moment. It is truly horrific to see the increasing numbers of obese children on our streets. I would love to see them becoming more aware of what goes into their bodies and what they need to be eating to grow up strong and healthy and happy. I would love to see children learning about and experiencing the actual growing of the food they eat, so that they can appreciate where it comes from, and what is entailed in producing the best quality and the best tasting food.

NOVEMBER

Nollaig ❧ Christmas

The Month of the Winter Solstice

HIS IS THE MONTH of rebirth, symbolised by the infant Jesus in the manger, who is remembered on 25 December or when the Sun is 'reborn' after the shortest day, the Winter Solstice, on 20 or 21 December. Nollaig is derived from the Latin *natalicia* or 'nativity'. The English language 'December' is less logical. Why Julius Caesar, as Roman Emperor, did not alter December (meaning tenth month) to mean twelfth month is bizarre. Soon after he set January to be the first month instead of March, he was assassinated. So perhaps he had intended correcting the confusing titles of other Roman months before Brutus brutally intervened.

The shortest day is also the beginning of the druidic Yuletide, which lasted twelve days, 20 to 31 December. Yuletide was celebrated by many peoples, from the Celts to the Scandinavians and from the Romans to the Hopi Indians of North America. This was the time when the druids believed the sun stood still, hence 'solstice' from Latin *sol* (sun) and *sistere* (to stand still). The Anglo-Saxons called the month Yule monath and they believed that the sun god was reborn in the underworld at this time. To celebrate that food could be grown under a new brightening sun in the year to come, gifts were exchanged from the preserved or stored harvest and homes were decorated in preparation for celebrations, now that any doubts about the sun's return were dispelled.

The Romans called this time of year Saturnalia, which lasted a week or more in honour of the god Saturn, who was the son of Caelus, the sky god (from where the word 'celestial' comes) and Terra, the earth goddess. The Greeks called this same earth goddess Gaia.

In the 1970s, Gaia's name was used to popularise the theory devised by chemist James Lovelock and co-developed by microbiologist Lynn Margulis. The Gaia theory says that the earth strives to maintain a stability of habitability by self-regulating oceanic salinity and global surface temperatures, etc. The Gaia theory is now applied to research in earth system science, biogeochemistry and climate change.

Whatever belief systems those who grew food in the past held, they all had respect for the earth in common. This respect was sometimes expressed as fear, as in the Irish expression, 'Ní fuacht go Nollaig' (At Christmas the real cold begins). So thank God for the warmth of the Yule log and the warm symbolism of the Christmas wreath, the tree, the holly and the ivy, not to mention the romance of the mistletoe – *Beannachtaí na Nollag*/Happy Christmas!

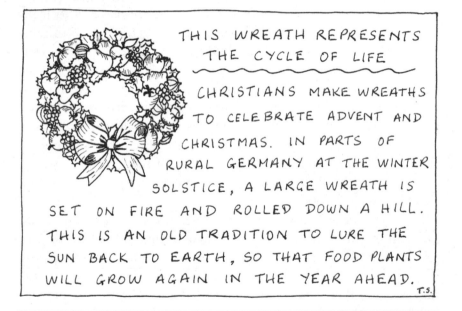

THIS WREATH REPRESENTS THE CYCLE OF LIFE

CHRISTIANS MAKE WREATHS TO CELEBRATE ADVENT AND CHRISTMAS. IN PARTS OF RURAL GERMANY AT THE WINTER SOLSTICE, A LARGE WREATH IS SET ON FIRE AND ROLLED DOWN A HILL. THIS IS AN OLD TRADITION TO LURE THE SUN BACK TO EARTH, SO THAT FOOD PLANTS WILL GROW AGAIN IN THE YEAR AHEAD. T.S.

An overview of the work ahead in the garden this month:
Plant: it's not too late to plant garlic cloves.
Harvest: swedes, winter cabbages, Brussels sprouts, spinach, celery, leeks, parsnips, endive, kale, cauliflowers and Jerusalem artichokes

DECEMBER

🍁 FIRST WEEK IN DECEMBER 🍁

Enjoying home-grown seed sprouts
– a healthy winter crop

'Wanted! A vegetable that will grow in any climate, will rival meat in nutritive value, will mature in 3–5 days [and] may be planted any day of the year…'

(Dr Clive M. McKay, Professor of Nutrition, Cornell University, USA)

A T this time of year, I set up a three-tier seed sprouting kit on the kitchen windowsill and buy a packet of mung beans in a local health food store. There are still cabbage leaves and leeks outdoors in the garden and I have stored vegetables like onions, garlic and potatoes in the shed. Pickled beetroot and frozen beans and peas are on standby also.

With stocks running low, it was surprisingly easy for me to learn how to augment the produce from the garden with bean sprouts grown in the kitchen. Certain seeds, like mung beans, chick peas and lentils, are very easy to sprout. Basically, sprouting means regularly rinsing your chosen seeds with drinking-quality water, letting them grow for a few days in the kitchen, and then harvesting this healthy fresh food.

And what about the incidents in Germany in 2011 where E-coli poisoning was traced back to a commercial bean sprout production? Well, the German authorities must follow up any suspicions they have. Meanwhile, no Irish bean sprouts have ever been suspected of being anything other than health-enhancing and delicious.

SUGGESTIONS FOR COOKING BEAN SPROUTS

🍁 Stir fry with other vegetables (alfalfa, clover, radishes, mung beans, lentils).

- Stir into soups or stews for a couple of minutes before removing from the boil (mung beans, lentils).
- Combine in hot rice dishes (fenugreek, lentils, mung beans).
- Steam and serve with butter (mung beans, lentils).

HOW TO SPROUT BEANS AT HOME WITHOUT A KIT

Equipment needed:

- Large clear glass jar (an old empty coffee jar perhaps)
- Nylon or muslin porous cloth and elastic to secure it like a lid
- A fine sieve and running water fit for drinking

A HEALTHY WAY TO SAVE MONEY

WATER FILLS THE TOP, FILTERS DOWN, COLLECTS IN RESERVOIR AT THE BOTTOM.

SOME SEEDS ARE GOOD FOR SOWING BUT NOT FOR SPROUTING. FIRST, BUY SEED PACKETS PRODUCED WITH SPROUTING IN MIND.

A 3-TIER SPROUTER KIT IS USEFUL FOR NEAT SUCCESSIONAL BEAN AND SEED SPROUTING.

RINSE THE BEANS TWICE A DAY AND LIE THE JAR ON ITS SIDE TO HELP SPROUTS.

MUSTARD AND CRESS GROW WELL ON DAMP TISSUE OR KITCHEN PAPER.

T.S.

Put a handful of seeds or beans in the bottom of the jar and cover them with plenty of water. Leave them to soak overnight. In the morning, pour the seeds into a sieve and rinse well with water. Be sure to remove any dead or broken seeds or pieces of debris. Return the rinsed seeds to the empty jar, secure the cloth lid and leave the jar on its side on the windowsill. Every morning and evening, rinse the seeds in the sieve and return them to germinate in the jar, remembering to replace the cloth lid each time. When white shoots appear from the germinated seeds, in three or four days, the harvest is ready.

HOW TO SPROUT BEANS WITH A KIT

Most health food stores sell kits for sprouting beans. The kit I bought is three tiered. Each tier is designed to grow a handful of bean sprouts at intervals of, say, two days, so that the kitchen always has a succession of fresh sprouts for salads or for cooking. The kit makes it easy to maintain this growing of sprouts in succession. Each morning the bowl on top of the kit is filled with fresh water. This water cascades through holes, rinsing each tier of germinating beans in turn. This water collects in a container below the lowest tier of beans. Then this used water is discarded in readiness for the repeat process that evening. And so it goes until each layer is ready for harvesting.

Before using a sprouting kit or a jar, follow the same routine – soaking the beans overnight, and rinsing and cleaning the beans in a sieve before setting about the process of sprouting.

SOME SEEDS AND BEANS WHICH SPROUT WELL

Seed Name	Ready In...	Growing Tips and Notes
Alfalfa	5–6 days	Rich in organic vitamins and minerals
Fenugreek	3–4 days	Have quite a strong 'curry' taste. Best mixed with other sprouts.
Aduki beans	3–5 days	Have a nutty 'legume' flavour
Chick peas	3–4 days	Need to soak for eighteen hours to fully swell. Renew water twice in this time.
Lentils	3–5 days	Try all types – red, green, brown and Chinese. Good eaten young.
Mung beans	3–5 days	Soak for at least fifteen hours. Keep in the dark for a sweeter sprout.

OTHER JOBS FOR THE WEEK THAT IS IN IT:

🍂 Firm the soil around Brussels sprouts and remove yellowing leaves as a precaution against grey mould.

🍂 Put nets in place over brassicas to prevent hungry pigeons wreaking havoc. However, do put out food for the birds. A good bird population in the garden helps to control snails, leather-jackets and aphids, etc.

🍂 Pot up some roots of mint and chives and bring them into the greenhouse or a sunny porch to lengthen their growing season – so as to have some more fresh herbs over the winter months.

The Bigger Picture:
Sprouts have a footnote in naval history

Ancient manuscripts from about 3,000 BC refer to bean sprouts not just as a food. The Emperor of China reportedly made medicinal claims for bean sprouts as being a treatment for muscular cramps, digestive disorders and weakness of the lungs. Even today, Chinese and other Asian communities, especially in mountainous areas, rely on sprouted seeds and beans as sources of fresh vitamins, enzymes and energy in winter. By this time of year, the stores of the autumn harvest have often run low.

Historically, the Europeans had a poorer awareness of nutrition than their Asian contemporaries. Clear evidence of this was the poor diets which caused the menace of scurvy for four hundred years before the late eighteenth century, especially among sailors when sea voyages began to be extended to two or three years. Scurvy is caused by a lack of ascorbic acid (vitamin C) and is first recognised by a lowered resistance to infection and a tendency to bleed easily. In severe cases it leads to weakness, weight loss, painfully swollen joints, bleeding gums, loosened teeth, bleeding under the skin, and a severe sensitivity to sounds and smells.

DECEMBER

Explorer Vasco da Gama lost two thirds of his crew to scurvy on his way from Portugal to India in 1499. Fellow Portuguese explorer Ferdinand Magellan lost 80 per cent of his crew to scurvy crossing the Pacific. A four-year British expedition, led by Sir George Anson in 1740, began with nearly 2,000 sailors. It finished with just 600. Of the 1,400 who died, 4 died in battle, a handful from injuries and the rest from scurvy and other vitamin deficiencies.

As a result of these horrific losses at sea, various measures were introduced to give sailors a better diet. Fruit and vegetable gardens on the decks of ships were tried, but were inadequate. Then unpasteurised beers and ales were administered – leading to several navigational errors! It was the Scottish naval surgeon James Lind (1765–1823) and Captain James Cook (1728–1779) who devised a specially formulated malt made by cooking sprouted seeds like cress and mustard at a low heat to boost the health of sailors on long sea voyages. Thanks in part to bean sprouts, Captain Cook succeeded in circumnavigating the globe in three years without losing a single sailor to scurvy. After that, lemons and limes were found to also prevent scurvy. Large supplies of limes were procured from the British tropical colonies, which duly replaced the need to prepare bean sprouts on board.

Meanwhile, on land, scurvy continued to be an issue. During World War I, British and Indian soldiers fighting in Mesopotamia (mainly Iraq today) also succumbed to scurvy. It was found that dried leafy vegetables and legumes were no help because they were not fresh. However, fresh pea and bean sprouts did prevent scurvy. Beans and seeds for sprouting were also easier to transport to the front than citrus fruits. Back at the hospitals, British doctor John Wiltshire found that bean sprouts also cured scurvy faster than citrus fruits. Research since then has increased our knowledge of the value of eating sprouted seeds, not just as a good source of vitamin C and other nutrients, but also, according to Dr Clive M. McKay of America's Cornell University, to stimulate the body's inherent self-cleansing and self-healing abilities. McKay has done considerable research into the nutritional merits of bean sprouts.

🍂 SECOND WEEK IN DECEMBER 🍂

For peat's sake, collect fallen leaves to make leaf mould

'Leaf mould: a nitrogen-rich material consisting of decayed leaves, etc., used as a fertilizer.'

(Collins English Dictionary, 2009)

IT is natural for me to want to tidy up the garden a bit, with Christmas not far away and with it the prospect of a visitor or two bringing season's greetings. It is notable how some visitors tend to have a keen interest in looking around the garden for exactly the time it takes to smoke a cigarette! For whatever reason, now is a good time to sweep and shovel up leaves which are surplus to requirements, on pavements and on the lawn. Remember not to disturb any pile of leaves which may be a home to a hibernating hedgehog.

MAKING GOOD USE OF FALLEN LEAVES TO MAKE LEAF MOULD

Leaf mould takes one, two or sometimes three years to go from being a collection of damp leaves to a friable brown loam. This is an excellent and attractive mulch or soil enhancer and in appearance it resembles moss peat. Making leaf mould is much slower than a compost heap of mixed organic materials, which tends to heat up and is ready to be dug into the soil within a year.

Leaves are slower to rot because they contain lignin, which is difficult for bacteria to break down. Lignin is broken down by fungi which work slower than bacteria. Hence leaves are best kept separate from the compost heap, once they are collected together.

Having a small garden, I collect the leaves in jute bags or a big thick plastic bag (which I can re-use year after year). I then tie the top

DECEMBER

311

and stick a few holes in it so air can come and go. The minimum transformation time is about a year or longer, depending on the toughness of the leaves in question. Well-decayed beech leaves produce a slightly alkaline loam. Leaf mould consisting of oak leaves takes considerably longer to break down and will give an acid loam.

In a larger garden, it is a good idea to build a simple leaf-mould container. The most common arrangement is to have four wooden posts in the ground and to surround them with chicken wire tied to the posts to form retaining sides. Two or three of these containers are handy so each year's leaf fall can be gathered in a space and left undisturbed for a couple of years to rot down before it is needed in the garden.

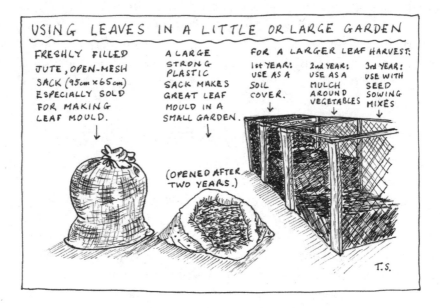

USING LEAVES IN A LITTLE OR LARGE GARDEN

FRESHLY FILLED JUTE, OPEN-MESH SACK (95cm x 65cm) ESPECIALLY SOLD FOR MAKING LEAF MOULD.

A LARGE STRONG PLASTIC SACK MAKES GREAT LEAF MOULD IN A SMALL GARDEN.

(OPENED AFTER TWO YEARS.)

FOR A LARGER LEAF HARVEST:

1st YEAR: USE AS A SOIL COVER.

2nd YEAR: USE AS A MULCH AROUND VEGETABLES

3rd YEAR: USE WITH SEED SOWING MIXES

T.S.

USES FOR MATURE FRIABLE LEAF MOULD

🍂 Mulch around trees, shrubs and plants. Apply a layer 8–10 cm (3 inches) thick to make an effective weed suppressant.

312

🍂 Improve soil structure before planting shrubs, hedging or trees. Dig in and mix leaf mould with the soil.

🍂 Make a potting or even a seed-sowing compost.

COMFREY AND LEAF MOULD POTTING COMPOST

1. This recipe is printed in Joy Larkcom's authoritative *Grow Your Own Vegetables* and was developed by organic gardener Terry Marshall. The main ingredients are leaf mould and comfrey, preferably using the Russian comfrey cultivar 'Bocking 14'.
2. Cut the leaves of well-established comfrey plants in early autumn.
3. Take a strong plastic sack and put in a layer roughly 7.5 cm (3 inches) deep of well-rotted leaf mould, ideally twelve to eighteen months old.
4. Cover with a similar thickness of comfrey leaves, pressed down lightly.
5. Alternate comfrey and leaf mould layers until the sack is full.
6. Tie the sack at the neck, make a few ventilation holes with a garden fork and leave in a sheltered place until spring, when it will be ready for use.

NOT USING PEAT TO MAKE POTTING COMPOST – PRESERVING OUR BOGS

The old Victorian gardeners had a preference for leaf mould made from beech leaves as an ingredient for making potting compost. It was really only in the 1940s when the international reliance on horticultural peat taken from bogs took off. About 2 per cent of the earth's landmass is the type of bog which is also called peatland. Finland has the largest peat bog area, followed by Canada, Ireland and Sweden. The Irish Peatland Conservation Council (www.ipcc.ie) represents the views of many people who value bogs for their unique wildlife habitats, as carbon sinks (natural reservoirs) and as sponges to control water flows and prevent flash flooding. They ask gardeners to sign a pledge not to use peat in their gardens. I signed up and so far, so good! However, I do not get around to making up seed and potting compost every time. Luckily the garden centres do stock peat-free composts as the protection of peatland habitats is important for many of their customers now.

OTHER JOBS FOR THE WEEK THAT IS IN IT:

🌿 Lift any remaining carrots and swedes for use or storage.

🌿 Sow winter salads in a protected place – in a polytunnel, greenhouse or under a cloche.

🌿 Make sure compost bins are covered to prevent rain leaching nutrients away. A cover over the compost of cardboard and old carpet is also a way of keeping the temperature up so that the microbes can more quickly work at decomposing the organic matter.

The Bigger Picture:
Organic farming – an encouraging report

Every September I like to go along to the National Ploughing Championships held on a large farm somewhere in Ireland. The dominant impression is created by the big and (temporarily) shiny farm machinery sending out the message that increasing the size of the (conventional) farm is the only way to go. The big picture worldwide is far more diverse. Eighty-five per cent of farmers worldwide are what we might call smallholders, farming without chemicals. Over 1.5 billion small-scale farmers have farms which are less than 2 hectares (about 5 acres) in size (Kathmandu Declaration, Nepal, April 2009, www.landcoalition.org).

In 2005, the UN, the World Bank and the World Health

Organisation, plus others like the UN Food and Agricultural Organisation, and the governments of 110 countries, co-sponsored an exhaustive study to set out the best way in which we can all feed humanity and achieve environmental sustainability. The study (the International Assessment of Agricultural Knowledge, Science and Technology for Development (IAASTD) report) involved 400 scientists and 580 authors, and the finished report runs to 2,500 pages.

It has been endorsed by fifty-eight countries so far, including Ireland, the UK and France. The report has a number of key messages:

- Small farmers are key to global food security.
- There is an urgent need for a major shift towards ecological agriculture.
- Multi-functionality in farming is important to ensure a resilient food supply.
- Food sovereignty is not enough as a goal; the aim must be safe food as well.
- Women will be as vital in agriculture in the future as they were in the past.
- Research must be practical.

These messages are an encouragement for farming that is organic and mixed. Some of the GM commercial companies like Syngenta did not support the conclusions. However, other big players like Unilever remained involved. Some pro-GM governments like Australia, Canada and the USA had reservations but did welcome the IAASTD report in the end.

Never before has the UN endorsed as strong a report advocating the need for organic agriculture. To quote Dr Hans Herren, co-chair of the IAASTD report, 'The question is not can organic farming feed the world. When all is said and done, we now know that organic farming must feed the world.'

☙ THIRD WEEK IN DECEMBER ☙

Gardening with Yuletide decorations and a festive tree in mind

'A society grows great when people plant trees
in whose shade they know they shall never sit.'

(Anonymous)

IHAVE always liked the idea of having an evergreen tree growing in the garden, which I could pot around this time every year and take inside, rooted and living, to be decorated, returning it to the garden after Christmas. Having a garden too small for a full-sized tree brings another meaning to the well-known quote above. The Christmas tree in my garden is too small to have anything other than a small cat sit in its shade.

BUYING A CHRISTMAS TREE IN A POT WITH A VIEW TO MAKING IT A GARDEN PLANT

Garden centres and mail order companies make it relatively straightforward to purchase a Christmas tree in a pot. Most of these 'baby trees', left to their own devices in open ground, would eventually grow up to 40–70 m tall, in the case of the Noble Fir (*Abies procera*), or 25 m for a Scots Pine (*Pinus sylvestris*). The growth rate can be rapid too. The European (Norway) Spruce grows at a rate of one metre a year, for example. These traditional festive tree varieties are not really suitable as long-term plants for the small garden, but they could be used for a second Christmas before being moved on to a bigger garden or a woodland environment.

A DWARF VARIETY

For a long-term tree which grows outside after Christmas, get a dwarf variety. The dwarf Christmas tree growing in my garden has no name, as it was a present and came without a label. However, it is conical, with blue-green pine needles, and lends itself to being decorated once it is indoors. For eleven months it grows (slowly) in the soil at the end of the raspberry patch beside the path.

To move a dwarf Christmas tree indoors

First acquire a clean black bucket (I use one similar to those used by florists to display bunches of flowers in water). You will also need a sharp spade. Put 3 cm (1 inch) or so of soil into the bottom of the bucket. Water this soil so it is damp and will act as a cushion for the tree roots. Dig straight down around the roots of the tree within a circumference no bigger than the bucket. Carefully, using the spade to lift and the other hand to hold the root ball together, place the tree, with the soil surface just below the level of the rim, in the bucket. Fill up the gaps with soil so the tree is secure and looking well in the black pot or bucket. Clean the bucket of soil on the outside and bring the tree indoors for decorating.

Buying a semi-dwarf pine tree

Cross-breeding the European Black Pine *Pinus nigra* with the Japanese *Pinus densiflora* has resulted in a cultivar called 'Pierrick Brégeon'. It has been sold since 1990 under the name 'Brepo'. Because it grows so slowly, it can be planted in a tub or pot for the patio. It is hardy enough to survive winter frosts, even in a pot. It can also be planted in open ground, where it will eventually grow into a 1m in diameter globe. Decorating a globe-shaped Christmas tree would make a change from the Victorian norm of a conical-shaped tree.

USING GARDEN GROWTH FOR CHRISTMAS DECORATIONS

Before Queen Victoria and her husband Prince Albert made Christmas trees popular, the Irish tradition was to bring foliage, mainly holly, into the house as decorations. In pre-Christian times, evergreen foliage symbolised the hoped-for return of spring. The Romans had a similar tradition using laurel and bay.

If my garden was bigger, I could grow a holly tree (*Ilex aquifolium*) like the one in my brother's suburban garden. This is a medium-sized tree growing to fifteen metres tall. Folklore records that the fairies get annoyed if a person misuses holly, such as by tying a bough to a rope to drag it down the chimney to remove soot. It seems the fairies would prefer if we used gorse for that task! The Irish name for holly, *cuileann*, is found in many placenames, such as Ballycoolin, the 'homeland of the holly'.

What I do have in abundance is ivy (*helix*). In fact, this time of year provides a good opportunity to cut back and control the spread of ivy. The best of these cuttings can be used over Christmas for decorations – around picture and door frames, in wreaths and to decorate a Yuletide candle or table centrepiece.

It is interesting to note that Christian authorities did not permit ivy in the house long ago because of the strong connection it had with pagan celebrations. Later on, however, ivy became a symbol for people who cling to God for support, just like the ivy clings to other plants and structures to reach the light.

OTHER JOBS FOR THE WEEK THAT IS IN IT:

- You know the soil is too wet to dig if it sticks to your boots. If this is the case, perhaps tidy the garden, store and check stores of produce, work in the greenhouse, repair woodwork and tools, and cut and stack firewood – until the sun and wind dries the soil enough to be workable again.

- Continue to collect fallen leaves and store them away in a chicken wire pen or in bags, plastic or hessian, to break down into next year's leaf mould.

The Bigger Picture:
How your kitchen garden can save you money

During recessionary times, it is not unusual to meet people or to be someone who is facing the horrible choice of whether to pay an instalment of the interest-only mortgage or put food on the table. A householder speaking on the radio recently said his aim was always to protect his family and keep the 'wolf from the door'. Now he only has dry breakfast cereal to feed his children. 'To tell the truth,' he said, 'the wolf is now in the house.'

Hopefully, this week at least some small money can be saved in households by using garden and hedgerow growth like ivy as Christmas decorations. Christmas is an expensive time and more significant savings are possible for many people if a frugal approach is taken to shopping, storing, preserving, cooking and kitchen gardening.

The Irish book *Waste Not, Want Not – Beating the Recession in the Home* by Rosemary Ryan gives good advice: 'If you find your income has reduced and you have to be more selective when shopping, plan your shopping wisely. Look out for bargains and ask for a discount. Make a list before you go…And, finally, leave the credit card at home' (p. 5).

You could save even more money if your garden or allotment (and not the shop) is the first place you visit when your kitchen cupboard is bare. This may seem obvious, but it is worth thinking about what extra the garden, the balcony, the window box or the bucket could grow. I am told by visitors to China that re-useable containers of all sorts are used as food growing spaces in urban and rural dwellings over there.

Historically, in wartime, the resourcefulness of people in producing healthy food is now seen as being as vital a factor in victory. In 1943 the British Ministry of Food published a booklet called 'Wise Eating in Wartime'. The turn of phrase in the following is a bit dated but the advice is still valid: 'An ounce of vitamin C is worth an inch of lipstick. It not only gives the skin a glow, but it helps it to heal. It keeps away infection, particularly from the so-called mucous membranes, such as the lining of the mouth…For a daily supply of vitamin C we must look first to raw cabbage leaves, raw broccoli and raw Brussels sprouts, made up in salads.'

The Environmental Protection Agency tells us that at least 30 per cent of food bought ends up being wasted. The Victorian food writer Mrs Beeton once wrote: 'Great care should be taken that nothing is thrown away, or suffered to be wasted in the kitchen, which might by proper management be turned to good account.'

Great care could equally be taken in the kitchen garden. The outer leaves of certain vegetables are often discarded, generally because people don't realise that they are edible and because they look less attractive than the parts normally eaten. I recall steaming leafy home-grown turnip tops and being surprised at how delicious they were with a bit of butter and some grated nutmeg or a dash of soya sauce; likewise with the leaves of beetroot and broccoli. Pods of peas and broad beans are perfectly good for making a vegetable stock, and leek tops, once cooked and liquidised, make a delicious ingredient in soups.

However, the growing of food does require an outlay of cash normally. This is why the booklet *Growing Organic Food on a Budget* by Jojo Norris was produced by Garden Organic in the UK (www.gardenorganic.org.uk). It is full of do-it-yourself tips to save money growing it yourself, such as:

- Put an ad on a local shop or library notice board looking for plant pots.

- Try food processing or drinks factories for plastic containers that make good water butts.

🌿 Make plant labels by cutting yoghurt pots or old Venetian blinds into strips.

🌿 Use urine/water (1:20), nettles or grass cuttings as a compost activator.

🌿 Make your own newspaper pots.

MAKE PAPER POTS TO START SEEDS

① WRAP A FOLDED PAPER STRIP AROUND A CARDBOARD ROLL WITH ENOUGH PAPER OVER-HANGING TO FORM A BASE

② EITHER TWIST LOOSE END OR ADHERE WITH A PAPER STICKER TO SECURE THE BASE.

③ PAPER PLANT POTS CAN GO STRAIGHT IN THE GROUND AS THEY DECOMPOSE AS ROOTS GROW.

AND... MANY CONTAINERS CAN BE RE-USED AS PLANT POTS.

... OLD VENETIAN BLINDS CAN BE CUT UP AS LABELS.

... PAPER AND CARDBOARD CAN BE A MULCH.

T.S.

DECEMBER

Time to cut and store firewood for use next year

'Oak logs will warm you well, if they're old and dry.
Larch logs of pinewood smell, but the sparks will fly.
Beech logs for Christmas time, yew logs heat well.
Scotch (pine) logs it is a crime, for anyone to sell.
Birch logs will burn too fast, chestnut scarce at all.
Hawthorn logs are good to last, if you cut them in the fall...'

(Michael Viney quoting Douglas Gageby for 'Another Life',
Irish Times, December 2003)

SOME years ago, I realised a dream of buying and installing a wood stove. These come in various sizes, but they are all far more heat efficient than an open fireplace. My stove burns logs about 25 cm (10 inches) long, so it is compact enough for an average three-bedroom semi-detached house. If I had some land (other than my garden), I would plant deciduous trees and use the thinnings and prunings for firewood. At present the prunings from the garden are useful as tinder to start up the fires in the stove. However, nothing would beat the 'buzz' of seeing wildlife thrive in the richly diverse habitat of a mixed broadleaf wood. Speaking of buzz – woodland would be the perfect location for a few honey bee hives too, of course.

If I had a patch of land, I would plant the following tree species. I list these trees in both Irish and English because of the connection between Irish placenames and the names of trees in Irish. There are thousands of Irish place names associated with trees, for example, Doire – Derry; Cill Chuilinn – Kilcullen; Cluain Sceach – Clonskeagh.

- Dair ghaelach agus D. ghallda — Sessile and pedunculate oak
- Fuinseog — Ash
- Crann silíní — Cherry
- Feá — Beech
- Seiceamóir — Sycamore
- Crann castáin — Spanish chestnut
- Crann teile — Common lime
- Beith — Birch
- Cuileann — Holly
- Coll — Hazel
- Crann fia-úll — Crab apple
- Caorthann — Rowan or mountain ash
- Sceach gheal — Hawthorn

Before planning a woodland, it is an idea to get advice from experts such as:

- The Tree Council of Ireland (www.treecouncil.ie)
- Crann (www.crann.ie)
- Teagasc (www.teagasc.ie)
- A farmer with mixed woodland or a forester

For example, advice may include mulching around newly planted trees to avoid grass choking the young saplings, and how to protect them against grey squirrels, rabbits, hares and deer. There is a certain amount to learn about how to thin and shape young trees with a hand secateurs annually, so that, on maturity, the timber will be of optimum value.

DECEMBER

CREATING A PLACE IN THE GARDEN FOR STORING LOGS

I have memories of cycling on holidays in the Dordogne region of France and seeing stacks of logs in fields. These were protected from rain by a sheet of corrugated iron. Other than that, the firewood was open to the wind, which is a key factor in seasoning those logs. I used to keep the firewood in the garden shed until my trip to France. On my return, I got help to build a lean-to roofed wood store. Now the wood stays dry but is stacked and open to the wind and sun for at least a year. The longer the logs are stored like this, the better. In their second year of storage, the logs turn blue grey when consumed by flames in the stove. This is a good sign to indicate the logs are seasoned and ready to burn cleanly, warmly and continuously. Logs which are not seasoned enough turn black when put into a lit stove.

BUYING LOGS TO STORE

Perhaps you have a good supply of firewood if you are lucky enough to own some woodland, and you pay to have the wood cut into logs with a chainsaw or you cut it yourself. If, like me, you have to buy firewood from a third party, then a Google search of 'Firewood' will yield a good list of suppliers. Before you buy any variety of wood, ask if it is seasoned and where it hails from. My supplier, Peter Barry of www.logonfirewood.ie, has his own woodland and a long track record of proper woodland management and timber seasoning. He sells whatever quantity his customer needs delivered to the door.

However, be warned: logs sold in plastic bags are a serious waste of money as they are generally damp and unseasoned. Worse still, unless they are properly seasoned for about two years, they will coat the chimney with creosote, like all unseasoned wood if it is prematurely burned in a stove or fireplace.

THE KNOCK-ON BENEFIT OF A WOODSTOVE FOR GARDEN SOIL FERTILITY

Wood ash in small quantities can be added to compost or sprinkled on soil, but turf or coal ash is not recommended as a soil additive as it is quite acidic. Wood ash, on the other hand, contains useful amounts of potash. However, one can have too much of a good thing. Hence I am glad the logs are well aged, as seasoned dry wood creates much less ash than freshly cut wood, when burned. As the allium family like potash, I often sprinkle some wood ash on the soil before putting in garlic, onions, leeks, etc. Otherwise the cooled ash is mixed in with the compost as one more ingredient, along with other kitchen and garden organic waste materials.

CREATE AN OPEN DRY AREA TO SEASON FIREWOOD AND TINDER

THIS WOOD STORE MAY LOOK BIG FOR A SMALL GARDEN, BUT THE LOGS ARE ONLY A FOOT (30cm) DEEP TO FIT INTO THE SMALL WOOD STOVE. THE METAL AND WOOD STRUCTURE IS 4 METRES LONG, BUT NARROW. PRUNINGS BECOME TINDER IN TIME.
T.S.

OTHER JOBS FOR THE WEEK THAT IS IN IT:

🍃 On any sunny days, ventilate the greenhouse to prevent moulds becoming a problem.

🍃 Take hardwood cuttings of soft fruit like gooseberries and red, white or black currants. For blackcurrants, take 20–25 cm (8–10 inch) shoots from this year's growth. Insert into the fertile soil half way, leaving on all buds. For other fruit bushes on the list, a 30–38 cm (12–15 inch) cutting is required.

The Bigger Picture:
A healthy, easy New Year's resolution

The celebration of the New Year is the oldest of all holidays. Ironically, New Year resolutions tend to be some of the shortest commitments people make. Few continue to keep their resolutions beyond the end of January. So, before wishing all within earshot *Bliain nua fe mhaise dhuit* or Happy New Year, consider a more interesting resolution, which will:

- Require the briefest visit to the garden each day.
- Improve health and vitality.
- Raise awareness about the edible nature of wild as well as cultivated plant parts.

This resolution is, of course, to add some raw food from the garden to your diet each day.

At this stage I am in the habit of tasting, as well as looking at, listening to and smelling what is growing in my food-growing patch. When it comes to making a sandwich or a salad, or just having a bit of garnish to decorate the top of a bowl of soup, there is generally something growing in the garden to add a bit of interest and to create a connection between the kitchen and the garden, between my food and the soil with which I am most familiar.

I have much more to learn about all the wild plants which could pop in for dinner, so to speak! Meanwhile, the 'old reliables' come and go depending on the time of year. Generally, the younger the plant, the tenderer and more tantalising it is. Here are a few which add a satisfying raw and wild quality to 'regular food':

- **Dandelion:** the young leaves make a handy leafy layer in a sandwich.

- **Rocket:** this salad plant seeds itself and adds a spicy flavour as well as looking pretty.

- **Lamb's lettuce:** these mild-flavoured plants self-seed and appear in December– January to fill a gap.

- **Fennel:** the feathery leaves and aniseed flavoured seeds add an exotic flavour, which I love.

- **Nasturtium flowers and leaves:** the leaves in sandwiches and the flowers in salads are peppery.

- **Borage:** this blue or white flower is known as 'fish and cucumber sandwich' as this is, strangely, the taste it evokes when it is eaten.

- **Rose petals:** an organic garden means petals are healthy to eat.

- **Clover, red or white:** the young leaves and flowers are both edible, if clean of course.

- **Broadleaf plantain:** the young leaves can be eaten in salads.

Given that the New Year is the oldest holiday we still celebrate, it seems particularly appropriate to resolve to follow in some of the footsteps of our earliest ancestors who harvested and picked their way through their landscape, not just for food, but for remedies, love potions, dyes, and so on. First let us concentrate on food.

Thoughts from other kitchen gardeners

SÉAMUS SHERIDAN

A founder of Sheridans Cheesemongers in 1995, Séamus Sheridan, along with his colleagues, has since expanded the business into the best-known cheesemongers in Ireland (see www.sheridanscheesemongers.com). Séamus is passionate about good food, helping growers and farmers to be commercially viable, and ensuring Ireland and the world is food secure in the future. Séamus also has a role as Agriculture Spokesperson for the Green Party (An Comhaontas Glas).

Describe the location in which you grow your own food:

The space which we cultivate at home is a small north-facing back garden in a Galway housing estate, where I planted a few small trees, one being a dessert apple tree bought from Irish Seed Savers, in Scarriff, Co. Clare. Apart from that, we mainly grow fresh herbs and some vegetables for cooking, both in the garden and nearby in the local community garden.

Which food do you look forward to harvesting most and why?

The children look forward to the apples, but I mostly cherish the herbs – thyme, rosemary and oregano. We grow some carrots and parsnips, but not enough to make a memorable harvest. The community garden on the estate is quite productive. I have planted herbs there also.

Which garden tool do you value most and why?

Sunshine! In the West of Ireland, we appreciate all the sun we can get.

What motivates you to undertake the work involved in growing food?

Well, my parents were great kitchen gardeners, so growing food brings back memories of a very happy childhood in inner city

Dublin. My main motivation is therefore to pass this love for food and growing to my own children.

What advice would you give to a person considering growing their own food?

Make a start, and get advice on how to go about it from an experienced market or kitchen gardener. Other gardeners are often generous enough to share some seedlings and seeds, as well as advice, which all help greatly in getting started.

Have you an aspiration for the future in relation to food?

I see fantastic potential for Ireland to grow the full range of foods for a healthy diet, especially more fruit and vegetables. I also look towards the day when all nations will co-operate to ensure food security for all humanity.

ÁINE NEVILLE

It takes huge energy and enthusiasm to work and live in Dublin City centre, while managing a kitchen garden near Wexford town. Áine has the determination to make this arrangement work, and is an amazing example of the lengths people can go to grow some of their own food.

Describe the location in which you grow your own food:

I garden in the fields around my mother's home in Curracloe which look over the flat expanse of Wexford's North Slobs, winter home to the noisy Whooper Swans and Brent Geese. Often the only other sound is of waves crashing on the beach, which is hidden from view behind the kettle and kame hills and the 'plantation' at Raven's Point. The soil on the gentle south-west slope where I have dug out vegetable beds and pitched a polytunnel is generally sandy and fine, though blighted with scutch grass and creeping buttercup. The manual control of them probably keeps me out working longer than I would otherwise need to be….every cloud has a silver lining!

Which food do you look forward to harvesting most and why?

Every year it's something different. My first globe artichokes brought back wonderful memories of the sheer joy of eating and sharing food that I had experienced living in Italy. Broad beans – a childhood horror – have become such an adult pleasure that they have me monitoring assiduously for black fly. And next spring is the magic year three for my asparagus when I hope to finally, finally harvest some spears. I simply can't wait.

Which garden tool do you value most and why?

My young niece Ailis – she's a natural in the garden and is much less squeamish than I am when it comes to dealing with slugs, snails and caterpillars. In terms of conventional tools, I'm a new convert to dibbers, having received a wooden handmade one as a present from Ailis's brother Shane.

What motivates you to undertake the work involved in growing food.

Working in my garden always gives me a great sense of contentment and peace. I grew up with vegetables growing in the garden and it seems the most natural thing in the world to have fresh, seasonal, chemical-free fruit and vegetables available; also, the very idea that I would have to restrict myself to what I could buy in supermarkets fills me with despair. And I find it incomprehensible that we have to transport food halfway round the world when we can grow so much here in Ireland.

What advice would you give to a person considering growing their own food?

Just do it (to borrow a phrase)! Do it with a child. Start small and seek out a GIY group (www.giyireland.com).

Have you an aspiration for the future in relation to food.

I hope that, through organisations like GIY Ireland, the practice of growing our own food will become commonplace once more, in homes, in schools and in communities.

Eanáir ❧ January

The Month of Janus

A VISIT TO BOA ISLAND in Lower Lough Erne, Co. Fermanagh, gave me a chance to stare into the face of Janus, or, in fact, the two faces of Janus. This stone statue, in the ancient graveyard of Caldragh, is seen by many people as a rare pre-Christian image of Janus or Ianuarius, the Roman god of new beginnings, the god of the doorway and the god who sees forward while also seeing backwards.

Eanáir or January is named after Janus and, being the first month in most people's New Year, it is often ushered in to the strains of 'Auld Lang Syne', even though few people singing it know the original lyrics! Other peoples such as the Saxons called the month 'Wulfmonath' and in Scots Gaelic it is 'Am Faoilleach', both of which roughly translate as 'the month of the wolf'. Charlemagne, preferring to be literal, called it 'Wintermanoth'.

THE MYSTERY OF THE JANUS FIGURES

THE STATUE ON BOA ISLAND, CO. FERMANAGH, IS CALLED A 'JANUS FIGURE', BUT JANUS WAS A ROMAN GOD, THE GOD WHO COULD LOOK BACKWARD AND FORWARD. THIS IMAGE IS CELTIC AND MORE LIKELY TO BE A CELTIC GOD. CELTS BELIEVED THE HEAD WAS THE CENTRE OF LIFE-FORCE. THIS WAS THEREFORE A POWERFUL GOD, MOST LIKELY REQUIRED TO ENSURE FERTILITY FOR CROPS, ANIMALS AND PEOPLE.

T.S.

January is not a busy time in the garden. In many ways, it is the ideal time to take a break if you can. I have discovered the hard way that summer is probably the worst time for the kitchen gardener to take a holiday, when the garden needs daily harvesting, weeding and watering.

An overview of the work ahead in the garden this month:

Plant: garlic, shallots
Sow under glass: onions, celeriac
Harvest: winter cabbages, Brussels sprouts and other brassicas
Indoor work: If you are lucky enough to have a heated seedbed under glass or a bright windowsill, then use module seed trays to start off winter varieties of lettuce such as Valdor or Troubadour. Also sow White Lisbon spring onions and Giant Winter or Grodane varieties of true spinach. Sow Sutton, the dwarf broad bean variety, for an early indoor crop.

🍂 FIRST WEEK IN JANUARY 🍂

The garden sleeps but planning and preparations go on

'The cold smell of potato mould, the squelch and slap
Of soggy peat, the curt cuts of an edge
Through living roots awaken in my head.
But I've no spade to follow men like them.
Between my finger and my thumb

The squat pen rests.
I'll dig with it.'
(Seamus Heaney, from 'Digging', Death of a Naturalist, 1969)

WHETHER you are a poet or not, the pen is probably more useful than a spade at the beginning of January for the kitchen gardener. The priority is to check what seeds are needed so you can be ready when the spring temperatures are high enough to sow seed.

To check your existing seed stocks alongside seed catalogues and order seeds, you need to:

🍂 Clear a table and gather paper, a pen, a seed catalogue(s) and packets of seeds from storage.

🍂 Decide which packets of seeds are still useful and which are not worth keeping.

🍂 Do a rough diagram of the growing area, showing the location of vacant plots.

🍂 Look through the catalogues (online or in hard copy) and choose seeds to order.

🍂 Note the plant type for each plot on the garden plan (observing the need for crop rotation).

JANUARY

333

🍃 Order the seeds and put back in cool dry storage the seed packets kept from last year.

SEEDS LAST LONGER IN THE FRIDGE

SEEDS ARE BEST STORED IN DRY, DARK, COOL CONDITIONS — SO A FRIDGE WITH SPARE SPACE IS IDEAL FOR STORING SEALED SEED BOXES WITH LABELS. SEEDS WHICH ARE SOWN 'LITTLE AND OFTEN' ARE EASIER TO ACCESS IN SCREW TOP JARS, e.g. CRESS AND RADISH. T.S.

ORDERING ORGANIC OR NON-ORGANIC SEED?

Trevor's Kitchen Garden has organic certification. This requires that only organically certified seed is sown in that garden. Even if the garden was not certified, I would choose organic seed for the following reasons:

🍃 The parent plant did well organically, so it stands to reason that the offspring will do well also.

🍃 Organic seed carries resilience to a wide range of environmental conditions as it is bred to manage without recourse to agri-chemical treatments.

🍃 Buying organically is a way of supporting a seed producer's decision to farm organically.

🍃 To achieve organic certification, all seed must be free from genetic modification.

WHAT IS THE CONNECTION BETWEEN NON-ORGANIC SEED AND GENETIC MODIFICATION (GM)?

At present, the non-organic seeds sold in Ireland are GM free. However, it is worth checking who owns the non-organic seed companies. The top ten seed companies in the world control 67 per cent of global seed sales. The top three – Monsanto, DuPont and Syngenta – all pro-GM, control almost half of all seed sales (47 per cent). The number one seed company is also the top GM-promoting biotechnology company worldwide, controlling 23 per cent of worldwide seed sales. That company is Monsanto, which continues to take over smaller seed companies at every opportunity.

There is evidence from this consolidation of a strategy at work among the large GM food companies to control more and more of the global food supply chain, starting with control of the seed industry. It is clear to me that our global food system is far from safe when we have a preponderance of genetic resources controlled by institutions whose primary goal is to concentrate on control of the food system for profit.

Organic seed products are by definition GM free. Producers of organic seed struggle against the dominant marketing of the large pro-GM seed companies. With the lack of mandatory GM-free labelling, the only guarantee that seed products are not genetically modified is to grow organically, using organic seed.

SOME OF THE ORGANIC SEED OUTLETS I LOOK AT WHEN ORDERING SEED OR RELATED PRODUCTS

Brown Envelope Seeds, Ardagh, Church Cross, Skibbereen, Co. Cork. This company also runs courses on seed saving.
Tel: +353 28 38184; email: seeds@brownenvelopeseeds.com; www.brownenvelopeseeds.com

Irish Seed Savers, Capparoe, Scarriff, Co. Clare; tel: +353 61 921866; email: info@irishseedsavers.ie; www.irishseedsavers.ie

The Organic Centre, Rossinver, Co. Leitrim; tel: +353 71 98 54338; email: seeds@theorganiccentre.ie; www.theorganiccentre.ie

Fruit Hill Farm (for seeds and tools), Bantry, Co. Cork; tel: +353 27 50710; email: fhf@eircom.net; www.fruithillfarm.com

For the adventurous gardener looking for an even wider range of international organic seed, there are mail order companies in the UK. Garden Organic (www.gardenorganic.org.uk), for example, carries a stock of flower seeds which is more extensive than that of the Irish seed companies. The Garden Organic catalogue is available at www.organiccatalogue.com. Tamar Organics in Cornwall caters for the professional organic grower, but has a gardeners' website too: www.tamarorganics.co.uk.

In the USA there is a vibrant organic seed sector supplying the many backyard growers (as kitchen gardeners are often called there). Examples of this are Johnny's Selected Seeds, which produces the largest seed catalogue I have ever seen. The company is also committed to sustainable and non-GM agriculture. Visit www.johnnyseeds.com. Another American seed company catering for garden growers of organic and heirloom crops has the interesting name of the Irish Eyes Garden Seeds Company. Visit www.irisheyesgardenseeds.com.

OTHER JOBS FOR THE WEEK THAT IS IN IT:

- Inspect any fruit and vegetables in storage, removing any that are beginning to rot.

- Using some rough wood from the woodpile, make up an insect 'hotel' which can be hung on a wall or a tree. This 'hotel', which looks a little like a bird box, should be packed with hollowed, dry stems. This should attract many beneficial insects, including bees, wasps and lacewings, which are either pollinators, predators or both.

The Bigger Picture:
Knowing the law for getting an allotment

According to the Collins Compact Dictionary, an allotment is 'a small piece of public land rented to grow vegetables on.' The folk memory of allotments is often associated with war and national solidarity, especially in Britain, Germany and the USA. Hopefully we can satisfy the growing demand for allotments into the future without a war as a catalyst. To quote C.H. Middleton, the iconic gardening broadcaster during World War II: 'Won't it be grand when we can sit on the old garden seat and listen to the birds instead of the sirens.'

Listening to the radio these days, it is fair to say that uncertainty over the future of finance, fuel and associated food supplies is a subtext to many of the breaking news stories. Whether our food supplies are interrupted by financial bombshells or the explosive metal ones, the availability of allotments will need to increase as an important element of future food security.

The Allotments and Cottage Gardens (Compensation for Crops) Act 1887 created the basis in Ireland and Britain for amateur allotmenteering, since from then on local authorities were obliged to provide plots if the public demand was strong enough in a given area. The UK Small Holdings and Allotments Act 1908 enabled further allotment provision. With the food scarcity caused by World War I, the number of allotments in Britain jumped from 600,000 to 1,500,000 by 1917. It was said at the time that, as well as feeding many families, the allotment movement also steadied that nation's nerve.

Following the War of Independence and the Civil War in Ireland, the new Irish Government maintained the allotment tradition with the Acquisition of Land (Allotments) Act 1926. Section 2 is entitled 'Local Authorities May Provide Land for Allotments', and states:

> 2(1) Whenever a local authority is of the opinion, as a result of representations made to them or on their own motion, that there is a demand for allotments in their area…such local authority may resolve to provide land for such allotments under this Act, and may thereupon carry such resolution into execution under and in accordance with this Act.

The Act defines an allotment as 'a piece of land containing not more than a quarter of a statute acre, let or intended to be let, for cultivation by an individual for the production of vegetables, mainly for consumption by himself and his family'.

The 1926 Act has since been superseded by the Local Government Act 2001, but the import of the 1926 Act is retained in Section 67 (1) of this Act, which states:

> a local authority may take such measures, engage in such activities, or do such things (including the incurring of expenditure) as it considers necessary or desirable to promote the interests of the local community in relation to the matters indicated in subsection (2).

The Act goes on to include allotments as one of 'such things'.

MAKING A CASE FOR THE LOCAL AUTHORITY TO PROVIDE ALLOTMENTS IN YOUR AREA

Making effective representations to, and engaging with, local authority members and management is the key to making your dream of an allotment a reality. Before approaching the council, it is important to gauge the number of like-minded would-be allotmenteers in your locality. Better still, call a meeting to form a local allotment association. Elect a steering committee, print up a logo and letterhead, and, to paraphrase Seamus Heaney, start 'digging' with your pen or computer.

The existence of an allotment association can be a key factor, especially if the local authority is short of finances. Due to staff shortages, a local authority may ask the association to effectively act as an administrator for any allotment land set aside by the local authority. This could mean ensuring the gate is kept closed and other such duties. Allotment associations in the UK, in my experience, are often delegated responsibilities by the local authority, to ensure allotments operate smoothly. In correspondence with any officials or public representatives, refer to the relevant legislation so as to highlight the legitimacy of the allotment campaign.

Before long there may hopefully be a new Allotments Act in Northern Ireland. Recently, the Bill was promoted by the appropriately named Sam Gardiner, an Ulster Unionist MLA.

🍁 SECOND WEEK IN JANUARY 🍁

Using an electric propagator to sow onions and other seeds

'January opens
The box of the year
And brings out days
That are bright and clear.'

(Dr Leland B. Jacobs,
American educationalist and poet, 1907–1992)

S EVERAL chats with expert vegetable growers at local horticultural shows convinced me to invest in an electric seed propagator. Mine cost less than €30 in a garden centre. It has yet to pay for itself, but I am hopeful that, over the course of a few years, it will.

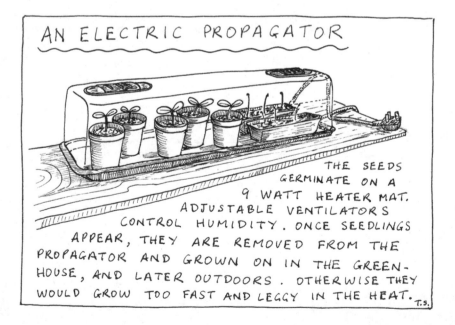

AN ELECTRIC PROPAGATOR

THE SEEDS GERMINATE ON A 9 WATT HEATER MAT. ADJUSTABLE VENTILATORS CONTROL HUMIDITY. ONCE SEEDLINGS APPEAR, THEY ARE REMOVED FROM THE PROPAGATOR AND GROWN ON IN THE GREENHOUSE, AND LATER OUTDOORS. OTHERWISE THEY WOULD GROW TOO FAST AND LEGGY IN THE HEAT. T.S.

Anyone who has been to a horticultural show will certainly remember seeing onions entered in the competition. They tend to be huge compared to anything sold in the shops or markets. I am told that a big reason for this is that the onion seed is planted in October or November in a specially lit, fertilised and heated growing medium in a greenhouse. The seeds get the impression that the winter months are really more like a mild summer, hence their abnormal growth. Show onions are bred to look good, but the downside of this cosmetic objective is they are disappointing to eat and lack flavour.

My priorities are taste, wholesomeness and as long a season for harvesting as possible. A heated electric propagator facilitates seed germination of edible red or white onions or even leeks in January, when seeds in an unheated greenhouse might otherwise struggle to germinate. Likewise, I like to grow sweet-pea flowers among the edible legumes. Sweet-pea seeds are often sown in a propagator around now. I shall keep experimenting. Next I would like to see if I can germinate parsley seeds, which are often slow to get started.

USING THE ELECTRIC PROPAGATOR FOR SEED SOWING OR ROOTING CUTTINGS

🍃 Locate the propagator in an area of natural light such as a windowsill or greenhouse, away from intense heat or draughts, and alongside a thermometer and a container of seed compost. Bring some cold compost indoors to warm it up to room temperature for a day or two before filling propagator pots or trays.

🍃 Cover the heat mat in the base of the tray with a thin layer (about 0.5 cm or a quarter inch) of damp horticultural grit or sharp sand.

🍃 Sow seeds in the small trays or pots provided with the propagator kit. Some people improvise, using a small module seed tray to fit the space so that seedlings can be more easily removed at transplanting stage.

🍃 Once the seeds are sown and the compost gently firmed down, place the seed tray or pot in shallow water, removing it when the compost is fully moist. Drain for a few minutes and then place it in the propagator. Put the lid on the propagator and close the vents. Switch on the propagator. If you are using a variable temperature model, adjust the temperature to that advised on the seed packet.

🍃 A soil temperature of 15–20°C (approx. 60–70°F) is generally recommended for seed germination. If the ambient temperature rises, prevent over-heating of seeds by switching the propagator off until temperatures drop again.

🍃 The propagator creates a humid growing environment. Use your judgement to open vents or remove the Perspex cover occasionally for 2–3 hours to allow foliage to dry off and to avoid seedlings 'damping off', i.e. death by any number of fungal diseases which are fatal to seedlings if conditions are overly humid.

🍃 Remove the propagator lid as soon as the seedlings appear, and transfer each one to a larger pot when they are large enough to handle.

🍃 Smaller seedlings can be spaced out in rows in seed trays; larger ones can be transferred to individual 7.6 cm (3 inch) pots, using multi-purpose compost. Handle the seedlings very carefully, holding them by a leaf (never by a stem), and lever them out of the compost using a dibber or a kitchen fork.

🍃 Make a hole in the new seed tray or pot of compost, pop in the seedling and firm the seed compost around the root ball. Water it well and place it in a warm, well-lit spot.

OTHER USES FOR AN ELECTRIC PROPAGATOR

In spring and early summer, softwood cuttings can be propagated and they generally root in six to eight weeks. Suitable herbs from which to take softwood cuttings would be, for example, marjoram, rosemary, sage, thyme and lavender. Once rooted, these new plants can be overwintered in a warm, well-lit spot indoors. Houseplants can also be propagated from leaf cuttings when the parent plant is growing strong during the summer.

OTHER JOBS FOR THE WEEK THAT IS IN IT:

🍃 Once the greenhouse glass is cleaned and the seedbed is made ready, early radish and carrot seed can be sown in the greenhouse. Minimal watering is needed as there is less evaporation in winter than during the summer. However, keep the watering can in the greenhouse topped up so that the water is at the same temperature as the soil in which the protected crops are growing.

🍃 Sharpen, lubricate and/or clean the lawn mower, spade, hoe, shears and any other important tools in preparation for spring work. An oily rag rubbed over metal surfaces will help to prevent rust and make the physical garden work slightly easier.

The Bigger Picture:
Year-round production – an old trick?

Producing a continuous supply of food in my garden for every day of the year is my goal. This goal is like an Olympic gold medal or the Sam Maguire trophy – it can be elusive or difficult to achieve. Having enough food growing to harvest all the time also means avoiding a glut of any one crop. The walled gardens on the big estates in the nineteenth century in the UK and Ireland demonstrated the potential to extend productivity and the diversity of fruit, vegetables, herbs and flowers to satisfy the cook and the kitchen, every day of the year. The head gardener also had the responsibility to keep staff and employers fed in the absence of supermarkets or imports, other than a few exotic luxuries like tea, coffee and sugar.

Apart from greenhouses, what else helped to give year-round fresh food production in the walled garden?

🍃 The walls: apart from being a boundary to keep out livestock, the walls around the old gardens served to both slow down as well as speed up the growth rates of various plants. The south-facing wall was warmest and against it were grown the fruits from warmer climates like peaches and nectarines. The west-facing wall got the warm evening sun and suited sweet cherries and plums. The east-facing wall got the crisp morning light first and suited native pears and apples. The north-facing wall protected summer salad plants (whose wild relations grow in woodlands) from strong sunlight. The dark Morello cherry apparently grew well against the north-facing wall to yield a later crop. Often specimens of the same fruit trees were planted against different walls to delay or speed up the ripening time.

🍃 Walls could be built up to twelve feet high, and were made of stone for strength but were faced with red brick in order to soak up the sun's warmth and radiate it back into the garden at night, like a storage heater. A very extravagant wall could have fireplaces and chimneys in it, so that fires could be set to further warm tender fruit trees and climbers.

🍃 The hotbed: before electric propagators, the warmth created by manure and other organic matter composting was harnessed to germinate seeds in cold weather. It seems the Arabs pioneered the first hotbeds and Westerners, returning from the Crusades, brought back the idea. When they ruled in Spain and Portugal, the Moors also used hotbeds.

🍃 In Victorian walled gardens, a brick walled seedbed was filled

344

to 4 ft with a mix of horse manure and leaves. It was then capped with a 10 cm (4 inch) layer of soil. A stick pushed into the mix was removed and tested for warmth after a few days, indicating the hotbed was ready for sowing cucumbers, early carrots or radishes, etc. Once sown, the glass lid (or 'light') was put in place to retain as much heat as possible.

WHAT HOPES HAVE WE OF PRODUCING FRESH IRISH PRODUCE TO SATISFY YEAR-ROUND DEMAND?

With all the talk of imported fruit and vegetables in the shops, it is heartening to come across excellent professional growers who have perfected their craft to supply the shops 365 days a year. For example, David Langan in Rush, Co. Dublin supplies butterhead lettuce all year, and it is impressive to see him gauge the growing time of a lettuce in winter compared to one sown in the summer. Likewise, John Gormley, a farmer in Garristown, Co. Dublin, grows turnips for a big supermarket all year round. Farmers like this have to predict accurately the optimum harvest date for each crop, taking account of variable light levels, soil fertility, temperature, moisture, etc. Trying to replicate such skills in my garden brings home this challenge and the immense skill and long experience it takes to produce fresh food all year round.

Preparing the ground for a plum, an apple and a fig tree

'He that plants trees loves others beside himself.'
(Thomas Fuller, English churchman and historian, 1608–1661)

IF the ground is not too wet or frozen, then thoughts can turn to planting deciduous hedging like hornbeam, beech or fruit trees. I find that organically grown fruit is not just very flavoursome, but it comes with the reassurance that it has not been sprayed with any poisonous chemicals. If I had a bigger garden, I would plant two of each fruit tree at least, so that cross pollination could increase the harvest. Meanwhile, if you are reading this and you live near me, please plant fruit trees too so we can pollinate each other's fruit trees and bushes!

PLANTING AN APPLE TREE

If I had not already planted an apple tree in the garden, this would be the time of year I would be preparing a site for a new tree. As with most trees, the apple appreciates good sunshine, good space and good drainage. See the Third Week in November for the varieties of apple tree.

❧ Dig the site thoroughly, working in compost to increase rooting depth, assist drainage and improve soil structure.

❧ Apples do well in a slightly acid soil, so a pH of between 6.2 and 7.2 is desirable.

❧ Trees up to three years old transplant well, and most are now sold in pots.

🍃 Dig a hole larger than the pot.

🍃 If the tree is sold without a pot, dig a hole to fit the root. Bare-rooted saplings, once they arrive in the garden, should be heeled in and stored in damp soil until planting time.

🍃 Have compost or leaf mould and a full watering can alongside you when you are planting.

🍃 Drive a stout stake into the ground as a support, on the side where the strongest wind blows, to avoid chafing of the bark.

🍃 Be careful to ensure the surface of the soil in the pot is level with the surrounding soil. Take care to keep the union (the swollen piece on the stem which indicates the junction between the root stock and the stem) at least 10 cm (4 inches) above ground.

🍃 Use a broad tie to secure the tree stem to the stake so that the bark is not choked or cut.

🍃 Mulch the surface around the new tree with newspaper weighed down with a natural weed-free material like leaf mould, grass clippings or bark.

PLANTING A PLUM TREE

I had a lovely generous Victoria plum tree, but I made the mistake of pruning it during this dormant period before spring. As a result, it contracted silver leaf disease and had to be dug up. It is now chopped up and stacked in the wood store! I have another space up against the west-facing wall where I will plant a new plum tree.

Plum trees work well as fan-shaped trees against a sunny sheltered wall.

🍃 Dig the site and incorporate organic matter.

🍃 Fix a trellis to the wall before planting.

🍃 Follow the same procedure for planting as for the apple tree (above).

🍃 Wait until the summer before pruning any awkward branches. Tie good branches to the trellis, which will form the fan-shaped tree in years to come.

PLANTING A FIG TREE

This ancient Mediterranean fruit tree, often mentioned in the Bible, is used to sunshine, so I hope it will thrive in my garden along the west-facing wall. A friend living nearby has a very successful fig tree, as does Ardgillan Castle's walled garden between Balbriggan and Skerries, which is open to the public and run by Fingal County Council. One advantage of my restricted half-barrel shaped planting site at the wall is that figs do better when their roots are restricted. If I was planting the fig tree in open ground, I would look for an old washing-machine drum, which is full of holes, and plant the root ball in this buried confined area.

While loamy soil is good, the fig does not need the soil to be too rich. Too much compost encourages excessive leaf growth at the expense of good fruit. However, the fig tree does need sufficient water between May and August, as it can be prone to drought since its roots are a little restricted in their reaching for moisture.

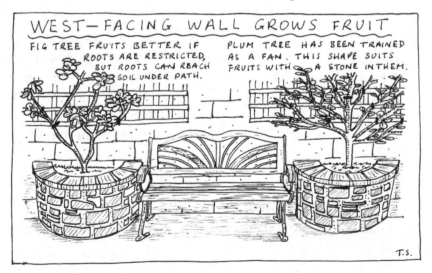

WEST—FACING WALL GROWS FRUIT

FIG TREE FRUITS BETTER IF ROOTS ARE RESTRICTED, BUT ROOTS CAN REACH SOIL UNDER PATH.

PLUM TREE HAS BEEN TRAINED AS A FAN. THIS SHAPE SUITS FRUITS WITH A STONE IN THEM.

T.S.

The planting procedure is similar to that outlined for the apple and plum trees above. To train the fig tree as a fan requires a spacing of 5 m (16 ft) along the wall. The leaves are big and bold, but nothing beats the luscious flavour of a fresh organically grown fig. Good varieties to grow are Brown Turkey, White Marseilles or Brunswick.

OTHER JOBS FOR THE WEEK THAT IS IN IT:

- Cut down all newly planted raspberries to 23 cm (9 inches) and cut excess canes to leave the remainder 10 cm (4 inches) apart.

- Plant rhubarb crowns. Cover them with a layer of manure or compost to create fertile conditions for healthy growth.

The Bigger Picture:
Gardening as a window on the arts

Imagery and ideas that have begun in a kitchen garden are to be found in a multitude of artistic expressions, from the evocative words of Biblical psalms to the protest songs of Billy Bragg, from ornate stucco ceiling plasterwork to the stunning camera work on television programmes like *The Victorian Kitchen Garden* (1987; BBC2). Art is often a reflection of life, but, as often as not, it can also be an escape from the mundane side of life. The kitchen garden can be essential, as during wartime, as well as an escape to the kind of tranquillity that W.B. Yeats evokes in his poem 'The Lake Isle of Inisfree'.

In the years to come, the real prospect of food production levels plummeting when fossil fuels are not so affordable or plentiful will require the growing of food to become as normal as preparing food to eat. A good motivation starting point might be the artistic and very effective posters from 1940s wartime 'Dig for Victory'

JANUARY

349

campaign in Britain. Those iconic posters epitomise a sense of national solidarity expressed by encouraging the widespread growing of food. It is doubtful whether the campaign would have taken off as it did had the artistic communications not been so brilliantly effective and inspirational.

Below are some examples of art which has spurred me on and empowered me to grow more food:

- The 'Dig for Victory' poster (see photograph section)
- W.B. Yeats' poem 'The Lake Isle of Inisfree'
- Carol Ann Duffy's poem 'Bees'
- Billy Bragg's song, 'The World Turned Upside Down'
- Peter, Paul and Mary, 'The Garden Song'
- Louisa Jones's book *The Art of French Vegetable Gardening*
- Carl Jones' painting 'Still Life Vegetables' (on view in my garden!)
- Psalm 65: 'Thou visitest the earth and waterest it...'

Meanwhile, an additional pleasure in having a kitchen garden is the way it becomes a social meeting place as well as a source of food. To date, my garden has been a venue for musicians and singers, artists and poets. Long may those summer sessions continue, but I would ask anybody else visiting to try not to fall into the pond (as has happened one or two unfortunates in the past!).

Digging out mature compost and making a new batch

'A good compost heap is the gardening equivalent of the gold standard – a huge reserve of biological wealth to bounce your horticultural economy along, stave off cyclical depressions and encourage growth.'

(Peter Harper, the Centre for Alternative Technology, Wales, 2001)

WHEN planning my garden, I decided the composting box or 'compost cooker' should be in the centre of the garden, as the pivotal transformer around which everything growing literally and metaphorically revolves. Every six months, this box is emptied of friable brown compost, and immediately filled up again with layers of woody prunings and hedge clippings inter-layered with accumulated kitchen waste and wilted weeds. Each kitchen waste layer is dusted with a thin layer of wood ash before the next woody layer is added. Once full, the front of this three-sided brick box is closed up, and an old carpet piece is put on top of the contents to keep heat in and prevent it drying out. The lid is put back and, apart from mixing it up from time to time, the contents are left to break down. Six months later, the size of the heap can be naturally reduced to a tenth of the size of what it was at the start.

See the Third Week in April for the basics of composting.

COMPOSTERS YOU CAN BUY:

☙ **The green cone:** I have seen this model sold in garden centres – it looks like two cones joined. The bottom cone is like a washing basket and is designed to be buried in the soil. Above ground is the lined plastic cone with a lid. I have found it works for small amounts of organic matter, but emptying it is awkward so it does not really suit the needs of a gardener who wants to use the mature compost around the garden.

🍂 **The free-standing cone:** this model is widely sold by local authorities. If the ratio of more carbon to nitrogen material is correct, then it can work, but very few people are interested enough to check it is working properly. Hence, the main complaint I hear is that the contents are too wet due to an overload of kitchen waste (nitrogen). Mixing in more paper or woody material (carbon) would solve this problem.

🍂 **The compost tumbler:** this is my favourite free-standing plastic composter. Each time a kitchen caddy of vegetable peelings, egg shells, tea bags and newspaper lining is tipped into the tumbler, the lid is screwed back on and the barrel is tumbled twice on its axis. This ensures that there is plenty of air in the mix. The tumbling also ensures no rodent will investigate a regularly moving object. After six months the contents are virtually composted. However, to make a soil-like friable compost, the tumbler contents can be used as the nitrogen layers in the traditional box composter (see below), where the carbon and nitrogen components 'cook' for a further six months to become a usable friable earthy compost. In the absence of a 'box compost maker' (which I tend to call a 'compost cooker'), a second tumbler would be handy, so that the first one is left to cook while the second one is filled over the subsequent six months.

🍂 **The compost box:** once this 'compost cooker' is filled with ingredients, the compost layers of ingredients are left to cook in the oven. This process can be speeded up if you mix the green and brown contents in the course of the six months when it is cooking. A cleverly designed compost aerating stick avoids the need for any forking or digging, while mixing and aerating the compost nonetheless. The picture below hopefully shows what a compost aerating stick looks like.

WAYS TO MAKE ORGANIC GARDEN COMPOST

GREEN CONE
ATTACHED TO
A BURIED
BASKET. THE
WORMS 'COME
AND GET IT',
BUT NOT FAST
ENOUGH FOR
ME!

COMPOST STICK
ONE-WAY
PLUNGER
WHICH MIXES
+ AERATES
COMPOST
WHEN
PULLED OUT.

PLASTIC COMPOSTER
NOT AS RODENT
PROOF AS THE
TUMBLER (SEE
3rd WEEK, APRIL),
WHICH I PREFER.

COMPOST BOX
HOMEMADE, BRICK
BUILT WITH SLAB
ROOF. MAKES GOOD
COMPOST IF MIX
LEFT FOR 6 MONTHS.
HAMMER HANDY FOR
PULPING STALKS.

T.S.

WHERE DOES THE MATURE COMPOST GO?

Two of the four plots in my vegetable rotation get a helping of compost each winter around this time. Where the peas and beans grew last summer has now been cleared in readiness for the brassicas in the coming spring. As brassicas are hungry feeders, they will benefit from well-rotted compost being dug in prior to planting.

Likewise, onions are quite hungry, so the patch which grew beet last summer, and where the onion sets are due to be planted when frost has passed, will get a couple of centimetres of compost. The surplus compost can be used as a mulch around the fruit trees, under hedging and where bedding plants will be going in the coming spring.

OTHER JOBS FOR THE WEEK THAT IS IN IT:

🌿 Arrange in a shallow box first early seed potatoes, eyes uppermost, and store them in a bright, cool frost-free place, so the seed will have sprouted when the frost-free weather for sowing arrives.

🌿 Complete the pruning of apple and pear trees, being careful not to prune any trees producing stone fruits, for example, plums, gages, damsons, cherries, peaches, nectarines or apricots.

The Bigger Picture:
The moon affects how nature works

The whole basis of organic farming is to work with nature. However, we never stop learning better and better ways of doing this, as the organic sector grows and more and more research is undertaken.

I still have to get to grips with and try my hand at biodynamic growing, for example. In a way, I understand it better if I call it lunar gardening, as it involves tapping into the gravitational energy cycles of the moon to grow better flowers, fruit and vegetables. The theory was first rationalised for Western consumption in the 1920s by philosopher Rudolf Steiner.

The moon has four phases, each lasting about seven days. Each quarter has different levels of moonlight and moisture, making certain weeks better than others for planting certain crops. For example, there are 'leaf days' and there are 'root days'. Research in Germany and the UK shows that potatoes sown on root days have a 30 per cent better yield, carrots sown on root days have a 21 per cent better yield and lettuce sown on leaf days are 50 per cent bigger and less likely to bolt.

Here is a rough guide to how the lunar calendar can influence biodynamic kitchen gardening:

🌿 The week before the new moon: good for root and leaf growth. Plant lettuce, spinach and cabbage.

🌿 The week after the new moon: good for leaf growth. Plant beans, peas, tomatoes and squash.

🌿 The week before the full moon: good for root growth. Plant carrots, onions, potatoes and beetroot. Also good for perennials, biennials, bulbs, pruning and transplanting.

🌿 The week after the full moon: the best time to harvest, transplant and prune.

WHERE TO FIND OUT MORE

Internationally, biodynamic farming is known by the trademark Demeter, named after the Greek goddess of agriculture, fertility and harvest. The first international Demeter association was founded in 1928. Today, biodynamic farming is practised in over fifty countries. Find out more about this global movement at www.demeter.net or email info@demeter.net.

In Ireland, the Biodynamic Agriculture Association of Ireland can be contacted at Watergarden, Thomastown, Co. Kilkenny; email: bdaai@indigo.ie.

The British Biodynamic Association has an excellent website (www.biodynamic.org.uk). I found the section called 'Getting Started with Biodynamic Gardening' in the 'Farming and Gardening' section, which is based on the personal experience of the writer, very practical.

Thoughts from other kitchen gardeners

STIOFÁN NUTTY

A qualified horticulturalist, broadcaster and business mentor, with a keen interest in forestry, ecology and growing food for his family organically, Stiofán can be seen on TV and heard on the radio speaking about gardening, the business world and meteorology. He closely studies climate change and posts a reliable weather forecast daily on his website: www.stiofannutty.ie.

Describe the location in which you grow your own food:

My garden is situated in Garristown, Co. Dublin. The growing season is two to three weeks shorter than in coastal Dublin locations due to the altitude and inland location. It is 125 m above sea level and gently slopes to the south. As we are on top of a hill and the air circulates freely, frosts are less severe than in surrounding lower points. The soil is a heavy clay loam soil that drains reasonably well. Unusually for North Dublin, the pH is neutral and the top soil averages about 30 cm in depth. In short, it's a good garden for growing food!

Which food do you look forward to harvesting most and why?

My two favourite crops are potatoes and peas. Sowing the potato seed marks the real start of spring, and the race to harvest before blight might strike reminds me of the 'life and death' challenges that faced our forbearers. Success or failure with this annual 'struggle' fascinates me and I get a great sense of gratification when my family sits down to share the first new season pot of spuds. Opening the first ripe pea pod is simply a magic moment in the vegetable grower's year.

Which garden tool do you value most and why?

If I was confined to having just one garden tool, it would have to be a long-handled fork. It can break up, aerate and aid the drainage of the soil. I use it to spread and mix in homemade compost. It's great for lifting tap-rooted weeds and, when it comes to harvesting potatoes and root vegetables, it's the tool to use. Last but not least, when I need to day dream, the long-handled fork is an ideal prop to lean on.

What motivates you to undertake the work involved in growing food?

I've always had a strong urge to provide at least some of my own food. Apart from the sheer pleasure and relaxation I get from the physical work, I believe that we are living in a time of transition. Much of the food we consume is directly dependent on the availability of oil. As oil availability declines, I fear that food will become more scarce and expensive. So I like the small comfort of knowing I could at least provide some food for my family should we really need to do so.

What advice would you give to a person considering growing their own food?

Don't hesitate; give it a go. Once you do, you're likely to keep at it, as it delivers great satisfaction, relaxation and superbly tasting food. To start, think small. Choose one (relatively easy) crop that you'd like to grow. Radishes, for example, are almost cast-iron certainties to succeed. They can be grown in the soil or in pots and harvested within six weeks. As you achieve and gain experience, gradually increase the number of crops you grow. You'll find experience makes it ever easier for you to grow more crops and manage a larger plot.

Have you an aspiration for the future in relation to food?

Yes, I want to introduce some small-scale livestock to my food growing. I'm lucky to have a wood. It would make an ideal home for a couple of pigs. All I need to do is to fence off the boundary, decide what type of pigs I'd like to raise and get a 'herd number' from the Department of Agriculture, Food and the Marine. They do need proper care and attention but are relatively independent and seemingly easy to look after. Then I'll have to consider doing a butchery course!

DARINA ALLEN

Darina Allen is famous worldwide for Ballymaloe Cookery School, and as a chef, broadcaster and author – not to mention as Myrtle Allen's daughter-in-law and Rachel Allen's mother-in-law. Darina is also passionate about growing food. This passion takes her from school gardens to farmers' markets and to conferences at home and abroad, where she demonstrates practically that the freshest natural produce makes for the best and tastiest results in the kitchen.

Describe the location in which you grow your own food:

I have a 100-acre organic farm just north of the village of Shanagarry close to the sea in East Cork. We have extensive organic vegetable and fruit gardens and an acre of greenhouses – a relic of a horticultural enterprise which has operated since the 1930s.

Which food do you look forward to harvesting most and why?

A very difficult question – I look forward to every food in season. First, young spears of pink rhubarb in spring, green gooseberries and elderflower, new potatoes, broad beans, peas in the pod, the first tiny cucumber…where do I stop?

Which garden tool do you value most and why?

My gardener!

What motivates you to undertake the work involved in growing food?

It is virtually impossible to have a constant supply of freshly picked vegetables for my family and cookery school unless we grow our own.

What advice would you give to a person considering growing their own food?

Don't be too ambitious. Start with a small area. Buy organic seeds and plants and share them with your neighbours.

Have you an aspiration for the future in relation to food?

I would like to see a vegetable, fruit and herb garden in every school in Ireland. It's totally essential to reconnect children with the reality of nature and how food is produced – they absolutely love it and the skills they learn can change their lives.

Epilogue

A Summer's Plot (not by Agatha Christie)

Lorcan Farrelly

His broadcast DNA on well-worked
  nurtured clay,
Where seeds well sprung,
Now raised beds filling up to falling
  out
With cabbage, kale and Brussels
  sprout.
There's rhubarb chard,
Courgettes and runner beans,
With many heads of lettuce,
From ruby reds to greens.

A busy time for mother earth,
Now giving birth,
As pomme-de-terres
Come spilling out.
Allotments full with happy sounds,
As disembodied chit chat fills the
  air.
A busy body on the move,
Where food for thought is talk of
  food.
The swallows overhead well fed
On flies from probing

Spades now fled,
As down below that purple beet,
A prostrate pimpernel, now
Peeping out from side of bed
Reveals its dainty scarlet head.
The redshank cranes its neck
Above that canopy of broccoli,
As that honeyed smell of sweet pea
Envelopes all around.
This palette sure to please all eyes,
Attracts the ladybirds,
The bumblebees and butterflies.

The plot man Michael Burke
Is happy with his lot.
That TLC and talk of NPK
Now bearing fruit.
No furrowed brow,
No taxing thoughts he will allow.
Contentment written on that face.
His motto being, GIY for better
  taste!
Today the trophy is nature's bounty,
His bouquet to embrace.

5 SEPTEMBER 2011

359

Acknowledgements

Thanks to all farmers and growers, those who have advised me in any way about food and farming, and those who continue to inspire me to keep learning. Helping us all to rise to the challenge of a post-oil society is SEED, the network of organic educational centres around Ireland. Thanks to them for their work.

I'd like to especially thank Bord Bia, Agri Aware, the Organic Trust and the IOFGA; also, agronomist Johnny Hogan, Colin Warren, Denis Harford, Dave Langan, PJ Jones, Jenny McNally, Michael Grimes and Dominica McKevitt of GIY Balbriggan. Thanks also to Luc Van Doorslaer, Laura Turner and Geraldine O'Toole and all at Sonairte, and to Hans and Gaby Wieland and all at the Organic Centre.

Among the inspirational growers I want to thank are the guest writers in this book, who have enhanced the book by relating their own experiences. Likewise, thanks to Lorcan Farrelly for the use of his poetry.

To Judith Chavasse, Kathryn Marsh, Geraldine O'Toole and Laura Turner – thank you for reading parts of the book and giving valuable feedback. A special thanks to Fionnuala Fallon for her advice and to Richard Johnston for the cover photograph. Thanks also to Brenda Fitzsimons and the *Irish Times* and to Steve Humphreys and the *Irish Independent* for photographs reproduced inside.

For the website out of which this book grew, www.trevorskitchen garden.ie, I owe a huge debt of gratitude to computer wizard Lorcan O'Toole and expert photographer Ciarán Finn.

Thanks to Orpen Press for encouraging me to write the book in the first place and for their editorial and marketing support.

Thanks to my long-suffering friends and family, especially my parents Mildred and Harry, my brother Derek and sister-in-law Sylvia, and my niece Neidín. I hope to get to see them more, now that the book is out.

In particular, 'Grazie mile, amore mio' to Áine, for sharing all the highs and lows of the project, for being a rock of wisdom and common sense, and for being an inspiration, not just to me, but to the wider GIY community.

Useful Books to Read

Beeton, Isabella (1861), *Mrs Beeton's Book of Household Management*, London: S.O. Beeton Publishing.

Bell, Jonathan and Watson, Mervyn (2009), *A History of Irish Farming 1750–1950* , Dublin: Four Courts Press.

Carson, Rachel (2000), *Silent Spring*, London: Penguin Classics.

Hooper, Ted and Taylor, Mike (1988), *The Beekeeper's Garden*, London: Alphabooks.

Jones, Louisa (1995), *The Art of French Vegetable Gardening*, New York: Workman Artisan.

Laitenberger, Klaus (2010), *Vegetables for the Irish Garden*, Milkwood Publishing.

Larkcom, Joy (2002), *Grow Your Own Vegetables*, London: Frances Lincoln.

Larkcom, Joy (1986), *Vegetables from Small Gardens*, London: Faber and Faber.

Lawrence, Felicity (2008), *Eat Your Heart Out*: *Why the Food Business is Bad for the Planet and Your Health*, London: Penguin.

Laws, Bill (2006), *Spade, Skirret and Parsnip: The Curious History of Vegetables*, Gloucestershire: The History Press.

Myers, Adrian (2005), *Organic Futures – The Case for Organic Farming*, Devon: Green Books.

Norris, Jojo (2002), *Growing Organic Food on a Budget*, Coventry: HDRA Publishing.

Pack, Charles Lathrop (1919), *The War Garden Victorious*, Philadelphia: J.P. Lippincott Company.

Peterson, John (2006), *Farmer John's Cookbook – The Real Dirt on Vegetables*, Utah, USA: Gibbs Smith.

Pfeiffer, Dale Allen, *Eating Fossil Fuels: Oil, Food and the Coming Crisis in Agriculture*, Canada: new Society Publishers.

Pollan, Michael (2008), *In Defence of Food – The Myth of Nutrition and the Pleasures of Eating*, London: Allen Lane.

Ryan, Rosemary (2009), *Waste Not, Want Not – Beating the Recession in the Home*, Dublin: Gemini International Ltd.

Schumacher, E.F. (2011), *Small is Beautiful: A Study of Economics as if People Mattered*, London: Vintage.

Seymour, John (2009), *The New Complete Book of Self-Sufficiency*, UK: Dorling Kindersley.

Fruit, Vegetable and Plant Index

N

nasturtiums 34, 231
nettles, uses of 32–33
nicotania 116
night-scented stock 116

O

onions
  autumn sown 133
  in crop rotation 24–26, 100–102
  drying out 171
  Electric 231, 237
  growing sets 262–263
  harvesting 231–232, 246
  planting sets 41, 69, 231, 237, 246
  Radar 231, 237
  sowing 29, 41, 75, 98, 188, 332
Oriental salads
  planting 182
  sowing 98

P

Parsley 281
  sowing 130
parsnips
  harvesting 276, 305
  sowing 29, 41, 98
pears 232
  pruning tree 354
peas
  Early Onward 19
  Excellenz 231
  harvesting 130
  planting 231
  saving seed 236–237
  sowing 16, 65, 75, 98, 133
  tending 73
peppers, sowing 41, 103
plum tree
  planting 347–348
  pruning 202–203, 240–241, 354
potatoes 46–48
  chitting seed potatoes 47
  in crop rotation 24–26, 100–102
  growing in bags or buckets 47–48, 42–144
  harvesting 130, 160, 240, 246
  planting 65
  planting early varieties 41
  sprouting 19
  tending 72–73
pruning 23–24
pumpkins, harvesting 276
purple sprouting broccoli, *see* broccoli

R

radish
  harvesting 98
  planting 114–116, 182, 225–226
  sowing 16, 65, 98, 130, 188, 222, 246, 343

raspberries
  Glen Moy 203
  planting 52
  pruning 44, 203–204, 293
  tending 73, 138
redcurrant, planting cuttings
    326
rhubarb 296–299
  'forcing' 17–18
  growing 297
  planting 349
  removing flowers, 69
  removing forcer 49
rocket
  planting 225–226
root vegetables in crop rotation
    24–26, 100–102
rosemary, planting cuttings 182
runner beans 246
  harvesting 160, 188
  preparing ground for
    planting 44
  sowing 65, 88
  tending 171

S
sage
  dividing 44
  planting cuttings 182
  potting up 138
salsify
  sowing 65, 75
shallots, planting, 332

spinach
  Crocodile 231
  Giant Winter 332
  Grodane 332
  harvesting 65, 98, 130, 160,
    246, 276, 305
  planting 182
  sowing 16, 75, 98, 160, 222,
    231, 246
spring onion
  harvesting 65
  sowing 231
  White Lisbon 213, 332
strawberries 42–44, 167–171
  conditions for growth 167–
    168
  lifespan 170
  planting 168–170
  planting runners 269
  protecting 171
  what to plant 42–43
  when and how to plant 43–
    44
swedes
  harvesting 305
  lifting 314
  sowing 130
sweet pea
  sowing 250
sweetcorn
  harvesting 188
  sowing 65
Swiss chard
  sowing 192

367

T

thyme
  planting cuttings 182
  propagating 91
tomato
  harvesting 188, 246
  as a pollinating vegetable 286
  sowing 29, 41, 88
  supporting 132–133
  tending 73, 177
trees, varieties for planting as
    woodland 323

turnips
  harvesting 130
  sowing 16, 41, 65, 75, 98,
    160, 188

W

weeds
  as food 103–106
  as soil indicators 103–104
whitecurrant cuttings 326
winter salads, sowing 314